OUR FIRST LADIES

By the Authors

PRESIDENTS OF THE UNITED STATES

OUR FIRST LADIES

By Jane T. McConnell

FAMOUS BALLET DANCERS

CORNELIA

OUR FIRST LADIES

*From Martha Washington
to Pat Ryan Nixon*

JANE AND BURT McCONNELL

Portraits by Isabel Dawson

NEW YORK

THOMAS Y. CROWELL COMPANY

Published in Canada by Fitzhenry & Whiteside Limited, Toronto

Manufactured in the United States of America by the
Vail-Ballou Press, Inc., Binghamton, New York.

LIBRARY OF CONGRESS CATALOG CARD NO. 78-89992
ISBN: 0-690-60454-8

Thirteenth Printing

PREFACE

AMERICA has been richly blessed in the character of its women; their patriotism, courage, resourcefulness, and integrity have helped to shape the history of our nation. In this book we have tried to avoid the legends that have accumulated through the years, and to present the facts concerning our First Ladies, together with an informal account of their personal lives— what they looked like; what they wore; how they brought up their families, performed their domestic and social duties, and met the challenge of their particular era.

Only one President of the United States was a bachelor. In the background of the lives of all the others were the wives who, directly or indirectly, influenced the thoughts and actions of our Chief Executives.

Abigail Adams, most articulate of our early First Ladies, advocated equal rights for men and women and the complete abolition of slavery as early as 1777. Dolley Madison, who saved the Declaration of Independence from destruction when the British burned Washington, won many political victories for her husband in the drawing room. And President Rutherford Hayes once said: "Mrs. Hayes may not have any influence with Congress, but she has a lot of influence with me."

Mrs. Franklin D. Roosevelt, whose speech before the Democratic convention swung the nomination for a third term to her husband, and whose active participation in political affairs broke all precedents among First Ladies, has become internationally famous.

Other wives, like Mrs. Calvin Coolidge and Mrs. Herbert Hoover, quietly exerted their influence and left the imprint of their personality upon the period during which they presided over the White House.

The story of the wives of the Presidents also contains the story of the family lives of the Chief Executives themselves. The two are inseparable; there is no dividing line in human rights and strivings. From earliest times, men and women have worked together for a better civilization.

In paying tribute to our First Ladies, this book pays tribute to American womanhood as a whole—to all those whose moral worth, courage, patriotism, vision, and interest in the welfare of our nation have helped to make it great, and are helping to keep it great. Each in her own sphere, in her home and in her community, shares the privilege and the responsibility of exerting an influence for good in upholding and preserving the highest ideals of our United States of America.

JANE AND BURT McCONNELL

CONTENTS

CONTENTS

CONTENTS

Martha Dandridge Custis Washington

THE FIRST FIRST LADY

THE Royal Governor's mansion at the colonial capital was ablaze with mirrored candlelight. The grand ballroom, with its luxurious hangings of silk and damask, its polished mahogany furniture and its glowing fireplaces, was filled to overflowing with the "first families" of Tidewater Virginia. Williamsburg was a quiet village for the greater part of the year, but during the session of the House of Burgesses it became the social center of Virginia.

Elegant ladies, sparkling with jewels, with their hair powdered and curled, rustled about in their tight-bodiced gowns and high-heeled satin slippers. Gentlemen, resplendent in white wigs, fine ruffled shirts, bright waistcoats, glove-fitting knee pants, silk stockings, and silver-buckled shoes, moved gracefully among the company, bowing low over the hands of the ladies. The Governor, a striking figure in his scarlet suit heavily embroidered with gold, was their host.

No heart in that crowded room beat with more pleasant excitement than that of Martha Dandridge, demure and pretty in her square-necked bodice and flowered petticoats. There was a gay twinkle in her hazel eyes as she acknowledged the attentions of the bewigged officers on the Governor's staff, handsome in their brocade coats and silken breeches. Her heart, as well as her tiny feet, was dancing tonight, as she went through the stately measures of the minuet. For tonight marked the beginning of her social life. Not yet sixteen, and little more than a child in appearance, Miss Dandridge was being presented at the viceregal court of Williamsburg. Gravely, gracefully, she made her curtsy to the genial Governor.

This opening of the court season was a night that Martha would never forget. The little town, with its sandy streets laid out in the form of a "W" and an "M" in honor of William and Mary, was patterned as closely as possible after the English court of King George II, reigning monarch of Britain and ruler of the American colonies. Many of the Virginians were lords and ladies from the best families of the mother country. Their clothes, their furniture, and their manners were imported from England and France. On their rich Virginia estates they enjoyed all the comforts and luxuries that were available at that period. Their sons were sent overseas to school, and their daughters were carefully reared at home. For girls, book learning was considered less important than the social graces.

Into this world of good breeding and gentle manners, at the family plantation on the Pamunkey River, Martha Dandridge was born on June 2, 1732. As the eldest child of a large family of brothers and sisters, she was capable and mature beyond her years. On her mother's side, she came of a line of scholars and divines; her father and his immediate ancestors were planters.

Martha's girlhood days were not spent in idleness; they were filled by lessons in sewing, housekeeping, cooking, dancing, and music. She was awakened not long after the slaves began to stir; for at six she had a lesson in reading and writing. Until dinnertime in mid-afternoon she practiced sewing, knitting, spinning, weaving, and cooking. She learned to embroider, and was introduced into the mysteries of jelly and pickle making. For hours at a time she hemmed and looped and overseamed, did tent-stitch, satin-stitch, and cross-stitch. At the age of seven or eight, she was set, no doubt, to making a carefully designed sampler, with its embroidered alphabet and its quaint birds and flowers, complete with her name, age, and the date.

By the time Martha was fifteen, she was an accomplished needlewoman and musician, and mistress of all the house-wifely arts. She had a neat little figure, pale skin, and light brown hair. At eighteen she was married to Col. Daniel Parke Custis, who was several years her senior, and went to live at the Custis plantation on the Pamunkey River. There were visits back and forth to neighboring estates; there were dinners, tea parties, and hunt breakfasts. Eventually there were four children, two of whom did not live. The surviving youngsters, John Parke Custis and Martha Parke Custis, were the pride and joy of their parents. But in 1757, Col. Custis died, leaving his young and very attractive widow with two children and vast estates.

It is said that, after a decent interval for mourning, many suitors called upon the Widow Custis. But Martha quietly went her way alone, managing her household and her estates as best she could, until a tall young soldier of Virginia rode into her life. He was Col. George Washington, recently returned from the Braddock campaign. Washington lost no time in telling Mrs. Custis how sweet and charming she was. They met at the plantation of Major Chamberlayne, where she was visiting. By the merest chance, the Major caught sight of Washington at the ferry, hurried down to the water's edge, and invited him up to the house.

The young soldier insisted that he could stay only a few minutes; he was hurrying to Williamsburg on official business. But he did not ride on to the capital; he stayed for dinner. In fact, the Major persuaded him, without too much difficulty, to stay all night. Shortly afterward Washington paid a formal call on the Widow Custis at her home, White House. When

4

he left, they were engaged. It was love at first sight, people said. And, while this is quite possible, Martha undoubtedly took her children's future welfare into consideration, together with the security, peace, and comfort which she was sure she would find with George Washington. He was a Virginian, tall, strong, young, forceful. He was well-mannered, smart in the management of estates and the appraisal of the lands to the westward. She had every right to believe, from the reputation he bore throughout the colony, that when she married him she could turn over to him the management of her property. Her children liked and admired the Colonel from the very first, and that probably counted heavily with Martha.

There were other considerations: both were independently wealthy; they moved in the same social circles. Both came from good families. They liked to ride to hounds, and were quite content with their lot as planter and housewife.

Washington was gone all summer with the expedition against Ft. Duquesne (now Pittsburgh). He returned in December, and on January 6, 1759, they were married. It was the union of two fine, strong natures. The wedding took place at her own home, with friends and neighbors coming from miles around. Then a coach and six horses, guided by liveried postilions, carried the little bride to her home in Williamsburg. Beside the coach rode the bridegroom, with an escort of officers and friends.

In his wedding suit of blue cloth, the coat lined in scarlet silk and trimmed with silver, Washington made a handsome figure. At his side hung his dress sword. Martha, so short that she could stand under Washington's outstretched arm, looked more like a young girl than a widow with two children. Her soft brown hair was arranged simply and ornamented with pearls. Her necklace, earrings, and bracelets were also of pearls. Her white satin dress, with its quilted petticoat, was of the finest imported material; and her over-skirt of heavy corded silk was threaded with silver. Diamonds twinkled in the buckles of her satin slippers.

Martha and her husband spent their honeymoon in the social atmosphere of Williamsburg, at her home, Six Chimneys. They remained for several months while the House of Burgesses (of which Washington was a member), was in session. Martha was nicknamed "Patsy"; and Washington also used the same nickname for Martha, the little Custis girl.

There have been many discussions as to whether the marriage of Martha and George was one of convenience, rather than true love. As the Royal Governor's most dependable officer, Washington had made a name for himself, even at twenty-seven. There was also the fact that he had declared his devotion to more than one Virginia belle; and it was well known that Martha had not lacked suitors. The real test of their romance is found in a life companionship of forty years, at home in Virginia, in military posts, in travel over dusty and muddy roads, and in the artificial social atmosphere of New York and Philadelphia. During those forty years, there were admiration, helpfulness, sincerity, fondness, and consideration on both sides. Both were swept along by events, but in their hearts they preferred the simple life of the plantation owner.

Certainly the sixteen years immediately following the marriage of Martha Custis and George Washington were happy ones. Washington had inherited Mount Vernon from his half-brother, Lawrence, who had served under Admiral Vernon and had named the estate in the Admiral's honor.

On the journey to Mount Vernon, with the Custis children,

they visited Washington's sister Betty (Mrs. Fielding Lewis) at her home in Fredericksburg, and made a trip across the Rappahannock so that Martha could meet Washington's mother. And they called upon other relatives and friends on the way.

Nowadays it is difficult to imagine how Martha Washington and other women of the period were able to manage their large households and entertain the relatives and friends who constantly came and went from one plantation to another. Martha's day started at sunrise. Almost always, there were guests for breakfast; and she presided graciously, making the tea and coffee herself. She thoroughly enjoyed running the establishment, and was devoted to her two children. Washington, having no youngsters of his own, lavished the affection of his generous nature upon them. In his carefully kept records we find him, year after year, sending orders to London and Paris for clothing, furniture, silks and satins, handkerchiefs, gloves, stockings, and shoes. For little Patsy there were fans, bonnets, dresses, and toys. Once the master of Mount Vernon ordered "six little books for children beginning to read, 10 shillings' worth of toys, and a box of gingerbread toys and sugar images or comfits."

As part of her dower, Martha Washington brought 150 slaves to Mount Vernon. These, with the slaves already on the estate, came under her particular care. With the exception of the field hands, they were taught to spin and weave; to knit and sew, to cook and serve. The new mistress supervised and directed all this. There were servants to relieve her of manual tasks, but the training and direction of these domestics probably left Martha few idle hours.

The duties of a Virginia plantation mistress of that period included everything from ordering the meals to directing the

7

cooking and setting the table. Then there was the garden. It was she who decided where the "pease" were to be sown and the herbs planted. She also looked after the spinning of yarn, the weaving of cloth, and the making of clothing for the family and the horde of slaves. At one time Martha Washington had sixteen spinning wheels in operation. There was set aside, for her use, a special spinning house equipped with looms, wheels, flaxbrakes, reels, and other domestic machinery. Much of the raw material was produced on the plantation.

Like many other housewives, Martha Washington made wine, cordials, shrub beverages, syrups, medicinal waters, wormwood tonic, spirits of mint, perfumes, perfumed powder "for the hayre," and even a powder to keep the teeth clean and white "and to fasten them."

Mount Vernon had its own carpenters, bricklayers, cabinet makers, blacksmiths, distillers, and millers. The estate consisted of some 8,000 acres, of which about 3,500 were under cultivation. The entire domain was one of serene and stately proportions; and the plantation, with its growing tobacco, ripening corn, and waving grain, with cattle grazing in the green fields and flocks of sheep with their lambs, must have provided a restful picture.

Breakfast was served at seven in the morning. Washington, as a rule, asked for hoecakes, honey, and tea; but he placed no restrictions upon his family and guests. They were served the generous southern breakfast that we sometimes find today— thin, crisp bacon or fried ham, scrambled eggs, corn cakes with plenty of butter or honey, tea, and coffee. Sometimes there were fried apples; and often there were fresh fish, crisp and golden brown.

The dinner hour was three o'clock in the afternoon. For

this occasion, Washington and his guests changed their clothes. Martha took her place at the head of the table, with her husband at her left. The roasts, the "pyes," tarts, preserves, jellies, cakes, and other delicacies were all prepared in the outside kitchen, which was connected with the mansion by a breezeway. With fourteen house servants, things ran smoothly.

The cooking was carried on under conditions of considerable difficulty. Stoves, of course, were unknown; everything —boiling, stewing, broiling, and baking—was done in the huge fireplace. The cook knew which kind of wood to use to produce a quick fire, a long-lasting blaze, or a "lazy" one. Canning, as we know it, was an unknown art.

The cookbook used at Mount Vernon was compiled by the mother of Martha's first husband, and presented to the bride. The quantities mentioned in some of the directions are staggering—twenty eggs, two pounds of butter, a quart of cream, and so forth. We don't know exactly how Martha made ice cream, but it was on the menu. Perhaps she followed the recipe that was printed in 1789; although Washington bought his "cream machine for ice" in 1784. The recipe was brought from France by Thomas Jefferson. We may gather that Washington was no spendthrift from the fact that, while he provided coffee for his family and guests, he considered it too expensive for daily use.

Life at Mount Vernon was a placid and uneventful existence for many years. Then little Patsy died at the age of seventeen. Jacky, the survivor of the four Custis children, had engaged himself to Eleanor Calvert when she was fifteen and he nineteen. Washington, as the step-father of the impetuous youth, suggested to the girl's father that they be prevailed upon to wait a few years—and Jacky was packed off to King's College (now Columbia University) in New York. The untimely death of his sister brought about his return to Mt. Vernon. By this time, "Nelly" Calvert was a young lady of sixteen, and they were allowed to marry.

Resentment on the part of the colonists, which had been smoldering since the Stamp Act agitation of 1765, now broke out into the flames of war. Washington rode off to the meeting of the General Congress at Philadelphia in September, 1774. The battles of Lexington and Concord opened the Revolutionary War on April 19, 1775. Then came the Declaration of Independence and Washington's appointment as Commander in Chief of the Continental Army. All through the struggle, Martha Washington put aside private desires, security, and comfort. In November, 1775, she journeyed by coach from Mt. Vernon to Cambridge, Mass., with her son as escort and his wife as companion. The roads were bad; the weather cold. It was the first of many such journeys. She made visits to the General's different headquarters again and again, keeping house, mending his clothes, nursing the sick, knitting socks for the soldiers, and cheering them on by her presence at the front.

Smallpox was playing havoc with the American forces near Boston, so Martha had herself inoculated against the disease. She was a good campaigner, and never admitted that the war was going against the colonists. She comforted the General when Philadelphia was taken over by the enemy, and when he was obliged to retreat from New York. Washington's army lived through Valley Forge; and Martha lived through it with them. In writing to her women friends, she described the winter huts as fairly comfortable; the Army as "healthy as can be expected"; and their own quarters "small, but better than they were in the beginning." She spent other winters at Morristown and Newburgh, never uttering a word of complaint.

In all, Martha Washington spent eight winters with her husband, wherever he happened to be. Later she told her grandchildren that she had "heard the opening and closing shot of almost every important campaign in the war." Her presence bolstered the morale of her home-loving husband. Her fortitude, determination, and courageous spirit put heart into the officers. She helped to keep the tattered, outnumbered Army together. Moreover, her patriotism was matched in all the thirteen states by the Daughters of Liberty, who banded together in groups, refusing to use tea or other goods from England; spinning, weaving, and sewing for the soldiers; declining to listen to suitors who had not answered the call to their country's defense. This was heartening to the men who were doing the fighting, but not novel; brave women, down through the centuries, have backed up their soldiers, and the women of the Revolutionary War were no exception. Hating war and bloodshed, fearing for their homes and their dear ones, they never wavered in their stand against tyranny, never admitted defeat.

Martha Washington lost her only remaining son during the Revolution: Col. John Parke Custis was stricken with camp fever and died on November 5, 1781. Two of his children were formally adopted at once by General Washington. Finally the Revolutionary War came to a successful end. On Christmas Eve, 1783, General Washington returned home.

Life at Mount Vernon, in the days following the war, was not as quiet and peaceful as the master and mistress had fondly imagined it would be. Their home became the gathering place of travelers, soldiers, statesmen, historians, painters, and sculptors. They wanted to see the great General who had vanquished England, the most powerful nation on earth. To meet these many demands on their hospitality, the General and his wife found it necessary to add more and more rooms to Mount Vernon, until it was nearly doubled in size.

Through all this excitement and disorder, Martha Washington moved serenely, managing her large household, watching over her grandchildren, and playing the part of gracious hostess. She taught her little granddaughter, Nelly, to play the harpsichord; and, since music was hard to come by, the mistress of Mount Vernon copied with her own hands sheet after sheet of music by Mozart, together with marches, dance music, and songs. Nelly was rewarded for her industry by the gift, from Washington, of a harpsichord which cost a thousand dollars—a large amount of money in colonial times.

This was a calm and unruffled period, in which crops were plentiful and goods were shipped in the plantation's schooner, from their own dock, to Philadelphia rather than to England. But the tranquil era came to an abrupt end when Washington was elected President of the United States. Both for him and Martha, the congenial life of Mount Vernon had to be put aside in the interests of the new nation. For the mistress, the break was quite difficult; for the master, it meant at least four years of financial sacrifice. His absence from the plantation during the war years had cost him at least $50,000; and he had not yet had time to recoup. In fact, he was behind in his tax payments (for he had refused to accept a general's pay for his services during the Revolution); and was obliged to borrow the money to pay his way to the inauguration. Yet Martha did not fret and fume; after all, the country had been saved!

Washington went on ahead, leaving Martha to make her domestic arrangements. In due time, she followed in the family coach; but there were so many stopovers along the route that she did not arrive in New York (then the nation's capital) until after Washington was inaugurated as the first President of the United States!

She found that the President had taken over one of the finest houses in the city, and that it was ready to receive her. Some of the furniture belonged to the couple; the balance was government property.

Martha Washington made a gracious and dignified figure as the wife of the Chief Executive. She derived considerable pleasure from the honors heaped upon her "old man," as she called him. She also enjoyed the consideration which was shown her as the First Lady of the land. Yet public life, at times, palled on her. She was not happy in the capital, and once wrote to a friend: "I never goe to any public place—indeed I think I am more like a State prisoner than anything else." Nevertheless, she dutifully held her Friday evening receptions, and presided at state dinners. There were parties on the rivers and almost daily drives about New York. Now and then Washington took her to the theatre.

During Washington's two terms, he engaged a steward to preside over the household—under Martha's orders. In the summer of 1790 they moved to Philadelphia, the new capital, where the family occupied the Robert Morris house, on Market Street. They furnished it handsomely; and on Christmas Day, a Philadelphia socialite reported: "There was held the most delightful occasion of the kind ever known in this country—the levee of the Washingtons." The levee, it may be added, ended at nine o'clock in the evening. For, as the First Lady explained to the guests, "the General always retires at nine."

Martha Washington seemed to thoroughly enjoy the social

whirl of Philadelphia. Either she was becoming reconciled to public life, or she preferred that city to New York. As mistress of the Executive Mansion, she had no precedents to guide her. But her knowledge of the social graces and her belief in the principles of democracy caused her to be loved and admired by the general public and emulated by the First Ladies who came after. She made the best of every situation. Soon after the end of the Revolutionary War she wrote to a friend: "I had anticipated . . . we should be suffered to grow old together in solitude and tranquillity. That was the first and dearest wish of my heart. Yet I cannot blame him for . . . obeying the voice of his country." This referred to Washington's election to the Presidency. In another letter, written at Mount Vernon, she said: "The General and I feel like children just released from school. . . . Nothing can tempt us to leave the sacred rooftree again."

It was wonderful to be back at Mount Vernon, she wrote to General Knox's wife, an old friend from Revolutionary War days: "I cannot tell you how much I enjoy home after being deprived of one so long. . . . I am again fairly settled down to the pleasant duties of an old-fashioned Virginia housekeeper, steady as a clock, busy as a bee, and cheerful as a cricket."

That was Martha Washington at sixty-six.

She had hoped, as a young widow with children and responsibilities, to settle down as the faithful and loving wife of a Virginia planter. But destiny brought crowded days and fame to her "old man"—a fame which filled her with pride and joy. Soon after they left the Executive Mansion and returned to Mount Vernon, the burden of housekeeping and entertaining grew to such proportions that Washington insisted on engaging a housekeeper to free his wife from petty details. The hospitality dispensed at the plantation was famous throughout the colonies; the host and hostess were so popular that they seldom had an opportunity to enjoy a quiet dinner by themselves. Once, Washington felt prompted to write in his diary: "Would anyone believe that, with 101 cows, I am still obliged to buy butter for my family?"

Martha and the General enjoyed two tranquil years at Mount Vernon after the exciting life of New York and Philadelphia. Then, early in December, 1799, Washington rode out over his land, as was his custom. He rode through rain, hail, and snow—as he had done on innumerable occasions. He faced a bitter wind. Returning at three in the afternoon, he complained of having taken cold. Two days later, on December 14, he died.

Washington's will stipulated, among other things, that upon the death of his wife, his own slaves were to receive their freedom. Upon learning this, Martha Washington relinquished her right of dower, thus emancipating her own slaves.

Three and a half years later, Martha realized that her own end was near. She found as many letters from her husband as she could, and destroyed them. She then sent for her clergyman, to take the last communion in the faith of her girlhood. Laying out her funeral dress, she calmly awaited the end. It came on May 22, 1802.

America's first First Lady was dead. She had lived a useful, eventful life during the most momentous years of the nation's history. In death, as in life, Martha Washington remains in the shadow of her illustrious husband. Yet it is a shadow which grows, rather than diminishes, as women are increasingly recognized for the tremendously important part which they play, and have played, down through the years —as the helpmeets of those who have shaped the destiny of the United States.

Abigail Quincy Smith Adams

ARDENT PATRIOT

ABIGAIL SMITH gave a final pat to her dark curls and turned toward the bedroom window. At nineteen, she was admired for her wit, intelligence, and tact, rather than for her appearance. But as she stood there, happiness so transformed her plain face, with its serious mouth and determined chin, that she looked radiantly beautiful. It was October 25, 1764—her wedding day. As she glanced out over the fields, she was glad the sun was shining. Around the little house in Weymouth, Massachusetts, a cold autumn wind whipped the dry grasses and rattled the doors and windows. But within all was warmth, bustle, and cheer.

Downstairs in the neat, prim parlor, relatives, friends, and neighbors were crowded. Young John Adams, uncomfortable in his wedding finery, thought he had never seen so many people in one room. Inwardly, he was as nervous as bridegrooms usually are. Outwardly, the short, stocky figure presented a calm, even imposing, appearance in his fawn-colored knee breeches, white satin waistcoat, and outer coat of fine blue broadcloth. When he saw his Abigail coming down the stairs, his stern face relaxed, and his eyes lighted. Abigail moved gracefully in her wide-skirted white challis dress, embroidered with tiny scarlet flowers. Her head rose proudly above the tight bodice with its square-cut neck.

Slowly the sacred words were recited, the marriage vows pledged, as Abigail and John were joined in a union of love and devotion that was to continue unabated throughout their lives. Everybody kissed the bride and shook hands heartily with the groom, and in the festivities that followed the future of the young couple was toasted roundly in mugs of punch. Then John mounted his horse, swung his little bride up behind him, and Mr. and Mrs. John Adams went riding down the road to Braintree, a few miles distant.

With her arms around her husband's waist, and her scarlet cloak flying in the breeze, Abigail was on her way to a new home and a new life. The world seemed very fair and the future filled with magic enchantment that October afternoon. Long afterward, she was to remember it as one of the very few carefree moments of a busy, eventful life, in which her influence as wife, mother, and intensely patriotic pioneer woman was to reach out over two continents and play an important role in the destiny of a new and struggling republic.

For Abigail Adams was one of the most remarkable women of her—or any—era. She was highly articulate, well educated, and possessed a rare amount of tact and judgment. Many have said that she was a better statesman than her husband, and that her keen intelligence and wise counsel were largely responsible for his success. Abigail herself would have laughed at any such suggestion. She was a sympathetic listener, and freely offered her opinions when John Adams discussed with her the problems that beset him. In the early years of their marriage she also helped him build up a highly profitable law practice, for she was related to half the socially important families around Boston.

There was nothing in Abigail Smith's childhood to foreshadow the part she was to play in American history. She was born in Massachusetts on November 23, 1744, the daughter, granddaughter, and great-granddaughter of prominent New England preachers. Her father was a Congregational minister at Weymouth. She was regarded as a delicate child and was never sent to school, yet she received an excellent education for a girl of that pre-Revolutionary period. Parson Smith encouraged his daughter to read and study his books. In her grandfather's house at Braintree, another fine library was at hand. There her grandmother, Elizabeth North Quincy, spent countless hours training the inquiring mind, sharpening the awareness, and increasing the understanding of little Abigail.

Years later in 1795, in a letter to her own daughter, Abigail wrote: "I have not forgotten the excellent lessons which I received from my grandmother at a very early period of life; I frequently think they made a more durable impression upon my mind than those which I received from my own parents."

It is easy to imagine Abigail as a child, demurely dressed in her stiff gowns, poring over spellers and readers, being petted a little, perhaps, as she dutifully drank the homemade herb teas, physics, and caudles of white wine with "six yelks of eggs" which her elders thought beneficial. They also believed that a change of air was good for her, so little Abigail often was driven from her home in Weymouth for a long visit with her grandmother at Braintree or with Uncle Isaac Smith and Aunt Elizabeth in Boston.

Boston was then the largest city in the colonies. Its busy port was an exciting contrast to the farm at Weymouth. In Uncle Isaac's warehouse on the wharf, there were enticing smells of coffee, spices, wine, tea, and molasses mixed with the sharp odor of salt fish. When, as a special treat, Abigail was escorted aboard one of her uncle's sailing ships lying at anchor in the harbor, the thrill of far places stirred her imagination. She gazed up at the tall masts, stared out over the expanse of blue water, walked the clean-scrubbed decks, and swayed happily with the gentle swing of the vessel on the tide.

But those were rare occasions. Much of her childhood was devoted to domestic tasks: weaving, knitting, sewing, spinning, cooking, soapmaking, candle-dipping. Abigail realized early that woman's work is never done. There were bread and meat-pies to bake; apples to be peeled, cut, and dried; and, swinging from the iron cranes in the wide fireplace, steaming pots of vegetables, soups, and puddings needed watching and stirring. Every New England housewife churned butter, pressed great cheeses, made the cider which the menfolks drank daily, tended kitchen gardens, dried herbs, and still found time for prayers, Bible reading, and regular attendance at church.

Abigail was also a prolific letter writer. In early missives to girls of her acquaintance she poetically signed herself "Diana." When she began corresponding with John Adams, she signed her letters "Portia" because he was a lawyer; and in those long letters to him she did not hesitate to express her opinions on public affairs.

Most of Abigail's friends and relatives disapproved of her growing friendship with John. Law was a new profession in the eighteenth century, and those who set out to make a living by settling the difficulties of others for a fee were regarded as a lazy, shiftless lot. Abigail did not share this view. When people said she was "wasting her time on that lawyer, John Adams," she only smiled. John loved her and she loved him, and that was all in the world that mattered.

They started married life together in a sturdy brick-and-clay farmhouse in Braintree. Its walls, sheathed in wood, were unpainted. The house, with a deep stone cellar, was built around a massive central brick chimney. There were enormous fireplaces and great brick ovens. Abigail's new home had already withstood more than fifty years of wind and weather, and, though it was plain and unpretentious, she loved it at once.

During the next ten years, Abigail was busy bearing and rearing their children. Nine months after the wedding a daughter was born. The proud father named her Abigail, but she was always called "Nabby." Later John Quincy was born, then Charles, then Thomas. In those ten years, the family moved often. In the spring of 1768 John's growing law practice made it necessary for them to move to Boston, where they rented a house in Brattle Square.

By 1773, the city was a hotbed of unrest. Some two thousand British soldiers were quartered there, and frequent quarrels occurred between the hated Redcoats and the colonists. John Adams had been among the first to speak out against the oppressive taxes called for by the British Stamp Act of 1765. Though he foresaw a long and bitter struggle ahead, he never for a moment considered anything but active resistance against the injustice of England's new commercial policy. Abigail, too, was quick to take her stand with the colonies. When, in December, 1773, British tea was dumped into the harbor by enraged patriots, she was jubilant. In a letter to her friend, Mercy Warren, she wrote:

> "The tea that bainful weed is arrived. Great and
> I hope effectual opposition has been made to the land-
> ing of it. The proceedings of our Citizens have been
> united spirited and firm. The flame is kindled and
> like lightning it catches from Soul to Soul . . ."

The women of the colonies were as deeply stirred as were the men at the constant injustice and growing tyranny of the British government. As early as the year 1766, a group of young women who called themselves Daughters of Liberty met and spun all day long for the public benefit. The ladies of Boston formed such groups, refusing to buy British goods, making American homespun cloth, and agreeing to drink no tea. This movement by patriotic women spread all through the colonies.

In June, 1774, John Adams was appointed a member of the Massachusetts Committee to the Continental Congress at Philadelphia, and on August 10, after moving his family back to Braintree, he set out for Philadelphia. "We live, my dear soul, in an age of trial," he told Abigail. "What will be the consequence I know not . . ."

From that time, except for a few scattered months, Abigail was separated for ten years from her beloved husband. And from that day, she made the farm at Braintree support the family. In the spring of 1775, the Revolutionary War swept almost to her doorstep; unfriendly Indians peopled the woods beyond her fields; there was danger on every side. Through all this, Abigail was magnificent in her fortitude and ingenuity. She gave the Minute Men her pewter spoons to be melted into bullets; helped make warm and substantial "county coats" for the soldiers; nursed the sick; supervised the farm; and did all in her power to obey her husband's request that she train her children to virtue—

> "habitate them to industry, activity and spirit; make them consider every vice as shameful and unmanly; fire them with ambition to be useful," . . . "and for God's sake, make your children hardy, active and industrious!"

Abigail, in the midst of war and want, went steadily about her tasks. She took her four children to be inoculated for smallpox; taught Charles and young Thomas to read; showed little "Nabby" how to sew and spin; and kept her eldest son, John Quincy, busy about the farm.

When her husband wrote her from Philadelphia: "in case of real danger . . . fly to the woods with our children," she set her lips firmly. No power on earth could force her from her home. The farm was all they had now. "I would not have you distressed about me," she answered. And again she wrote him:

"Courage I know we have in abundance . . . but powder, where shall we get a sufficient supply?"

This was Abigail, superb in spirit and action, equal to any emergency, with danger ever present. She was a monument of strength and faith—faith in God and in her country, faith in the ability of her husband as a statesman, faith in the land, faith in herself and her convictions.

With her young son, John Quincy, she had stood on Penn's Hill, spyglass in hand, listening to the shelling of Boston. A year later on that same hill, she was filled with joy when Washington's troops drove out the British. She rode into Boston to hear the Declaration of Independence which her husband had helped formulate, and that night she wrote to him:

"The bells rang, the privateers fired the forts & batteries, the cannon were discharged, the platoons followed & every face appeared joyfull . . . After dinner the kings arms were taken down from the State House and every vestige of him from every place in which it appeared & burnt. Thus ends royal Authority in this State. And all the people shall say Amen."

24

One can imagine Abigail setting down those words, her quill pen scratching, her cheeks flushed with excitement and elation. Her spirit and vitality were apparent, through the years, in her clear and vigorous letters.

> "By the way," [she wrote her husband in 1776] "in the new code of laws which I suppose it will be necessary for you to make, I desire you would remember the ladies and be more generous and favorable to them than your ancestors. Do not put such unlimited power into the hands of husbands. Remember all men would be tyrants if they could. If particular care is not paid to the ladies, we are determined to foment a rebellion, and will not hold ourselves bound by any laws in which we have no voice or representation."

Those words were doubtless written in fun. At any rate John accepted them as such: "What next?" he replied. "As to your extraordinary code of laws, I cannot but laugh!"

Abigail then wrote more seriously:

> "I cannot say I think you are very generous to the ladies; for whilst you are . . . emancipating all nations, you insist upon retaining an absolute power over your wives."

Freedom was always dear to Abigail's heart. Almost a century before the Civil War she expressed herself clearly on the subject of slavery:

"I wish most sincerely there were not a slave in the province. It always seemed a most iniquitous scheme to me to fight ourselves for what we are robbing the Negroes of, who have as good a right to freedom as we have!"

In the autumn of 1777, when things looked particularly dark for the ragged, struggling American army, and Washington had lost the battle of the Brandywine, Abigail sent off another characteristic letter to her husband:

"We are in no wise dispirited here. If our men are all drawn off and we should be attacked, you would find a race of Amazons in America."

Had the women been forced to defend the colonies, doubtless Abigail herself would have led them on to battle for their cause.

Loneliness was the only enemy she ever feared. Only in the long and heartbreaking separations from her husband was Abigail ever appealingly weak. There were melancholy hours, as she sat by her fireside late at night, when she felt she could not bear the separation from her "Dearest Friend," and then she wrote wistfully: "All the letters I receive from you seem to be written in so much haste that they scarcely leave room for a social feeling . . . I want some sentimental effusions of the heart."

Abigail hoped John soon would be reunited with his family. But in February, 1778, Congress sent him to France to be ready to negotiate the peace treaty that the members hoped would soon be needed to end the American Revolution. He sailed with his oldest son, John Quincy; and again Abigail was left to shoulder the responsibilities of the farm alone.

In June, 1779, she wrote to her husband:

> "Six months have already elapsed since I heard a syllable from you or my dear son, and five since I have had one single opportunity of conveying a line to you . . . Labor is at $8 per day . . . Linens are sold at $42 per yard; the most ordinary sort of calicoes at thirty and forty; molasses at $20 per gallon; sugar four dollars per pound; board at $50 and $60 a week . . ."

But Abigail managed somehow. John Adams had been sending remittances home in merchandise. She became a merchant, and sold the goods at a nice profit or bartered it for necessities. She kept the farm in good repair, paid the bills and taxes, kept out of debt, and fed and clothed her family.

In 1784, seeing little hope of being recalled to America, John Adams wrote Abigail to join him. With her daughter, Nabby, she sailed in June of that year on the *Active*. It was a rough crossing and the two were seasick from the start. Abigail, however, soon grew accustomed to the pitching and rolling of the vessel. By the end of the thirty-day voyage, her spirit of adventure was at high pitch, and her talk and her many letters to friends and relatives were filled with nautical terms. Being Abigail, she had learned all about the rigging and the steering.

Paris and its dance halls first shocked, then delighted Abigail. She enjoyed France, and was blissfully happy to be with her husband once again. There was pleasure, too, for Abigail in her close friendship with the Marquise de Lafayette. The aristocratic Frenchwoman and the preacher's daughter from New England found in each other a kindred spirit. They visited together by the hour, chatting over their knitting or embroidery, while the two children, Virginia and George Washington Lafayette, played at their feet. Benjamin Franklin often came to call on the Adamses, and Thomas Jefferson was almost like one of the family. Franklin was old and infirm and Jefferson was sick a great deal, so during that winter of 1784-1785 John Adams bore almost the entire responsibility of conducting American diplomatic business with the French court.

In May, 1785, letters from America notified Mr. Adams that he had been appointed the first American minister to the Court of St. James's, and he and Abigail went at once to England. In this extremely difficult post, Abigail once again demonstrated her tact and skill at getting along with people, and played a highly important part in the destiny of our young nation by keeping her husband from losing his temper. It was not easy for John Adams to meet face to face the King who had for many years regarded him as a traitor and a rebel. Both the American Minister and King George III were brusque, and made no attempt at friendship. John was stung by the King's hostility. It was Abigail—charming, pleasant, and calm—who acted as a buffer between the two men, urging her husband to use persuasion rather than open defiance. She herself resented the King's manner, but she realized that her husband was there as the official ambassador of the United States, and therefore they must put aside their personal feelings.

In her straightforward, intelligent, and gentle way, Abigail

28

proved to be a more valuable diplomat than John. For three years she made her curtsies, smiled in friendly fashion, and faithfully attended court balls and presentations. She was not humble before royalty, but her charm and good humor won her the admiration of all England. Later, in America, she was destined to occupy an even more important position, but never did she show more courage and diplomacy than during those three momentous years in London. With it all, she managed to enjoy herself. For, in her own words, she was "a mortal enemy to anything but a cheerful countenance and a merry heart."

During their stay in London, Nabby was married to a member of the legation staff; the daughter of Abigail Smith Adams became Abigail Adams Smith.

When at last John and Abigail went home, they had served their country well and had paved the way for the American ambassadors who would succeed them down through the years.

Abigail's heart sang when they returned in 1788 to her beloved Braintree. Now maybe they could settle down happily together. But America was beginning to recognize the integrity and mental capacity of John Adams. He was made Vice President of the United States, while Washington was the choice for President. When Washington retired at the end of eight years, there was a hotly contested election in which John Adams, by a slender majority, was made President; and Thomas Jefferson, Vice President.

Being the wife of the President of the United States did not worry Abigail in the least. She had lived in London and Paris. As the wife of the Vice President, living first in New York and later in Philadelphia, she was well schooled in the social requirements of a First Lady. She also had a good grasp of political affairs, domestic and international. John always discussed affairs of state with her. Often, listening to her opinions and forthright ideas, he saw conditions more clearly and was influenced by her sound judgment.

As Abigail Adams was the wife of the first minister to the Court of St. James's, so she was the first First Lady to live in the White House at Washington. Almost at the end of her husband's presidential term, early in November, 1800, the Adams family moved into the unfinished Executive Mansion. Washington then was little more than a wilderness. Not an avenue or street was laid out, and roads were either knee-deep in mud or buried in dust.

> "Surrounded with forests," [Abigail wrote,] "can you believe that wood is not to be had, because people cannot be found to cut and cart it? Only a few cords have we been able to get. This house is twice as large as our meeting house . . . Not one room or chamber is finished . . . To assist us in this great castle, bells are wholly wanting . . . not one single one being hung through the whole house."

But, as usual, Abigail's courage came to the fore. "If they will put me up some bells and let me have wood enough to keep fires, I design to be pleased," she declared genially. And she made a drying room of the great unfinished audience room, and hung out her washing!

She was now fifty-six years old, and sometimes not very well. She longed for the tranquillity of her New England home. Yet, because it was expected of her, Abigail plunged into the social duties of the President's Lady. The first New Year's reception was held in the White House on

January 1, 1801. Mr. and Mrs. John Adams received their guests in the Oval Room, which was made cheerful by the red upholstered furniture they had brought from France. The gleam of candlelight, and the glow and warmth from the fireplace (for which Abigail had managed to get sufficient wood) lent a festive air to the occasion, and Washington received its first sensation of being a society. That was the first of many social functions over which Abigail presided in those last few months of her husband's public life.

As President, John Adams was handicapped from the start. He succeeded a man whom the people loved and revered, and who had all the personal charm and tact that Adams lacked. He made the mistake of retaining Washington's cabinet, and three of the members turned out to be disloyal. Adams was also continually at odds with Alexander Hamilton, who had been Washington's chief financial adviser. The French monarchy had been overthrown and there was trouble with the new regime. Hostilities commenced upon the sea. Feeling ran high in the United States, but President Adams was determined to keep our new and struggling country out of war. For his failure to defend our rights—and for other reasons— he was widely criticized and disliked. Yet, in almost every argument in which John Adams was engaged, it is now generally admitted that he was right.

Abigail realized the difficulties of his position and sympathized with him in his problems. And she was relieved and happy when, at the end of her husband's term, they retired to private life and settled down on the farm in Braintree.

Though Abigail was ill most of the last few years of her life, she watched over her household as always, kept at her knitting, and continued to write hundreds of letters. Many of those letters went to her son, John Quincy, who was successively minister to Germany, Russia, and England. When, in 1817, President Monroe appointed him Secretary of State, Abigail's pride was intense.

She did not live to see her son become President of the United States. The only woman in our history to be the wife of a President and the mother of a President passed away in her sunny west bedroom in the home she loved. With her husband beside her—the husband with whom she had spent 54 years of happily married life—Abigail Adams died on October 28, 1818, less than a month before her 74th birthday. This most remarkable woman of a remarkable age had served her community and her country well. She had traveled a long way from the little farm in Massachusetts; her influence had reached out to help shape the laws of our new nation; she had acted as counsel and guide to two men who became Chief Executives of that nation. Her words of wisdom, handed down to us through her letters, are many. Perhaps there are no lines more fitting for her epitaph than those with which she reassured her husband when they returned from London to Braintree:

"I have learned to know the world and its value. I have seen high life. I have witnessed the luxury and pomp of state, the power of riches, and the influence of titles. Notwithstanding this I feel that I can return to my little cottage and be happier . . . and if we have not wealth, we have what is better—integrity."

Martha Wayles Skelton Jefferson

WHO DID NOT LIVE TO SEE THE WHITE HOUSE

IN the year 1760 when George III ascended the throne of England, there were no clouds on His Majesty's horizon. In British America, one of his colonial officers was living in retirement. A gawky, redheaded lad of seventeen had entered the College of William and Mary; and a young miss of eleven, at her home in an adjoining county, was no doubt making samplers and studying music. Yet events were moving swiftly. Within fifteen years, the sword of the retired officer, George Washington, was at England's throat; the red-haired stripling, Thomas Jefferson, was denouncing the King in blistering language that might well have cost him his head; and the carefree young miss, Martha Wayles Skelton, had become Jefferson's wife.

Martha's long white fingers moved deftly over the keys of her pianoforte. Thomas Jefferson, standing tall above her with his violin tucked under his chin, wielded a lively bow in the lilting music of a Bach chaconne. They made a charming picture, there in the candlelight. Through the open windows the soft autumn breeze stirred the white curtains. More than one caller, as he heard the music of Tom Jefferson's fiddle, pulled on his reins, stopped for a moment to listen, wheeled his horse, and turned back. For even the most ardent suitor realized that, with the young lawyer from Albemarle County calling regularly, he had no chance of winning Martha Wayles Skelton.

This was the first and only real romance of Thomas Jefferson. Martha had married Bathurst Skelton at the age of seventeen, had borne a son who did not live, and had lost her husband before she was nineteen. Now, at twenty-three, she had shining auburn hair, fair skin, and large hazel eyes. A little above medium height, she was also better educated than the average Virginia belle of that period. According to one of Jefferson's better biographers, Martha was slender and her intellect was keen. Unfortunately no authentic portrait of her is known to exist today. Nothing appealed more to Tom than Martha's love of music and her accomplishments as a musician. The two spent many happy hours together during the autumn of 1771.

Martha liked Jefferson's consideration for other people; it didn't matter whether they were slaves or plantation owners. She was charmed by his manners. His ancestors had lived in the colony for three generations, and he was now the ranking official of the county. As his wife, she would have a position of dignity and responsibility, for Peter and Jane Randolph Jefferson had left their son an established place in society and the means to maintain it.

Martha admired the liberal stand that Jefferson had taken on education, religious freedom, and a law forbidding the further importation of slaves. She was entranced when he told her that from Monticello, their future home, they could see, on a clear day, the distant Blue Ridge Mountains. She looked forward to attending court days at Williamsburg, when planters and farmers flocked to the seat of government, auctions were held, and slaves and lands sold. For this was the golden age of the slave-owners.

The freeholders of Albemarle County had elected Jefferson one of their two Burgesses; that would mean a long stay in the colonial capital during the sessions. One more reason, no doubt, for marrying the brilliant young lawyer from the hill country, with the third largest practice in Virginia, was that she loved him. He had done his share of flirting, strolling through the flowery lanes of Williamsburg, and dancing with the pretty daughters of the neighboring plantations. She found consolation, however, in the fact that Jefferson never had thought seriously of marriage until he met her.

They were married at her father's plantation, The Forest; the tall, thin, freckled Jefferson and the beautiful Martha. There were festivities at her own home and at plantations along the route to Monticello. They drove up the James River Valley to the Rivanna, then rode horseback the rest of the way. Before they reached Jefferson's home, they ran into a heavy snowstorm. Arriving late at night, they found no fire burning and no supper. The servants were asleep in their quarters, so the bridal pair made the best of the situation. Martha's constitution was not very rugged, but she considered her chill homecoming as something which one might expect on the frontier, and made a joke of it.

On their wedding day, January 1, 1772, Martha was twenty-three, and Jefferson six years her senior. He brought his bride to a simple brick building with parlor, kitchen, hall, bed-chamber, and study all in one. Jefferson was an important public figure, with responsibilities and a legal practice that often required his presence at Williamsburg, but he was able to spend a great deal of time at home. Martha was impressed when her husband's political views were sought by members of the House of Burgesses who were twenty or thirty years his senior. Her husband was at the height of his private fortune and personal happiness, and she looked forward to the time when his integrity, his enduring friendships among the solid citizens of Virginia, his unquestioned patriotism, and the clarity and forcefulness of his ideas would become the priceless heritage of their children.

Martha's father, a wealthy and influential member of the

Tidewater aristocracy, died not long after her marriage, leaving her considerable property. He had believed that young women should be useful as well as ornamental. His daughter was therefore taught to write a neat hand and to keep accurate accounts of plantation receipts and expenditures.

In the years that followed her marriage to Jefferson, Martha was to learn over and over again that life was not easy. Within nine years she bore five children, two of whom did not survive. Jefferson adored her, and she was spared hard physical labor, but he did not seem to realize that Martha was not the healthy, rugged, childbearer that his mother had been. Four of their six children died in infancy or childhood.

Martha had known from the beginning that her husband was a genius. Now he was engaged in drawing the plans for Monticello, the most elegant mansion in all Virginia. He was a musician, an architect, and a landscape gardener. He could sew up a wound, tie an artery, or set the broken leg of a slave. He was a mathematician, and had invented, among other things, a plow that won a gold medal at a French exposition. He had built the first section of his house and laid out the grounds; and no doubt much of the income from her estate, over a period of years, helped to pay the cost.

Her husband had strong principles and convictions, as he demonstrated in writing a pamphlet, "A Summary View of the Rights of British America." Jefferson, in this outspoken bit of logic, maintained that the American colonies had a right to govern themselves, through their own legislatures. She was proud and grateful when the oldest and wisest of the Virginia legislators depended upon the soundness of her husband's judgment and delegated him to write a reply to the British Prime Minister on the question of taxation without representation. He quickly became a national figure. When in March, 1775, a convention was called at Richmond, Jefferson was a delegate. It was here that his old friend, Patrick Henry, demanded action in these inspired words:

"Is life so dear or peace so sweet as to be purchased at the price of chains and slavery? *No! We must fight!* I know not what course others may take, but as for me, *give me liberty or give me death!*"

Martha remained at home while these stirring events were taking place. She kissed her husband good-by when he left for the convention in Philadelphia, and she was not greatly surprised when he was chosen to write the Declaration of Independence. Martha was not well at the time, and he returned to Monticello as quickly as possible after the convention adjourned—only to be recalled in September. He returned to the plantation in December. In May of the following year, duty called him to Philadelphia, and Martha was left to cope with a number of serious problems—the British attempt to lure the slaves into their camp, the shortage of crops, and inflation.

She sat in the bedroom and knitted, after Jefferson's return, while he prepared arguments for the separation of church and state in Virginia. His "office" was the alcove of their bedroom. In it he drafted his educational bills, setting forth the conviction that free government depends on knowledge and its dissemination among the masses of the people. His hostility to the combination of church and state, it should be explained, did not indicate a prejudice against either Catholics or Protestants; he fought to break the strangle-hold of the Church of England on the liberties of the conscience.

Jefferson had long been concerned about his wife's failing

health; it was one of the reasons for his retirement from Congress. He was constantly being asked to return to public life, but he always declined. Once he was offered an appointment to France; and at another time the honor of representing Virginia in Congress. He did, however, agree to serve as governor of his state in 1779, since he could then take his family to Richmond, the capital. Thus he was able to inaugurate reforms in the archaic laws of Virginia; and to find arms, men, money, and provisions for Washington's army.

The army never had enough of these necessities, however, and the British eventually advanced on Richmond. The Governor and his family were obliged to flee to Charlottesville. This ordeal, together with the birth of another child, drained Martha Jefferson's strength; she never quite recovered from it. During the weeks of her final illness, in the summer of 1782, Jefferson sat constantly at her bedside or at his writing table in the bedroom alcove. No matter what happened in the world, his place was at her side; her name was etched on his heart.

On September 6, 1782, Jefferson made this entry in his book: "My dear wife died this day at 11:45 A. M." At his death, 44 years later, locks of hair and other little souvenirs of his wife and each of his children, both living and dead, with words of endearment written in his own hand, were found in a secret drawer of a cabinet. Jefferson never married again, although he was a man who craved affection and attention.

After his wife's death, "Little Martha" became his constant companion. When finally he agreed to go on a government mission to France, he took Martha and her younger sister, Maria, with him. On returning to the United States to become Washington's Secretary of State, Jefferson left his two daughters at Monticello. Both were married when still in their teens, and only once did they pay their father, then President of the United States, a long visit. When Martha lost her husband, however, she and her six children went to live at the President's House in Washington. Meanwhile, Maria had passed on.

When Jefferson retired from the Presidency, after eight years in office, he took Martha and her children back to Monticello. The house had been enlarged from time to time, and now it was usually filled with visitors. People from all parts of the world wanted to meet and talk with the great Jefferson. For seventeen years, until he died, Martha was a devoted daughter, extending graciously the Virginia hospitality for which her father and mother had always been famous.

It would have pleased the elder Martha, had she lived, to know that he was the leader of his political party for a quarter of a century; that he was the mentor of Madison and Monroe, who followed him in office; that he became, in turn, minister to France and Secretary of State; that he insisted that the Constitution of the United States contain a Bill of Rights, and himself offered the first ten amendments; that, with the aid of John Adams, he negotiated a loan with The Netherlands which saved the credit of our new nation; that as President of the United States he purchased the immense empire of Louisiana, thus doubling the territory of the new nation; that both the loan and the purchase were consummated without the sanction of Congress; and that he sent Lewis and Clark on their expedition to Oregon.

On a simple shaft under a grand old oak at Monticello, where Jefferson was buried, his major achievements are set forth in his own words. He does not record that he was governor, foreign envoy, Vice President or President of the United States, or sponsor of the Louisiana Purchase. The three things which he wished the world to remember were that he wrote the Declaration of Independence, was the author of the statute for religious freedom in Virginia, and the founder of the University of Virginia. He might also have added that he was largely responsible for the design and the location at Charlottesville of one of the finest and most appropriate groups of buildings in the United States.

The list of his achievements is too long to record here. But we may be sure of one thing: Martha Wayles Jefferson would have been proud of him, had she lived.

Dolley Payne Todd Madison

MOST POPULAR FIRST LADY

NOT the slightest sound disturbed the Sabbath morning quiet within the Pine Street Meeting House. Not a flower or an ornament relieved the severe simplicity of its bare walls. At one side of the center aisle, on the long wooden benches, sat the women, stiffly straight-backed in their drab gowns and snow-white kerchiefs, their faces almost hidden by deep-scooped Quaker bonnets. On the other side, in their gray cloaks and breeches, sat the men. Both men and women were as motionless, almost, as those who rested in the unmarked graves of the Friends' Burying Ground beyond the dooryard.

Dolley Payne, fifteen, had not moved in more than an hour. She sat beside her mother and realized that she, too, ought to be meditating. Without meaning to do so, Dolley moved a restive foot under her long, wide skirt, and an old board creaked. A deeper scarlet mounted in her rosy cheeks. Her blue eyes flashed with mischief under their long black lashes. Her thoughts wandered, and she sighed. Why did a religious ceremony have to be so long?

In that year of 1783, Philadelphia was the most important city in the American colonies. To the Quaker girl from the backwoods of North Carolina, now almost a young lady, it seemed incredible that thirty thousand people could be crowded into one city. The neat brick houses, she thought, with their spotless white doorsteps and the shutters on the ground-floor windows, were very elegant. She even enjoyed scrubbing the steps of her mother's house, for then she could watch the parade of the beautiful ladies in silks and satins, and the gentlemen on their spirited horses.

Dolley had been schooled in the strict rules of conduct of

the Quaker faith, but she was anything but a Quaker at heart. She was as gay and lively a personality as ever lived. She longed for fine laces and jewels, even as she scrubbed the steps; she hoped that one of these days her mother would consider her grown-up, so she could have a beau. She hated the drab clothes and plain bonnets of the Quaker women. She wanted to dance, and laugh, and sing. She wanted to know the feel of silk next to her skin, and the smell of rich perfume. Yet Dolley was not an unhappy child, for always she lived in a colorful world of her own.

It had been so ever since she first opened her blue eyes to the pioneer life of the Friends in North Carolina. John Payne, her father, and other Quakers had settled among the New Garden group, and there Dolley was born on May 20, 1768. She was named Dolley (with an e)—not Dolly, nor Dorothy, nor Dorothea. That was the way her birth was entered on the records and in the family Bible; it was the way she signed her letters. It was so written on her marriage certificate, and so carved on her tombstone.

The Paynes left North Carolina when Dolley was less than a year old, and took the wagon trail to Virginia. Her childhood was spent happily on a small plantation, presided over by her busy mother and a faithful Negro mammy who was devoted to the little girl. Sometimes her Grandmother Coles came to visit them. Dolley was very fond of her grandmother, and very proud, in later years, of Patrick Henry, whose mother was the sister of Grandmother Coles. When Patrick Henry came to visit them, he poured hot melted butter over white fluffy popcorn, and toasted chestnuts in the fire, and they always had a candy pull.

In the spring of 1783, John Payne gave his slaves their freedom and moved to Philadelphia. Slaves brought from two hundred to twelve hundred dollars each in the market, and Payne owned fifty of them. But the Quakers were against slavery, and he realized that he could not keep slaves and remain a good Quaker.

In Philadelphia, no less a person than Thomas Jefferson called upon the Paynes; he and Dolley's mother had often ridden and danced together when they were much younger, and he had not forgotten "Molly" Coles.

The Paynes joined the Pine Street Meeting, and there Dolley met an earnest young Quaker lawyer, John Todd. It was a case of love at first sight on his part; and no doubt he persuaded Dolley that in time she would learn to love him. In any case, they were married in 1790, when she was twenty-two; her father died two years later.

John Todd was kind and considerate; he adored Dolley. And it was part of her happy disposition to adapt herself to circumstances. She was not inclined to introspection, but accepted what life brought. She was a good wife, a neat housekeeper, and a devoted mother to their little son, born two years after their marriage and named John Payne Todd. The couple were quite content in their little home on South Fourth Street.

After her father's death, Dolley's mother became the proprietress of a popular boarding house. Aaron Burr, the Senator from New York, boarded with her during the sessions of Congress, and Dolley—along with many less beautiful and more mature women—thought the dapper New Yorker was the most wonderful man she had ever met.

When a serious yellow fever epidemic struck Philadelphia, in 1793, John Todd bundled Dolley, their little boy, and the new baby off to another town, but he stayed in the city to look after his law business. It was a fatal mistake; the young

46

husband himself succumbed. Dolley also lost her baby. Dolley, with her little son and her thirteen-year-old sister Anna, returned to her home in Philadelphia. Her husband's estate was sufficient for her needs.

That winter Dolley Payne lived the retired life of the Quakers and soon recovered from her bereavement. She was a beautiful young widow, tall and statuesque, with blue eyes, dark curls, and rosy cheeks. Wherever she went, people gasped in admiration; the Quakers felt that no mortal person had a right to be so lovely.

For a time Dolley's masculine acquaintances were limited to her business and legal advisers and to Aaron Burr, who remained a good friend of the family. Dolley's heart must have skipped many a beat as she listened to his flattering remarks. The New Yorker was a widower; he was handsome, and he liked the ladies. But he was not one to tie himself down, even to the charming Widow Todd. And if Dolley ever loved him, the secret was never disclosed during her lifetime. It is, however, significant that in her will she named Aaron Burr as the sole guardian of her only child.

In one way or another, Aaron Burr exerted a tremendous influence in the young widow's life. For it was he who brought James Madison to call one evening. Madison was the young friend and political protégé of Thomas Jefferson, Washington's first Secretary of State and minister to France. Since Thomas Jefferson was one of her mother's old beaux, Dolley was quite flattered when Madison asked Burr to introduce him to the Widow Todd. So, with her friend Elizabeth Collins, she received the two distinguished men in her parlor.

The candlelight shone on rubbed mahogany and polished silver. Dolley herself was radiant in her mulberry satin, white kerchief, and lace cap. Madison, who was neither tall nor impressive, was shy, but his hostess quickly put him at his ease. She found that he had a fine sense of humor and a gentle charm. He, in turn, a confirmed bachelor, was convinced that here was the woman he wanted for his wife.

Dolley hesitated. There was, for one thing, the difference in their religion. There was also the fact that her husband had been dead less than a year. Madison was forty-three, and she was not quite twenty-six. There may have been the possibility that Aaron Burr would be prodded into asking her the same question. She knew, also, that without mutual respect, real love between man and wife cannot exist; and she had the highest regard for "the great little Madison," as he was known in government circles. At the Continental Congress and among the colonies, he was hailed as the "Father of the Constitution."

Soon after Dolley met Madison, she was summoned to Martha Washington's drawing room in the Morris House, which the President and his First Lady had taken over for the duration of their stay in Philadelphia. Dolley's hostess was most cordial. Over the teacups, the first First Lady asked: "Is it true, Dolley, that you are engaged to James Madison?"

Dolley blushed and hesitated. Perhaps she was thinking: *How did Martha hear the news so quickly—unless James himself asked her to intercede for him?*

"If it is true," Martha Washington went on, "don't be ashamed to confess it." Both she and the President, she assured her visitor, held Madison in the highest esteem, and she personally was sure that he would make Dolley a good husband.

Whether Dolley Payne Todd was actuated by her admiration and respect for James Madison; by the urgent protestations of Madison himself; or the approval of the President and his wife, may never be known. There was a rather re-markable similarity of temperament, and both Dolley and James had active and inquiring minds. She complemented Madison, who was small, serious, and once had studied for the ministry. He neither danced nor talked well, and he had little exterior charm of manner. He had been physically un-fit for military duty during the Revolutionary War. Now he needed someone with Dolley's overflowing charm and genu-ine interest in people. They looked on each other with eyes of mutual devotion. She may not have conceived a romantic passion for Madison, but she cherished a warm, sincere af-fection which lasted all his life. In the years to come, she was destined to win political victories over the tea table and the dinner table; to help her husband through many an un-pleasant political situation by making friends with his enemies and winning over their wives. One of the most charming things about Dolley was her devotion to Madison's mother, who lived at the plantation, Montpellier, to the age of ninety-seven.

Madison and Dolley (as everyone called her) were married at her sister's home by an Episcopal clergyman on Septem-ber 15, 1794. Dolley was, of course, "read out of" the Pine Street Meeting, but that did not seem to worry her; now she would be free to live her own life.

They drove in their coach to the family home in Orange County, Virginia, and spent a month with Madison's parents. Then they returned to Philadelphia for the session of Con-gress. Dolley's position in Philadelphia society was assured: was she not sponsored by no less a personage than President Washington's First Lady? Was she not also the wife of the "great little Madison"?

It was a magnificent Dolley who blossomed in this gay

social atmosphere. Except for morning use in her own home, she put away the drab garments of the Quakers. Then, powdered and curled, rustling in heavy silks, her laughing face framed by laces and ribbons, young Mrs. Madison lunched and dined and went to the levees and balls that were so popular during that period.

After three years there came a change of administration, and Dolley and James Madison returned to a quiet life at Montpellier. Both missed the stimulation and excitement which they had found in the capital city, but they adjusted themselves happily to the placid existence of plantation owners. From the beginning, Dolley was a great favorite of Madison's mother. But both were overjoyed when their friend Thomas Jefferson took office as President in 1801, and appointed Madison his Secretary of State.

During the previous administration, the capital had been moved to the new site on the banks of the Potomac River. So it was to Washington that the couple journeyed by coach. Jefferson received them warmly. He had been Madison's preceptor in politics and the law; and he and Dolley's mother had grown up in the same part of Virginia. So, as President Jefferson expressed it, Dolley was like a daughter to him.

Since the President and Vice President Aaron Burr were widowers, the wife of the Secretary of State was the logical person to act as hostess in the President's House. Unlike Martha Washington and Abigail Adams, Dolley Madison thoroughly enjoyed the prospect of presiding at teas, dinners, balls, and receptions. During Jefferson's two terms, with the exception of short periods when his daughters visited him, Dolley Madison was the hostess at all state functions. On New Year's Day and July 4th, the President's House threw open its doors to the general public. When the President was at his Virginia plantation, Monticello, the real center of Washington social life was the Pennsylvania Avenue home of James and Dolley Madison. There, rival senators, Cabinet members, and foreign diplomats met in the most informal manner.

Dolley was always tastefully dressed. The period called for short waists, narrow skirts, gold-leaf hair bands, turbans, ringlets, scarves, reticules, and jewelry. There was also, of course, Dolley's gold and enamel snuffbox! The offer of her snuffbox, she discovered, saved many an awkward moment. She ignored all controversy on political questions, and devoted herself to carrying on the tradition of Jefferson— warmth and friendliness, greeting everyone who came to the Wednesday receptions, and passing from one guest to another. Looking out of the windows, she could see the squalid little town, still in the process of building, sprawling on the banks of the Potomac, with pigs in the puddles and cows and goats grazing along the "streets."

We may be sure that while she was dispensing hospitality, Dolley Madison was not unmindful of her husband's best interests. Nor, for that matter, was she unmindful of her own, which were inextricably linked with those of James. When, at the end of his second term, Jefferson declined to run again, Dolley redoubled her efforts to put her husband's best political foot forward. She smiled at the right people and was seen everywhere. Foreign diplomats agreed that she would be an ornament to any court in Europe. She was beautiful, gay, witty, clever, charming. Political alliances for "the great little Madison" grew stronger as Dolley's warm friendliness and tact won over senators, representatives, and governors.

Madison richly deserved to be called the "Father of the Constitution." He could not be called an orator, yet he was an agreeable, eloquent, and convincing speaker. With the backing of Dolley and Jefferson, he was elected. Madison took the oath of office on March 4, 1809, and a week later he and his wife moved into the President's House. Dolley soon took over the job of renovating the interior, with the aid of the architect of the Capitol and the five thousand dollars which Congress had appropriated for the purpose. At her first levee, two months later, a thousand candles lighted the house. The Marine Band, in their scarlet uniforms, played sprightly music. Later, at a state dinner, she surprised her guests with a dessert new to the colonies—ice cream. Still later, she dumbfounded Washington by being driven through the streets in a chariot, built in Philadelphia at a cost of fifteen hundred dollars and drawn by four matched horses. She spent money freely, but this gave her husband a certain satisfaction. For the inauguration ball, he had presented her with pearls, and these were her only jewels. Madison himself, pale, thin, and retiring by nature, enjoyed seeing his Dolley the center of interest; he was quite content to remain in the background.

Some historians have given Dolley credit for introducing ice cream into the United States, but she never claimed that distinction. She knew that Martha Washington had served it at Mount Vernon and that Thomas Jefferson had obtained the recipe in France, carefully copied it in his own hand, and brought it home with him years before.

Dolley's one real worry was her son, John Payne Todd. Like his mother, the young man was sociable by nature; he enjoyed the gay whirl in the capital. But he had none of his mother's stability. He could have gone to Princeton, but he was too lazy to study. Lacking any sense of responsibility, Payne Todd apparently had no intention of trying to earn a living. The money which Madison gave him slipped through his fingers. It seemed to his mother that he was always in debt. One wonders how he could have been so unlike the plodding, honest, straightforward Quaker lawyer, John Todd.

President Madison had his worries, too. He had struggled to carry on Jefferson's peace policy and thus avoid an open conflict with England. He knew that the United States was not prepared to go to war with the greatest naval power in the world. He was determined to keep clear of foreign entanglements, as George Washington had advised; to maintain a position of neutrality and leave England and France to fight their own battles. But this was not easy. Both British and French naval officers preyed upon the ships and trade of American citizens. The two European nations were waging a war on commerce; both were on the lookout for munitions cargoes and blockade runners. Often British officers would halt an American ship on the high seas, search the vessel, and carry off sailors who, they claimed, were deserters from the British Navy.

Many American citizens—and the "war party" in Congress —wanted to declare war on Great Britain, but Madison hoped that the ends he sought could be gained at less cost by peaceful measures. This was a vain hope; on June 18, 1812, the President approved an Act of Congress declaring war against Great Britain. Thereupon, to the extreme satisfaction of Dolley, he was re-elected for a second term. Some critics of the administration, in fact, referred to the conflict as "Mrs. Madison's war."

In the summer of 1814, a British fleet entered Chesapeake Bay and put ashore a large landing party. They routed the opposing American forces, advanced on Washington, and burned the Capitol, the Library of Congress, the President's

53

House, and other buildings. At the time, Madison was away on a tour of inspection of American troops. When news reached Dolley that the British were marching on Washington, she was practically alone in the house with the servants. She proceeded methodically to collect her husband's papers; and, while waiting for couriers to bring her news of the enemy and for her husband's return, she calmly wrote a letter, vividly describing the situation, to her sister:

Tuesday, August 23rd, 1814.

"My dear Sister:

My husband left me yesterday to join General Winder . . . I have since received two dispatches from him . . . he desires that I should be ready at a moment's warning to enter my carriage and leave the city . . . I am accordingly ready; I have pressed as many Cabinet Papers into trunks as will fill one carriage; our private property must be sacrificed, as it is impossible to procure wagons for its transportation. I am determined not to go myself until I see Mr. Madison safe. . . .

"My friends and acquaintances are all gone—even Colonel C, with his hundred men, who was stationed as a guard. . . . French John [Sioussat, a loyal servant], with his usual activity and resolution, offers to spike the cannon at the gates, and to lay a train of powder which would blow up the British should they enter the house . . .

"Wednesday, 3 o'clock . . . We have had a battle near Bladensburg [Maryland], and I am still here, within sound of the cannon! Mr. Madison comes not; may God protect him! Two messengers, covered with dust, bid me fly; but I wait for him. . . . At this late hour a wagon has been procured; I have had it filled with the plate and most valuable portable articles belonging to the house . . .

"Our kind friend, Mr. Carroll, has come to hasten my departure, and is in a very bad humor with me because I insist on waiting until the large picture of General Washington is secured, and it requires to be unscrewed from the wall. This process was found to be too tedious for these perilous moments; I have [therefore] ordered the frame to be broken, and the canvas taken out; it is done—and the precious portrait placed in the hands of two gentlemen from New York for safe keeping.

"And now, dear sister, I must leave this house . . . When I shall see or write you, or where I shall be tomorrow, I cannot tell."

The original Declaration of Independence, framed and placed in a glass case, was taken along, as were some silver spoons from the dining room. Dolley bundled her Negro maid into the wagon, and they were driven off toward Georgetown. Both were dressed in clothing such as a farmer's wife and a servant would wear. They were accompanied by a civilian and a soldier, both armed but dressed like the humble beings they seemed to be. The roads were choked by the exodus from the burning city.

As Dolley left by one road, the enemy entered the capital by another. She spent the first night in a tent at a refugee camp, gazing out at the burning ships in the Navy Yard, destroyed by order of the Secretary of the Navy to prevent them from being captured by the enemy. The next day the party crossed the Potomac by the chain bridge into Virginia. Dolley and her maid found refuge in a house, and on Friday night the President himself turned up, along with several Cabinet members. No doubt he realized that his wife's quick decision and her bravery in carrying it out not only had saved the Declaration of Independence, the Stuart portrait of Washington, and some silverware, but also the invaluable records of his entire public career.

Three days after the enemy left Washington, the government returned. Of the many houses offered to the homeless Madisons, Dolley chose to live temporarily in that of Colonel John Tayloe. It was there, on the night of September 13, that Francis Scott Key came and asked to see the President. Madison, at his wife's request, gave Key permission to ask the British Admiral then attacking Fort McHenry to release a friend, a Dr. Beane.

Key watched the bombardment that night from the deck of the enemy ship, and when morning came he was so happy to see the American flag still flying that he sat on the deck and wrote the words to the "Star-Spangled Banner"—which became, in time, the national anthem of the United States. Without Dolley Madison's intercession, it is quite possible that the "Star-Spangled Banner" never would have been written.

Madison shrank from the task of rebuilding the devastated capital. He wanted to move the seat of government back to Philadelphia. His wife persuaded him to change his mind. It was unthinkable, she declared, that we should let the British drive the government out of the site chosen by George Washington for the nation's capital. Here we have another example of the influence that the wives of the Presidents have exerted upon them in the discharge of their official duties.

Within three years a new Executive Mansion was built on the site of the original structure. The blackened walls were painted white to cover all traces of the fire, under the direction of James Hoban, the original architect. People began calling it "The White House."

Meanwhile, Dolley Madison entertained lavishly at Octagon House, Colonel Tayloe's unique residence of imported brick at New York Avenue and Eighteenth Street. On the evening of February 14, 1815, her drawing room was crowded with guests when Henry Carroll, secretary of the American envoys at Ghent, arrived with the startling—and most welcome—news, seven weeks after the signing of a peace treaty, that the war with Great Britain was over. Peace had come just in time to save Madison's administration. He signed the treaty, then and there, in the Oval Room on the second floor.

In October the Madisons moved to the corner of Nineteenth Street and Pennsylvania Avenue, where they remained until the end of Madison's second term in March, 1817. The President was thin, pale, and worn to a shadow by his duties and responsibilities; Dolley was, if possible, a more striking figure than ever. She seemed to thrive on excitement. Throughout the nation, people talked of her bravery and resourcefulness during the war and of her coolness and good judgment. The Washington of 1817 was a bustling town, compared to the village which the Madisons had entered sixteen years before. Now there were actually streets and sidewalks.

John Payne Todd, Dolley's son, had failed in everything he had tried. But he did his mother—and the nation—one good turn when he told her that the children of ancient Egypt used to roll hard-boiled eggs, decorated in gay colors, against the base of the Pyramids. They had no Pyramids in Washington; but the Capitol grounds did have a nice lawn. So Dolley

Madison, wife of the President of the United States, with her own hands dyed hundreds of hard-boiled eggs and invited the children of Washington to an egg-rolling on the Monday after Easter. The youngsters came in droves, and the custom was continued through one administration after another, until egg-rolling in the nation's capital on Easter Monday became an American institution.

By the time James Monroe was elected President, Madison was a tired old man, eager to settle down at Montpellier and spend the rest of his days on the old plantation. Dolley regretted having to leave her friends and the gay life of the capital, but she cheerfully accepted the inevitable. The many visitors who came to Montpellier enlivened her rather monotonous existence. She was kept busy caring for her ailing husband and his 85-year-old mother. In 1829, at the age of 97, Madison's mother died; and the following year Dolley lost her sister.

She was now her husband's companion, nurse, and secretary. She read to him to spare his failing sight, wrote his letters, and even dressed and powdered his thinning hair. As rheumatism crippled him more and more, she waited upon him constantly. The years had developed in her a sincere affection for this quiet little man; it was mainly due to her tender care that he lived to be eighty-five.

Like his preceptor, Jefferson, Madison was almost bankrupt when he died. Sadly, the former First Lady returned to Washington to live. Sometimes it was necessary for her to borrow money, but she insisted upon living well. Her son's lavish spending caused her great distress; he seemed to be always in debt. Congress, as a special honor, voted her the franking privilege. She also was voted a seat on the floor of the House of Representatives, a distinction which had never before been granted a woman.

Her hair was white now, and wrinkles were difficult to hide, but Dolley Madison was still a distinguished figure. Her house, on the northeast corner of Lafayette Square, is still known as the Dolley Madison House. Here, within sight of the White House, she spent the last twelve years of her life. She had presided over, or been active in, Washington society for nearly half a century; her "reign" saw eleven Presidents of the United States come and go: Washington, John Adams, Jefferson, her own "little Madison," Monroe, John Quincy Adams, Jackson, Van Buren, Harrison, Tyler, and Polk. One of the greatest statesmen in American history chose her, from among all women, for his wife. Her prodigious contributions to the Jefferson-Madison political era are without parallel in our history. As our most popular and most glamorous First Lady, her place in history is secure.

Dolley Madison died on July 12, 1849. She was buried in the Congressional Cemetery; six years later her body was removed to Montpellier and laid beside that of James Madison.

Elizabeth Kortright Monroe

BELLE OF NEW YORK

THE picture we have of Elizabeth Kortright Monroe, wife of the fifth President of the United States, is not as clearly etched in history as those of her predecessors. It has been written that she was "a serene and aristocratic woman, too well bred to be visibly moved by anything —at least in public." Yet one individual act which highlighted her career establishes the fact that she had spirit and courage, as well as a tender heart. She was only 26 years old at the time, which was 1795; the place: a prison in Paris.

All of France, in those stormy days following the French Revolution, was in the grip of a reign of terror, as one group of radicals after another seized power. King Louis XVI had been put to death in January, 1793; in the autumn of that same year Queen Marie Antoinette was borne to the scaffold. Robespierre was executed. Lafayette had escaped across the border, and was in mild exile in Germany. When James Monroe, the American minister, and his wife arrived in Paris in 1794, they were shocked to learn that Madame Lafayette was being held at Le Petit Force prison, momentarily expecting that she would be put to death.

The indignities she suffered at the hands of the terrorists incensed James and Elizabeth Monroe, to whom the very name of Lafayette was sacred. As American minister, Monroe realized he had no right to interfere in the internal affairs of France, and he knew it would be dangerous to antagonize the forces then in power. Eliza, though she was young and inexperienced in foreign diplomacy, understood her husband's position; but she could not rest until something was done to rescue the wife of the beloved general. So the young couple made a plan, which probably was Eliza's idea.

A few days later the carriage of the American minister drove up with a flourish at the entrance of Le Petit Force prison. In the carriage, elegantly dressed, her figure stiffly erect, sat Elizabeth Monroe. While her liveried footman climbed down from his box, she sat quietly. She wanted to make certain that the prison guards who rushed forward recognized the official shield of the United States emblazoned on her carriage door. Her cheeks were flooded with color, but her violet eyes were serene and her voice was firm as she stepped out and demanded, in flawless French, to see Madame Lafayette.

The insolence of the guards changed to awe. Almost at once she was escorted to the cell of the prisoner, who was overcome with emotion when she saw that her visitor was not a messenger sent to lead her to execution, but a friend, an American. Quickly, in a whisper, Eliza Monroe explained her mission: Her husband was powerless to take direct action, but they hoped their concern for Madame Lafayette would impress the French government. Surely, the visit of the wife of the American minister would not pass unnoticed, and it was but a small gesture to show the gratitude of the United States to the great Lafayette!

The plan worked. A few days later, thanks to Eliza Monroe, the French government, as a mark of friendship for our country, released Madame Lafayette.

As for Eliza Monroe, the incident served to make her more and more popular in Paris. Wherever her husband and she appeared, "la belle Américaine" was greeted with cheers and noisy applause.

Eliza had been called "the Belle of New York" long before Paris hailed her as "la belle Américaine." She was born in New York city in 1768. Her paternal ancestors had arrived in

America from Holland more than a century before, their name then being Van Kortryk. Eliza's father, Lawrence Kortright, was a retired officer of the British army and was regarded as a mild Tory. Following the Revolutionary War (during which he lost much of his fortune) Captain Kortright decided to cast his lot with the colonies and became a loyal American. He was one of the founders of the New York Chamber of Commerce.

Friends were always warmly welcomed at the Kortright home on lower Broadway, and Eliza in her teens found life gay and amusing. Many of the most socially prominent young men in town were attracted by the aristocratic, talented Miss Kortright, and her acquaintances were sure she would make a brilliant marriage. Then, when she was eighteen, Eliza fell in love, and New York society buzzed with the news that she had consented to marry the "not particularly attractive Virginia Congressman, James Monroe."

Monroe knew the moment he met her that Eliza Kortright was the girl he wanted to marry. They were soon seen everywhere together—at dances, on sleigh-riding parties, and on picnics at the Battery. Under date of March 2, 1786, Monroe wrote to his uncle:

> "On Thursday I was united to the young lady I mentioned. To avoid idle ceremonies of the place, we withdrew into the country for a few days. We have been several days since returned to her father's house, since which I have as usual attended Congress."

James and Elizabeth must have made a handsome couple. She was eighteen, and he was twenty-eight. She was beautiful, with glossy black hair and violet-blue eyes; he was fair with light brown hair, and gray eyes which one critic of the period described as having "more kindness than penetration." She was slender and tall, but James was taller. Lean and erect, with soldierly bearing, he was just short of six feet.

Eliza was tremendously proud of her husband, who had crowded so much experience into his twenty-eight years. While still in his teens at William and Mary College, he had put aside his books to join Washington's army of volunteers. He had fought in most of the important battles; had been wounded in the battle of Trenton, and had spent a starving, freezing winter with the troops at Valley Forge. At twenty-two, he was studying law with Thomas Jefferson. Two years later he was a member of the Governor's Council, and before he was twenty-six he was a member of the Congress of the United States.

On his uncle's advice, the young couple decided to settle in Fredericksburg, and it was to his uncle's house that they went to live when his term in Congress ended. Eliza loved Virginia. She felt even more at home there than she did in New York. In Fredericksburg in 1787, their first daughter was born and Monroe wrote his friend Thomas Jefferson on July 27th: "Mrs. Monroe hath added a daughter to our society who tho' noisy, contributes greatly to its amusement."

In that same year, Monroe was elected to the Virginia legislature, and sent to the Constitutional Convention. Two years later he became a United States Senator, and on May 27, 1794, Eliza was tremendously excited over his appointment as minister to France. Neither she nor their little daughter was seasick on the forty-five-day voyage by sailing ship from Baltimore to Paris. It was on this visit to the French capital that Eliza Monroe was instrumental in securing the freedom of Madame Lafayette.

As Eliza was a favorite with the French people, so also was her husband. They liked him and he liked them. He showed so openly where his sympathies lay, in fact, that England complained to the United States, and he was recalled.

In 1803, however, after serving as governor of Virginia, Monroe was again sent to France, this time by Thomas Jefferson, who had succeeded John Adams as President. Monroe was to negotiate with France for the purchase of the isle of New Orleans; and Spain for the purchase of the Spanish territory east of the Mississippi.

The Monroes, with their two daughters, became at home in most of the courts of Europe. It was a happier, gayer Paris than Eliza had known on her previous visit. With her daughter Eliza in school at St. Germain, Mrs. Monroe often stayed in the lovely suburb on the banks of the Seine and enjoyed the French countryside. But when they went to London, Eliza longed desperately for home. Her calls on the ladies of the British court were not even returned; she suffered from rheumatism which seemed to occur more and more often in the fog and chill of London. To Eliza, England was unpleasant exile. No wonder she longed desperately for home! But it was years later, in December, 1807, before they finally returned to the United States.

Again James Monroe served in the Virginia legislature; again he was elected governor. Before the end of his term, he was summoned by President Madison to become his Secretary of State, and later to act also as Secretary of War.

Eliza yearned for peace and quiet and for the leisurely life of Virginia, but her husband was to assume a still higher office before they could retire to their home in the Blue Ridge

Mountains. In 1816, James Monroe was elected President of the United States.

Eliza Monroe was well fitted for the position of First Lady. Her years of entertaining and being entertained abroad in the most stately court circles had supplemented the social graces in which she had been trained as a girl. Though middle-aged, she was still a strikingly handsome woman. Ever since her marriage she had adjusted herself completely to the public life of her husband. She had adopted his politicial beliefs and ambitions; her patriotism matched his own. Because she loved him devotedly, she was eager to be known as a daughter of Virginia, his native state.

As First Lady she was unfortunate in following into the White House the lovable, energetic, and extremely popular Dolley Madison, who thoroughly enjoyed dinner parties, receptions, and balls. It would have been a difficult assignment for any woman. For Eliza Monroe, at the beginning of her husband's term of office, it must have seemed almost unendurable. She was often ill, and at such times her married daughter, Eliza Hay, appeared in her stead. Young Eliza was not as diplomatic as her mother. Accomplished, good looking, and educated abroad, the attitude of *grande dame* which had fitted the daughter of the American minister in France was resented by Washington society. Some historians say that the ladies began by boycotting Mrs. Monroe and her daughters, and that more than once the White House drawing rooms opened to empty chairs.

The First Lady increased her unpopularity by getting together with Mrs. John Quincy Adams, whose husband was then Secretary of State, on the matter of social precedence. Mrs. Monroe would neither pay calls nor return them; Mrs. Adams would return visits but would not pay first visits to anyone, regardless of importance. The two women were widely criticized at the time, but their firm decision established a social pattern that saved much time and energy for those who succeeded them.

Mrs. Monroe's first big task was to refurnish the White House. Almost destroyed by the British during the War of 1812, it was not completely in order when the Monroes moved in. Using her own furniture, silver, and various treasures picked up abroad, and ordering quantities of additional items from France (all of which the government later bought), the First Lady redecorated the Executive Mansion with a lavish hand. When it was thrown open to the public on New Year's Day, 1818, the hundreds of guests gasped with admiration at its splendor. Rooms and halls were blazing with candlelight which gleamed on massive mahogany, delicately carved French furniture, bronze ornaments, exquisite crystal chandeliers, and draperies and upholsteries of silk and brocade; along with expensive paintings, ornate clocks, and other objects of art. Against this magnificent background, Elizabeth Monroe moved majestically among her guests. Now fifty, and looking much younger, she was handsome in shimmering satin, pearls, and a plumed turban. White House society was impressed; the First Lady's reception was a success.

The younger daughter of the Monroes, Maria Hester, was the first daughter of a President to be married in the White House. At a quiet ceremony performed before a small group of relatives and close friends, she was married to Samuel L. Gouverneur of New York in 1820.

In that same year, James Monroe was re-elected with only one dissenting vote, this being cast for John Quincy Adams so that only Washington might have the distinction of unanimous election. Monroe's administration was designated the "era of good feeling." He secured Florida from Spain; took a strong stand for protective tariffs; and proclaimed to the world, in what became known as the Monroe Doctrine, that the United States would never tolerate "an attempt by any European nation to reduce an independent nation of North or South America to the condition of a colony." He also arranged to set aside each year money for reducing the national debt; he began a system of roads, canals, and other improvements; re-established the Bank of the United States; held out the hand of friendship to the Indians; and encouraged settlement of the West by selling the public lands to settlers at a fair price.

Eliza was proud of his achievements as Chief Executive; she was proud of his honesty and fairness. She knew that he might have been elected for a third term, but she was relieved when he refused to run again. He was sixty-seven, his face was lined by care and responsibility. He, as well as Eliza, was eager for the seclusion of their Virginia home. "Especially on Mrs. Monroe," he said, "the cares and burdens of my long public office have borne too heavily."

Oak Hill, the plantation home which Monroe had planned for his retirement, was built while he was President. Jefferson drew the plans for the colonial mansion in the Virginia hills, and Monroe himself planted locust, poplar, and oak trees around the house. A tree from each state in the Union was presented to him by Congressmen from the various states.

It was a happy day for Eliza and the aging Monroe when they left the White House and went to live at Oak Hill. Though she was not well, she was still active. When, in the autumn of 1828, her husband fell from his horse, she nursed him back to health. Again, the following spring, when he injured his wrist, it was his loving Eliza who waited on him, read to him, and did much of his writing for him.

On September 23, 1830, she died and was buried in a vault on the Oak Hill property; and on July 4 of the following year, James Monroe passed away.

Louisa Catherine Johnson Adams

ONLY FOREIGN-BORN FIRST LADY

BEFORE little Louisa Johnson was five years old, she chattered happily—and with equal ease—in French as well as in English. This perfect command of French was to play an important part in her survival many years later, but to the child in the friendly little seafaring town of Nantes, it seemed a perfectly natural means of expression, and that was all.

Louisa Catherine was born in London on February 12, 1775. Her mother, Catherine Nuth, was English; her father, Joshua Johnson, was the London partner of an American tobacco firm. Years before he had left his native Maryland to try his fortunes in the mother country.

Joshua Johnson, the American tobacco importer, found life in England unpleasant, to say the least, during the Revolutionary War. By 1777 he was convinced that he could no longer remain in business there and retain his loyalty to the Colonies. So he took his wife and children to France and settled in Nantes. There he could speak out for the land of his birth, where other members of his family were fighting for independence. He quickly found work to do, for Congress charged him with the duty of examining the accounts of American officials in France who were handling public funds.

Exactly when Louisa met John Quincy Adams for the first time is not certain. Probably it was when she was three, and he was eleven. For to Nantes, in 1778, came John Adams, bringing with him the young son who was destined to rank high in America's history. Nantes was a port of entry, and John Adams was an important American official, doubtless the two youngsters met at the Johnson home. Whether John Quincy, a precocious lad acting as his father's secretary, bothered to notice baby Louisa is a question; but he noticed her seventeen years later!

In 1790, Louisa's father was appointed American consul in London. The home of the Johnsons lay in the shadow of the Tower of London, and this house on the hill was always filled with young folks as well as old. Soon after Louisa's twentieth birthday, when she was pretty as a picture, with brown hair, laughing eyes, and a profile as perfect as a cameo, there came to call at the consul's house a young American diplomat. And Louisa's girlish heart did cartwheels! His gallantry, his sophistication, his smart appearance, and his knowledge of the world made all her English suitors seem boring. Young John Quincy Adams was in government service, and his father was Vice President of the United States!

John Quincy was charmed by Louisa, who played the harp and the spinet while he accompanied her on the flute. She sang well, sketched well, and wrote French verse. In fact, she seemed to him everything that the wife of an Adams should be!

An early portrait shows Louisa with brown curls framing a sensitive oval face, with large dark eyes and a pleasing gentle mouth. Part English, she looked definitely American.

On July 26, 1797, John and Louisa were married. John Quincy Adams told his bride that he loved her, but that he loved his country more. That statement probably didn't worry her much, for the truth was that Louisa was the only thing in the world that John had ever refused to sacrifice to his mother's judgment. Abigail was afraid that the foreign-reared girl might not be made of the stern stuff she desired for her brilliant, beloved son. In love, however, John was not to be swayed. Much later, as he expected, Abigail Adams and her husband agreed that Louisa was all any man could desire, and more. When John Adams was a very old man he wrote: "I have come to realize that his choice of a wife was the wisest choice of his whole career."

The young couple spent a happy honeymoon in England, while John Quincy waited for his next appointment. It came, and off to Berlin he went with his bride, as the first American minister to Prussia. There in April, 1801, Louisa's first son was born, and they named him George Washington. Then, when the baby was only a few weeks old, John Quincy Adams was recalled. Louisa was to see America at last!

After a fifty-eight-day voyage, they landed at Philadelphia. John took his wife at once to Washington, where she had a happy family reunion; her father was now Commissioner of Stamps in the nation's capital. There Louisa and her baby stayed for a visit while her husband went home to New England. A week later he returned for his family, and Abigail Adams took her new daughter and grandson to her heart.

Boston, as Louisa first saw it, was a town of wooden houses and cobbled streets which were unlighted at night. Life in America must have seemed very strange in those days to the young woman who had been born and brought up abroad. Years later, Henry Adams wrote that "try as she might, the Madam could never be a Bostonian, and it was the cross of her life."

On the fourth of July, 1803, a second son, John Quincy Adams, Jr., was born. The following autumn U.S. Senator Adams moved his family to Washington. There Louisa found plenty of social life, but she must have had her problems. Her husband—blunt, sometimes domineering, and stubborn in his dealings with political adversaries—made many enemies. He was unyielding and a poor mixer; his fiery integrity would not allow him to give up his independence of thought and action to the Federalists or to any other party. Louisa admired him for that; through the rest of his life she knew he would suffer for his uncompromising honesty, and she would stand by him proudly. There was a gentler side to John Quincy Adams, too, which Louisa knew well. She was in Boston on her thirty-second birthday, but her husband, then in Washington, was not too busy with politics to send her a special poem in honor of the occasion:

To LOUISA

"Friend of my bosom! Wouldst thou know
How, far from thee, the days I spend,
And how the passing moments flow,
To this short, simple tale attend."

The next stanzas told in rhyme how he rose early and went about his work; but the last three verses showed conclusively that his thoughts were always with his beloved family:

"As eve approaches, I ascend
And hours of solitude ensue;
To public papers I attend,
Or write, my bosom's friend, to you.

I see the partner of my soul,
I hear my darling children play;
Before me, fairy visions roll
And steal me from myself away . . .

Louisa! Thus remote from thee,
Still something to each joy is wanting
While thy affection can to me
Make the most dreary scene enchanting."

No doubt that tender message made Louisa hurry back to Washington and her social duties there. She and her husband were on excellent terms with President Jefferson and his family; they dined often at the White House. Then when James Madison was elevated to the Presidency, he named John Quincy to another high diplomatic post: minister to Russia. At the age of fourteen, Adams had been Minister Dana's secretary for a year; now he was going back to the land of the czar. By this time, Louisa had a third son—Charles Francis Adams, born in August, 1807.

Leaving the two older boys in Grandma Abigail's capable hands, Mr. and Mrs. John Quincy Adams and little Charles Francis sailed for Russia. At last, after a stormy voyage of two and a half months, they landed in St. Petersburg. Soon afterward Louisa Johnson Adams made her curtsies to the Empress Elizabeth and the mother of the czar. Both Mr. and Mrs. Adams were received cordially by Alexander I, but there were times when Louisa thought she could not bear to stay in Russia another day.

In the bitter cold of winter, she was obliged to huddle beside her charcoal brazier and paste strips of paper over the cracks in their draughty house to keep out the icy winds. Cooking arrangements were complicated. There were servants to bargain with and direct in a language of which she knew nothing; bathing and toilet facilities were crude compared to those in America; she rode in curious vehicles, attended churches where there were no seats, and struggled on the modest income of her husband to appear well-dressed at court functions. There were even times when she declined invitations because she felt that her appearance in an old gown might reflect upon the government which her husband represented.

Nevertheless, she enjoyed many sleighing parties, carnivals, civic fetes, Easter and May Day celebrations. There was no lack of gaiety in the lavish, jewel-and-fur-bedecked city of St. Petersburg.

Louisa and John Quincy Adams lived there for five years, and the American minister made good use of his opportunities. His correspondence with Secretary of State Monroe was lucid and convincing. It was Monroe, no doubt, who recommended to President Madison that Mr. Adams be ordered to Ghent to preside over the American Peace Commission at the end of the War of 1812. To John Quincy Adams, who had dedicated his life to public office, this was but another step in his career.

To Louisa, however, the move was heartbreaking. She had felt lonely in Russia before; with her husband gone, she was desolate. She had watched her fourth child, a girl born in this barbaric land, wilt and die after a few months. She had lost her mother, and a sister during her residence in St. Petersburg. Now she was left alone with her young son to cope, perhaps, with another Russian winter!

When at last the commissioners' names were affixed to the peace document, John Quincy sent a message to Louisa, directing her to take her official leave, close up the house, and meet him in Paris. It all sounded so simple; but it was midwinter, and two thousand miles of snow-covered roads lay between Louisa and her destination—a hazardous adventure for a lone woman and her seven-year-old boy!

Louisa's good qualities were now to be put to the test. She accepted the challenge, and thus began the most remarkable episode in her entire life. Hiring horses and a coach, she took with her a bag of gold and silver coins, and set out to travel across a disorganized Europe, devastated by war, with irresponsible soldiers on the loose, drinking, carousing, and singing their national songs. The Russian part of her journey was difficult enough, with the bitter cold. But worse trials were in store for Louisa. Her bag of gold and silver was stolen; she grew sick and faint; at Frankfurt her servants deserted her; she could not bribe them to go farther; poor little Charles Francis was terrified.

Louisa had been separated from her husband for many months; she had not seen her two older sons in America for more than six years. As she struggled desperately to continue her journey, she wondered whether she would ever see any of them again. Finally, as she drew nearer to Paris, she began to dream of reunion with her husband, but she was rudely awakened. Her carriage was surrounded by French troops, and noisy crowds, for it was rumored that Napoleon had escaped and was returning to Paris! And there sat Louisa and her little boy in a carriage which was obviously Russian, while women who hated the Cossacks shouted curses at her. Soldiers seized the horses and halted the coach. For a few moments it seemed that nothing could save Louisa and little Charles Francis. While French muskets were turned upon them and their drivers, Louisa remained calm, and her mind worked fast.

Suddenly, in the perfect French which had been almost a mother-tongue since her childhood, Louisa rose and called out in a clear, ringing voice: "Vive la France! Long live Napoleon!" Then, as the boisterous soldiers cheered, she quietly produced her credentials.

A short time later, at the Hotel du Nord in Paris, a weary but triumphant Louisa recounted her adventures to her husband. He was "perfectly astonished." Louisa Johnson Adams, like John Quincy, had accomplished her diplomatic mission! And her husband was so impressed that he asked her to write out the story of that forty-day journey for the family archives. Thus, in 1815, at the age of forty, Louisa had her wish; she had been admitted to the Adams clan—at last she had really become a New Englander!

In the days that followed, Louisa witnessed that frenzied interlude between Napoleon's return from Elba and his defeat at Waterloo. She watched boisterous crowds dancing in the streets of Paris. She went to the cathedral, and saw a crowd storming the doors in order to catch a glimpse of Napoleon at mass.

And then, in May, she was off with John Quincy and their little son for the Court of St. James's. Her husband and she found themselves in much the same uncomfortable position there that John and Abigail Adams had occupied thirty years before. Then the British King had been hostile because of the outcome of the Revolutionary War; now his descendant was unfriendly because of the War of 1812. But John Quincy and Louisa were happy in London. They were amiable and courteous, and finally the social atmosphere grew warmer. The Duke of Wellington called personally and invited them to his daughter's wedding, and the Duchess came to see Louisa. Best of all, she was back in the city of her birth, and, the two older boys having been sent for, her family was reunited.

In April, 1817, after two years in London, John Quincy received from President Monroe his appointment as Secretary of State in the new administration, and the Adamses left as soon as possible for the United States. To Louisa that was a real home-coming. She loved Washington; her people were there. She would have her own Tuesday evenings and give theatre parties! She even gave a ball for General Jackson, although the General was her husband's political rival, and that ball equaled in splendor and gaiety the merry regime of Dolley Madison. Louisa smiled to see this verse published in *The National Intelligencer*:

> "Wend you with the world to-night?
> Brown and fair, and wise and witty,
> Eyes that float in seas of light,
> Laughing mouths and dimples pretty,
> Belles and matrons, maids and madams,
> All are gone to Mrs. Adams'.
>
> Wend you with the world to-night?
> Juno in her court presides,
> Mirth and melody invite,
> Fashion points, and pleasure guides!
>
> Wit through all its circles gleaming,
> Glittering wealth and beauty beaming.
> Belles and matrons, maids and madams,
> All are gone to Mrs. Adams'."

Long after that brilliant evening in the F Street home, the city talked of the beautiful and hospitable Louisa Adams. And in 1825, when John Quincy Adams became President and they went to live in the White House, she remained the gracious charming hostess. Only failing health prevented her from entertaining as often and as luxuriously as Dolley Madison had done. Her son John and Mary Hellen were married in the Blue Room of the White House in February, 1828; and youthful laughter and song, flowers and ribbons, and pretty girls in high-waisted gowns with hoopless skirts and silk sashes brightened the mansion. The hair of the ladies was worn in curls then, piled high on the head, with a fillet or a jeweled band to bind them. For the men, long trousers of nankeen and fine cloths had taken the place of the old smallclothes (knee breeches); coats were shorter and tighter, and hair was no longer powdered.

The President, however, was not enthusiastic over his duties as the host in the White House; in that winter of 1828, he wrote in his diary:

> "This evening was the sixth drawing-room. Very much crowded. . . . The heat was oppressive and these parties are becoming more and more insupportable to me."

John Quincy Adams had other, more serious troubles, and, a disillusioned man, he went out of office in 1829. With a majority of the House and Senate opposed to his administration, and the Vice President and the Speaker of the House opposed to him, there was little opportunity for him to carry through a policy of his own. Now he was to be turned out of the public service to which he had devoted his life. Or, so everyone thought. But they reckoned without John and Louisa. She presided at the White House reception in December, and just before their departure she gave a dance! Abigail Adams was gone now; they had also lost old John Adams and their oldest son, George Washington Adams. But they carried on.

John Quincy, with Louisa again making a home for him in Washington, was not allowed to retire; he was sent by the people of Massachusetts to the House of Representatives and soon was recognized as the official orator for Congress on state occasions. Louisa shared his triumph and was secretly pleased to be back in Washington, with her books and her painting, her music and her garden.

For seventeen stormy years John Quincy Adams, his hands shaking, his voice cracking with age and emotion, battled for the abolition of slavery; addressed the Congress on behalf of the Smithsonian Institution; strove for good government as he envisioned it.

Late in February, 1848, Congressman Adams was in his usual place in the House. He started to rise and then pitched forward to the floor. Louisa came, grief-stricken, but she could no longer help the partner of her heart. John Quincy Adams died at the Capitol in Washington on February 23, 1848.

Louisa Adams was an old lady now, with silvery hair. But she was to outlive her husband by more than four years. Then, in the spring of 1852, in the Quincy house, she died as gently as she would have liked to live. They buried her in the Quincy churchyard, in the Adams family plot.

Rachel Donelson Robards Jackson

FIRST FIRST LADY FROM THE FRONTIER

IF the wife of Andrew Jackson ever read Shakespeare, she must have paused long over those words: "Done to death by slanderous tongues." For against her was waged the fiercest personal attack in our history.

As a child, Rachel Donelson was a true daughter of the frontier, as merry and spirited a girl as ever danced on the deck of a flatboat or seized the steering oar while her father took a shot at the Indians. Healthy, energetic, and imaginative, she belonged to that group of venturesome souls who push out beyond the mountains, finding in danger and hardship an added zest for living.

Rachel was only twelve when she set out with her family on a river migration from Virginia to Tennessee, a perilous journey of two thousand miles which lasted from November, 1779, to April of the following year. Her dark eyes sparkled with pride and excitement when she learned that her father, with a guard of thirty men, had been chosen to lead a party of one hundred and fifty women and children from Fort Patrick Henry on the western Virginia frontier to meet their menfolk who had gone overland to build homes and clear the land.

Colonel Donelson had served three terms in the House of Burgesses. He realized that piloting these women and children down the Holston River to the Tennessee, down the Tennessee to the Ohio, up the Ohio to the Cumberland, and up the Cumberland to a new settlement which was to be known as Nashville, was quite an undertaking. Nevertheless, with pioneer daring he started off, with a fleet of scows, canoes, and pirogues, carrying food, ammunition, clothing, and household goods. And no one can say the trip was without

84

adventure. They navigated swirling rapids and treacherous currents; they fought their way through the hostile Indian tribes of Kentucky; when they ran out of food, they paused to send hunting parties ashore. Bitterly cold winds and snow, weariness and privation were their portion.

Through it all, Rachel crouched quietly at her father's side, her quick eyes alert for Indians, her brown hands ready to reload the rifles. When the long journey was over, she went cheerfully to work, chinking log cabins with mud and moss; making quilts and deerskin clothes; trying out lard, smoking bacon, and fashioning her own linsey-woolsey dresses. She set her spinning wheel on a buffalo robe, near the cooking crane in the fireplace, and watched the pot boil while she spun flax and wool. At log-raisings, dances, and quilting bees, she was lively and gay.

Then, when she was seventeen, her father decided to move to "the settlements" in Kentucky. There, the black-haired, brown-eyed, rosy-cheeked Rachel attracted the roving eye of Captain Lewis Robards, a young Revolutionary War hero. To the backwoods girl, he was a handsome and romantic figure. After a brief courtship they were married. For the first few months they were quite happy, but Rachel, little more than a child, soon realized that her husband was moody, possessive, quick-tempered, and unreasonably jealous. Rachel could put up with his tirades; as a good wife, she tried to smooth over their quarrels; when he was drinking hard, she was patient and forgiving. It was something, as his own mother told her, that "the war had done to him." But she could not condone his infidelity. His intimate relations with one of his mother's house servants, a young mulatto, finally brought about their separation. Divorce was virtually unknown in that era of our history, separations a disgrace.

Nevertheless, Rachel returned to her home near Nashville. By then, her father had died, and the Widow Donelson was running a boarding house. It was there, one day, that Rachel answered a knock on the door, and found standing before her a red-haired, freckle-faced stranger who towered above her. When she looked up into his eyes, she thought they were the bluest she had ever seen. And when he explained that he and his friend, Overton, had entered into a law partnership, and wanted to rent one of her mother's cabins, Rachel was stirred by the kindly, deferential voice.

In the months that followed, Rachel's heart was like a bird on the wing. She was 22; her one romance had brought only sorrow and shame. Though no word of love passed between her and Andrew Jackson, the hard-riding, hard-fighting young frontier lawyer, she sang now as she went about the cooking and scrubbing. And on Sunday afternoons when her family, with Jackson and Overton, took their picnic lunches down to the river bank, life again seemed worth living.

It was while she was visiting at the home of Colonel Green, near Natchez, Mississippi, that Andrew Jackson brought Rachel stirring news: Robards had had a bill of divorcement introduced in the Virginia legislature, and the body had voted favorably upon it. Shortly after, an ardent and happy Rachel and an equally happy Andrew, passionately in love, were married in Colonel Green's drawing room.

The couple returned to Nashville and settled down. Time passed blissfully. Almost before they realized it, two years had gone by. Then came the crushing blow that was to haunt Andrew Jackson and his Rachel for the rest of their lives: Lewis Robards had challenged their marriage at Natchez! The report that the Virginia legislature had granted Robards a divorce was found to be untrue. What they had actually passed was an Enabling Act which merely gave Robards the right to plead his case before a judge and jury. Robards waited two years, until April, 1793, to do this.

It was the second petition of the kind to come before the Virginia legislature. Probably only a very few lawyers knew what the Enabling Act really meant. Every one appears to have assumed that a divorce had been granted. Rachel believed it; Jackson believed it, though he never stopped torturing himself with the thought that he should have investigated the matter and sent for a copy of the Virginia bill.

The fact remained that Jackson had been married for two years to another man's wife. Meanwhile, Robards had obtained a divorce in Kentucky; Rachel was branded as an adulteress, her beloved Andy was named as corespondent. As soon as they could, the couple secured a new license, and the marriage ceremony was again performed on January 17, 1794. Yet in all the years to come, Rachel Jackson, cherished by her husband far beyond the lot of most women, was haunted by the knowledge that the story of her disgrace was written in the records of the Kentucky courts. It changed her from a laughing, warm-hearted girl to a sad and bitter woman, stung by the unmerited accusations, frightened by the innuendo and gossip which pursued her. As for Andrew Jackson, his remorse and his fierce love for Rachel almost turned him into a monomaniac. Once, in a pistol duel, he killed a man who had cast aspersions on Mrs. Jackson's name. At another time he indulged in a brawl with the governor of the state, for the same reason. Rachel flinched when she met strangers. When her husband was elected to Congress and left for Philadelphia, she remained behind. She directed the field hands in plowing and planting the crops, made clothes for her little nieces and nephews, and prayed for her husband's quick return. When he did come, he brought lumber, nails, glass, and other materials for building the finest house of its kind in the Cumberland Valley. He furnished their new home, Hunter's Hill, with beautiful furniture, expensive hangings, and wall papers. There was nothing too good for his Rachel. Rachel, installed in the new house on the hill, foresaw that it would only attract more attention to them. More gossip would be whispered by the ladies over their teacups; more ribald jokes would be recounted in the bars and taverns of Tennessee.

Rachel's Christmas present from her husband that year brought tears to her eyes. Although he was in Philadelphia, and virtually bankrupt, he had not forgotten her. On Christmas morning, standing before her door, was a shiny black carriage of her very own, with a pair of handsomely matched iron-gray horses. Rachel stood there in the winter sunshine, angry with herself for allowing slander to wreck her life. As long as Andrew loved her and she loved him, they could stand together, hand-in-hand against the world! His many letters when he was away—and he was away a great deal—comforted her. Once he wrote her from Knoxville:

> "My dearest Heart:
> With what pleasing hopes I view the future when I shall be restored to your arms there to spend my days with you the dear companion of my life, never to be separated from you again. . . . I have this minute finished my business here, and . . . would not think of going to bed without writing you. May it give you pleasure to receive it. May it add to your contentment until I return. May you be blessed with health. May the Goddess of Slumber every evening light on your eyebrows and conduct you through pleasant dreams.

88

Could I only know you enjoyed peace of mind, it would relieve my anxious breast and shorten the way until I am restored to your sweet embrace, which is the nightly prayer of your affectionate husband."

Besides the ever-haunting fear of gossip, Rachel carried another sorrow under her heart. Andrew Jackson loved children, as she did; but they never had any of their own. She borrowed children from the neighbors, and became "Aunt Rachel" to all the youngsters of the countryside. In 1810, she took the baby of a relative who bore twins. The child was legally adopted and christened Andrew Jackson, Jr.

When Jackson resigned from the Senate and was elected to the Supreme Court of Tennessee, they felt that their private lives would be placed beyond petty gossip; no one would dare to talk about a judge or his wife. But again Rachel became the object of a whispering campaign. She was becoming resigned to it now, yet she was relieved when, because of lack of money, they were forced to sell the magnificent house on the hill and move across the river to a log cabin which once had been a trading post. Here, away from the public eye, Rachel was happy. When her husband became General Jackson, with the state volunteers under his command, twenty or thirty officers often descended upon him for a conference. Rachel set up long tables on the lawn and served refreshments. When the weather turned cold, she served them inside the cabin, with its long room and blazing fireplace.

With the coming of the war in the summer of 1812, she took over the running of the farm. When the General, with his volunteers, was ordered south, she rushed to the city and had a miniature of herself painted on ivory. For the rest of his life Jackson wore that miniature close to his heart, suspended around his neck by a strong black cord. Every night before lying down to rest, he propped up the miniature on a table beside him and read the Bible she had given him. That she was now a woman of forty-five, a little plump under the chin, went unnoticed by "Old Hickory."

When one of her nephews arrived with orders from the General for Rachel to join him, she joyfully began packing her trunks. Meanwhile, her husband was winning the famous battle of New Orleans. When she arrived there, he was the most widely acclaimed General of the War of 1812!

New Orleans was a city greater than any she had ever seen; a people with elegant manners, courtly speech, and warmth in their hearts. They liked Rachel. They gave her jewelry, brought dressmakers and hairdressers to her apartment, told her what to do in the social whirl which followed the occupation of New Orleans by the American forces, and showed her in many ways how splendid, loyal, and generous the Creole ladies of the city could be. Rachel was radiant as she drove along the streets, sitting beside her husband, with the crowds cheering as they passed.

At the grand ball which was given in their honor, she felt twenty years younger and looked many pounds lighter. Mrs. Livingston, social leader of both the French and American colonies, superintended the making of her costume. The violet gown of softest velvet, with its sheer lace bodice, enhanced Rachel's brunette beauty; and the lace mantilla draped over her head brought out the loveliness of her glossy black hair. She wore pearls and carried an evening bag made of the same velvet as her dress. Andrew told her that she had never looked more beautiful.

Rachel knew in her heart that this happiness could not last. Already the General was being mentioned as a presidential candidate. If they had been involved in scandal, accusations, and duels while Andrew was running for comparatively unimportant state offices, they would be crucified by the opposition party if he were to run for President! Yet she made no move to dissuade her husband. She even went with him on a trip to Washington, where they were entertained by President Madison, Secretary of State and Mrs. Monroe, and the Custis family at Mount Vernon. She sat, at the request of a well-known Washington artist, Anna Peale, for her portrait; looking serene and lovely in a dark blue velvet gown, with a soft lace collar and matching cap. But she longed for the seclusion of home; soon she was back at The Hermitage.

For a time, she need not worry about malicious gossip, for General Jackson made it very clear that he had no ambitions for the presidency, and he endorsed Secretary of State Monroe to succeed President Madison. Later, when President Monroe visited their section of the country, he enjoyed the hospitality of the Jacksons, who were then living in their new brick house.

In 1821, when General Jackson was appointed governor of Florida, Rachel accompanied him down the Mississippi and on to Pensacola. There she saw the Spanish flag lowered and heard her husband give the command to hoist the American flag in its place. In 1823, she went along with him to Washington, when he took up his duties in the Senate. In a letter to a friend, Rachel wrote:

> "We are boarding in the same house with the nation's guest, General Lafayette. When we first came to this house, General Jackson said he would go and pay the Marquis the first visit. Both having the same desire, and at the same time, they met on the entry

of the stairs. It was truly interesting. At Charleston, General Jackson saw him on the field of battle: the one a boy of twelve, the Marquis, 23."

The following year Rachel went with her husband to the capital of Tennessee, when the state legislature formally nominated him for the presidency. The national elections were three years away, but already the opposition party had found that she was the chink in Andrew Jackson's armor. The attack was not long in coming. A Cincinnati newspaper published an article in which this question was asked: "In September, 1793, twelve [Kentucky] men constituting a jury, after hearing proof . . . declared that Mrs. Robards was guilty of adultery. Ought a convicted adulteress, and her paramour husband, be placed in the highest offices?"

This was merely the beginning. In the next broadside, the Ohio editor claimed that Rachel and Andrew Jackson had never been married in Natchez! They had no written document of their marriage, which was nothing unusual in those times. The ceremony had been considered binding and legal by the Americans then living in the Spanish territory. Colonel Green and many of the guests were dead; the others were widely scattered.

Jackson, wild with rage and trying vainly to keep this slander from Rachel's ears, sent an emissary down the Mississippi to trace, and bring back copies of, the records. In Tennessee, his friend John Overton headed a committee of prominent citizens organized to examine the relationship and marriage of Rachel Robards and Andrew Jackson.

The calm and judicial report of the committee, published throughout the United States in June, 1827, vindicated the couple. Letters poured in to Rachel, congratulating her on her victory. But gossip, like fire, travels fast. Rachel realized that only too well. The Cincinnati newspaper still insisted she was not "a suitable person to be placed at the head of the female society of the United States." In other words, people should not vote for Jackson. They must forget, thought Rachel bitterly, that he had been a lawyer, judge advocate, attorney general, justice of the Supreme Court of Tennessee, representative, senator, major general, and that he had served his country long and well.

In all fairness, however, it must be noted that in the mud-slinging of the Adams-Jackson campaign, the rival candidates behaved much more scrupulously than did their political associates. In his diary, John Quincy Adams set down a fair, legal account of the divorce and referred respectfully to Mrs. Jackson. When Jackson learned that his followers were planning a wild counterblast accusing Adams of having lived with his wife before marriage, he insisted that no such charge should be made.

Crushed and hopeless when Jackson's emissary was unable to locate a record of their first marriage, Rachel sought sanctuary in the little church she had built on the plantation. Jackson was fighting mad; he swore she would stand at his side when he took the oath of office as President of the United States.

The governor of Tennessee brought them the news of Jackson's election in 1828. Rachel's heart pounded as she listened. When a friend congratulated her, she answered gravely: "For Mr. Jackson's sake, I am glad; for my own part, I never wished it."

For Rachel, the breaking point was near. Born to the hardship, toil, and danger of the frontier; disillusioned at eighteen by her first marriage; exposed to the tortures of slander;

93

caught, finally, in a surge of political forces she did not understand and could not control; Rachel suffered a heart attack on December 17, 1828, and died a few days later.

Andrew Jackson's hour of triumph became a time of mourning. He entered the White House alone, a shattered, gray-haired old man. Idolized by the people, he now stood at the head of a great nation; yet the two things he valued most in the world were the miniature of his wife and the Bible she had given him.

They buried her in the garden of her Cumberland Valley home, dressed in the gown of white satin which she was to have worn at the inauguration ball. Her grave is marked by a tablet which Jackson had placed there, inscribed with these words:

"Here lie the remains of Mrs. Rachel Jackson, wife of President Jackson, who died the 22nd of December, 1828, aged 61. Her face was fair, her person pleasing, her temper amiable, her heart kind. She delighted in relieving the wants of her fellow creatures, and cultivated that divine pleasure by the most liberal and unpretending methods. To the poor she was a benefactor; to the rich an example; to the wretched a comforter; to the prosperous an ornament. Her piety went hand in hand with her benevolence, and she thanked her Creator for being permitted to do good. A being so gentle and so virtuous, slander might wound but could not dishonor. Even death, when he tore her from the arms of her husband, could but transport her to the bosom of God."

Hannah Hoes Van Buren

FIRST FIRST LADY OF DUTCH ANCESTRY

SNOW swirled thickly around the girl and the boy who trudged through the December twilight, hand-in-hand. But Hannah Hoes and Martin Van Buren were accustomed to the cold stormy winters of the little village of Kinderhook, New York. For all of Hannah's thirteen years and Martin's fourteen had been spent in this sleepy Rip Van Winkle town where they were born.

They had been playmates ever since they could remember. Together, in bright scarves, knitted hoods and caps, warm mittens, and sturdy coats and shoes, they coasted down hill. Together, wearing iron skates which curved up at the toe, they fairly flew over the ice of Kinderhook Lake, cheeks glowing, eyes shining, their breath like smoke in the cold, clean air. Spring was exciting, too, with hoop-rolling, rope-skipping, and romping games of tag on the village green, and sometimes the children went off to the sweet-smelling pine woods to hunt for trailing arbutus and purple violets.

Now, on this December afternoon, their feet making no sound on the fresh-fallen snow, they chattered gaily in the language of their Dutch ancestors. "I am to be apprenticed to Mr. Frank Sylvester for five years. I will become a great lawyer," said Martin. He spoke decisively, as he always did about his future, and his blue eyes under the broad high forehead and thatch of bright hair were eager and clear. "I will become a great lawyer, Jannetje!" He squeezed her thin little mittened hand, as if to communicate some of his enthusiasm to the slender girl at his side.

Hannah smiled demurely, her own blue eyes wide with admiration and wonder. Mat was very smart, he knew everything; she was sure of that. Often she had listened to the wonderful tales he told of the great men in fine clothes who came to his father's tavern, and of their lively discussions about politics. Kinderhook was only sixteen miles south of the capital at Albany, and stage coaches frequently brought passengers for an overnight stop at the Van Buren Inn. Through Martin, Hannah heard about eminent lawyers, state senators, and other important men. Martin had even listened to Alexander Hamilton, Aaron Burr, and John Jay, as they chatted amiably with the ruddy-faced proprietor over their cider and hot toddy.

Of course Martin would become a great lawyer, but five years seemed to the young Jannetje like a very long time. "You will become a great lawyer and go away, and forget all about Kinderhook," she said dolefully.

Martin laughed gaily. "You know I won't," he answered softly. "I will never forget Kinderhook, and I will never forget you, Jannetje."

Martin Van Buren and Hannah Hoes were carefree children then, walking home from school. Yet each knew and always had known, it seemed, that they belonged together.

Hannah Hoes (the original spelling was Goes) was born on March 8, 1783, in the completely Dutch community of Kinderhook, on the east bank of the Hudson River. The entire region was populated by immigrants from Holland, who, even after the close of the Revolutionary War and for many years more, clung closely to the language, habits, customs, and dress of their fatherland. The white steepled church in the village was Dutch Reformed, and the Hoeses, Van Burens, Van Alens and all the rest observed the Dutch holidays and festivals in the manner of their ancestors.

In November, they built flaring bonfires for St. Martin's day; solemnly they went to church for the religious ceremonies of Christmas and New Year's; they enjoyed the merry pageants of May Day and the excitement of market day fun at kermis, the feast day of the local patron saint. But best of all, for Hannah and Martin, was the eve of Saint Nicholas, when, according to legend, the good saint came riding over the rooftops on his white charger, with gifts for good children and switches for bad. The Hoeses and Van Burens always spent the holiday eve together, and Hannah often helped her mother frost the little cakes, and make the marchpane paste for sweetmeats.

Then suddenly life became more serious for Jannetje; Martin went away to study law, and she walked home from school alone. It was not until the autumn of 1806 that she and Mat began discussing the date of their marriage. Hannah's brother, Barent, was courting one of Van Buren's sisters, and there must have been many skating parties, sleigh-rides, and gay gatherings of the family clans.

Hannah and Martin were married on the twenty-first of February, 1807, by the Reverend Peter Labagh. The wedding took place at the home of Hannah's married sister, across the river and a few miles south of Kinderhook. Martin was twenty-five, and Hannah was a year younger. Their wedding journey was the sleigh ride back home to Kinderhook, where they set up housekeeping in a modest little house. The following year the young lawyer was appointed surrogate for the county; so the Martin Van Burens packed up their belongings and moved to Hudson.

To Hannah, the busy shipbuilding center, with its population of more than three thousand, seemed elegant indeed. Its streets and squares were neatly laid out, and the waterfront was lined with warehouses, stores, and long wharves bustling with activity. Sailing ships and steam packets came and went, carrying passengers and freight up and down the river. And Hannah was much impressed with Hudson's water supply, which was then considered highly modern. Most of the houses had their own "acqueducts" which "conveyed water . . . from several springs, two miles distant." The main streets were lined with book stores, dry goods shops, merchants, tailors, apothecary shops, and taverns such as the little bride from Kinderhook had never seen before. She felt almost as if she were in a strange country, for while Kinderhook was like a small bit of Holland, the town of Hudson had been settled in 1783 by seafaring Yankees. The New Englanders were not overcordial to the Dutch, and Hannah was shy.

Inside their own house on upper Columbia Street, Hannah and Martin still talked together in Dutch, and it was several years before Hannah gained courage enough to join the First Presbyterian Church. There was no Dutch Reformed church in Hudson, and since religion was a needful thing, she attended services regularly and became accustomed to the reading of the scriptures in English. There is no record that her husband ever joined the church in Hudson, but almost always he sat in the pew by her side when she went to meeting.

Hannah's first baby, Abraham, was born in Kinderhook. During the nine years in Hudson, she bore three more children: John, in 1810; Martin, in 1812, and later, a baby which did not survive.

Despite the cold New England atmosphere, the years in Hudson must have been happy years for Hannah. She was proud of her three fine sons, and prouder still of her husband, who advanced steadily in his work. From early youth, Martin was absorbed in politics. Like Jefferson, he was often chosen to draft resolutions and speeches for others. In 1812, when he was only thirty, he became a state senator. Four years later, as one of New York state's leading lawyers, he decided to move to Albany.

For Van Buren, the move to the state capital was the beginning of a brilliant career which finally led him to the White House; but for little Hannah Hoes, born and raised among the green fields and cool hills of Kinderhook, it was a different story. Albany was then one of the largest and most important centers of the United States. There were splendid churches and school buildings. The Van Burens went to live in a neat little brick house not far from Martin's law office and just across the street from the impressive new academy where their two older boys went to school.

Great must have been Hannah's pride, as she stood on her spotless doorstep and watched her sons cross the street and climb the broad stone steps of the school building. She herself had never had much schooling, and her husband had lacked money enough for a college education. But in this big city her sons would have all the opportunities their parents had missed.

Even closer to Hannah's heart than the school was the beautiful church on Chapel Street which recently had been built at a cost of more than seventy-five thousand dollars. As soon as they were settled, Hannah presented her "letter." Albany, she felt, was more like home than Hudson, for many Dutch people lived in the state capital. Besides, the gifted young preacher whose parish she had joined in Hudson was now installed in the big new church in Albany, and she was warmly welcomed as a member.

It was the weather that made life difficult for Hannah Van Buren. The climate of the city did not agree with her; she longed for the fresh country air. Day after day, during her first winter in Albany, she shivered in temperatures below zero. In March the city suffered the severest floods in forty years. Hannah's health began to fail.

The following winter, she bore her fourth son. He was a fine, strong baby; but a few weeks later, on February 5, 1819, Hannah Van Buren died, in the thirty-sixth year of her age. She was the first to be buried in the newly opened burial ground of the Second Presbyterian Church. Later, her remains were removed by her husband to the old cemetery in Kinderhook, along with the original gravestone which told the passers-by: "She was a sincere Christian, a dutiful child, tender mother, affectionate wife. Precious shall be the memory of her virtues."

It was not until eighteen years after her death that Van Buren became the eighth President of the United States. Through all the years he treasured the memory of his Jannetje. He never married again, although he was a young man when Hannah left him to bring up their four sons. At the White House he stood alone to welcome his guests. No one took Hannah's place as hostess until their son, Major Abraham Van Buren, brought his bride, Angelica Singleton Van Buren, to the White House.

Perhaps destiny was kind in sparing Hannah those years in Washington, for they were stormy ones for the man from Kinderhook. Almost before he could get his administration going, the country was crippled by a severe financial panic. Oddly enough, it was the Erie Canal that led to the panic of 1837.

Opened in 1825, it made its investors wealthy. Other promoters were sure a similar canal—or a railroad—would make them all rich. In the wave of wild speculation which followed, millions of dollars were borrowed from the banks for the building of towns and villages for which there were no residents. Unimproved land was bought with borrowed capital. Then came the day when notes were worthless and New York banks suspended payments. Business after business went bankrupt. Van Buren could not check this rising tide which swept the country, though he called an extra session of Congress to urge the enactment of the Sub-Treasury bill, which would strike the chains of banks from the hands of government. Hannah would have been proud of her husband had she lived to share his burdens, for this was the outstanding achievement of his administration. The paper-money bankers, however, carried out a bitter campaign against him, and he was not re-elected. He returned home to Kinderhook, where he lived until July 24, 1862. He died in his 80th year.

Van Buren wrote his autobiography after his return to Kinderhook. In all its eight hundred printed pages, there is no mention of Hannah, doubtless because he considered his personal memories too sacred to be shared with strangers. With the exception of a few time-blurred records and dates written in faded ink, about the only memento left to the nation of the wife of President Martin Van Buren is an engaging portrait painted when she was a bride.

In a high-necked, full-sleeved, tight-bodiced dress, her amiable, round Dutch face framed by a deep, pleated, white frill, Hannah looks out demurely from wide blue eyes. Little golden-brown ringlets fringe her smooth forehead, and above them her hair is piled high in soft puffs. Dainty, small, and doll-like, as the artist has pictured her, she might have been a subject of Rembrandt. Studying this painting of Hannah Hoes Van Buren, we can well believe the words of an old biography which says she was "alike distinguished for beauty and accomplishments."

Anna Symmes Harrison

FIRST FIRST LADY FROM NEW JERSEY

ANNA SYMMES, who became the wife of the ninth President of the United States, lived longer than any other First Lady. She was born in the first year of the Revolutionary War, and died in 1864, during the Civil War. She was the wife of one President and the grandmother of another.

Shortly after Anna's birth on July 25, 1775, her mother died. When the little girl was four, her father, State Supreme Court Justice Symmes, took her on a journey she would never forget as long as she lived. Morristown, New Jersey, her birthplace, had fallen into the hands of the British, and in order to assure his small daughter a place of safety, Colonel Symmes disguised himself in a British officer's uniform and carried her on horseback and by boat to her grandparents at Southold, Long Island. Then he returned to his war duties, and Anna did not see him again until after the evacuation of New York in the autumn of 1783.

At the home of her grandparents in a prosperous community of farming and whaling, little Anna thrived. Doubtless she wandered happily under the apple trees in the well-kept orchard and went with Grandma and Grandpa to the meeting house at "the Fork" on Sundays. As soon as the war was over, the people of Southold township set about establishing Clinton Academy, "a school which should afford facilities for a higher grade of learning." Anna was sent to this school. Later, when Judge Symmes decided his daughter should have the best education possible, he enrolled her in what was regarded as the finest boarding school in the country—Mrs. Isabella Graham's school for young ladies on lower Broadway, in New York city. Anna Symmes thus became the first of the First Ladies to be sent regularly to school, and also to complete her studies in what we now call a high school.

While she was living contentedly with other young daughters of wealthy parents at Mrs. Graham's seminary, Judge Symmes began to think about the Northwest. His interests lay in the unexplored regions north of the Ohio River. As a Representative in Congress, he had voted for the ordinance of government covering the new Northwest Territory. Later, with a few associates, he bought almost half a million acres of wild land in Ohio.

In 1787, he was appointed justice of the Supreme Court in Ohio, with headquarters at the bustling little town of Losantiville, which in 1790 was renamed Cincinnati. Seven years later, he returned to New York for two reasons: he was going to marry again; and he planned to take his bride and his daughter, Anna, back to Ohio.

Moving from the fashionable city of New York and the sheltered atmosphere of Mrs. Graham's boarding school to the small settlement at North Bend, Ohio, with its fifteen crude houses and a few log cabins, must have been something of a shock to Anna Symmes. She, however, seems to have adapted herself readily to frontier life in the "commodious dwelling and blockhouse" her father had built. For one thing, she and her new stepmother liked each other at once. For another, it wasn't long before she met William Henry Harrison, a tall young officer stationed at nearby Fort Washington and a seasoned Indian fighter at twenty-two.

The third son of Benjamin Harrison, he was a member of one of Virginia's wealthiest and most influential families. At eighteen, he did what many young men were doing in those days of Indian uprisings—he joined the army, became an ensign, and set out for the settlement on the Ohio River, where the government had built Fort Washington. There he was promoted to lieutenant and served as aide to General "Mad Anthony" Wayne. In 1794 he was assigned to duty at North Bend; and in 1795, Anna Symmes came into his life.

Anna was nineteen then, a slender, not very tall girl with dark eyes and dark hair. Her mouth was full and generous, there was a captivating dimple in her chin, and later she was to be toasted by "Mad Anthony" as "the fairest bride in Northwest Territory." At first, Judge Symmes smiled upon the romance that quickly developed between his daughter and the young officer. Then, hearing some rumors, he sternly ordered the engagement broken. Anna, however, had a mind of her own. When, on November 25, 1795, her father rode off on a business trip, young Harrison (having secured the backing of his commanding officer), appeared to claim his bride. The young couple walked to the home of Dr. Stephen Wood, a justice of the peace, who read the marriage ceremony, gave them his blessing, and watched them ride off toward Fort Washington.

For a time, Judge Symmes would not speak to his son-in-law. When they did meet face to face at an army post dinner, the judge demanded: "How do you expect to support my daughter?"

"With my sword and my good right arm, sir!" young Harrison answered promptly. The response so pleased the judge that he was willing to forgive the young couple. Their marriage remained a love match through danger, hardship, tribulation; even through fame, adulation, and political success. Before their first child was born, Harrison acquired some land and built a four-room log cabin. In 1798, their second child was born. When the settlers elected Harrison to Congress, in 1799, the young couple with their two children made the journey to Philadelphia by horseback, keelboat, and stagecoach.

Philadelphia, then the national capital, was the gayest city in the United States. Proudly Anna watched her husband as he spoke in the House of Representatives. As the first delegate from a territory, he was an object of special attention. On his return to the wilderness in 1800, he had taken another step forward in his career, for he carried with him the appointment as Governor of Indiana Territory, with headquarters at Vincennes, a distance from Cincinnati, down the meandering Ohio River, and up the Wabash, of more than five hundred miles.

But Anna had thrown in her lot with the frontier and William Henry Harrison. She had brought back to North Bend a new baby, born at the home of an aunt in Richmond, Virginia. Her husband came from Vincennes to guide her on the westward journey.

On a large tract of land just north of Vincennes he built a brick house somewhat like those Anna had admired in Philadelphia, and this home became the center of social and official life in the territory. Men in fringed deerskin hunting clothes and coonskin caps, and women in homespun skirts and jackets journeyed to Grouseland for hoedowns and Virginia reels. The Governor was hospitable and affable; his wife was a gracious and charming hostess.

For twelve years Anna Symmes Harrison presided over that household; for twelve years she watched her husband in his unrelenting fight against the fur traders and others who contributed to the moral disintegration of the Indians by selling them whisky. Most of the territory under the governor's nominal control was still in the hands of hostile tribes, some of which were committing fearful ravages on the frontier. In addition to his worries over the Indians, Anna knew her husband had to be on guard against the "outs" who wanted to gain control of the territorial government machinery.

Harrison was a fair-minded Virginia gentleman, and a good administrator. The Indian Chief Tecumseh, with whom he had to deal, was a warrior and a realist, besides being a politician. Tecumseh had a single aim—to unite all the Indian tribes against the white settlers and land speculators.

While Harrison was making treaties with the Indians, Anna ran the plantation, thankful that Grouseland was something of a border fortress, with walls of solid brick eighteen inches thick. The upper stories were equipped with loopholes for defense and in the cellar was a powder magazine surrounded by massive masonry. A trap door led to a lookout on the roof. Secret passages ran from closet to closet. Anna had long been accustomed to the presence of Indians, and she scarcely noticed them as they beached their canoes near the bend in the river. They were frequent visitors when her husband was at home. But when he was riding out through the territory, as he often was, she was watchful.

It was during one of the governor's journeys that her baby, John Scott Harrison, was born. Dr. Scott, for whom the baby was named, traveled all the way from Lexington, Kentucky, to attend Mrs. Harrison. The child was destined to have a minor political career of his own in later years and to become the father of Benjamin Harrison, twenty-third President of the United States.

The time came at last when the settlers and their families at Vincennes were obliged to seek safety from the Indians. Anna, with her children and servants, fled east to Cincinnati.

There she took in and cared for her once-wealthy father. Her husband, now a brigadier general in the regular army, went forth to give battle, not only to the British, but to the thousands of Indian warriors whom the enemy had supplied with arms and ammunition. The War of 1812 was now in full swing in the Northwest Territory, and Anna could only wait and pray for the safety of her husband.

General Harrison's victorious campaigns brought him to the favorable attention of the American people and paved the way to his political successes. But more than a year of war had passed before Commodore Perry sent his famous message to Harrison, then a major general of the district: "We have met the enemy, and they are ours." Perry's destruction of the British fleet on Lake Erie, and Harrison's winning of the famous battle against the Indians at Tippecanoe broke the backbone of the enemy's resistance. Harrison became the hero of the hour.

At the end of the war, he and Anna were reunited at North Bend. With a wife and eight children to support, Harrison turned to farming. But he found time, in answer to a request by President Madison, to negotiate with the tribes of Indiana Territory over a period of two years. He went east to Washington, where his portrait was painted; while Anna remained at home, with another new baby and a dying father to care for. When Harrison was sent to Congress in 1816, Anna stayed behind to supervise the farm.

Almost before Anna realized it, her daughter Betsy was eighteen—old enough to marry. Household expenses increased, and the Harrisons had to mortgage some of their land. One after another the children married; by 1824 Anna had six grandchildren. Her husband now became a senator, and once more she remained at the North Bend farm while he spent part of the year in Washington. When, at the end of three years in the Senate, Harrison was sent to Colombia as the American Minister, there was no change of scene for Anna Harrison. The story of her life is the record of a good woman's devotion to her family and the sacrifice of her own pleasure for their welfare. One can imagine how pleased and excited she was when her husband returned from the faraway republic in South America, bringing her a brilliant macaw and seeds and plants for her garden.

By the year 1837, when Anna was 62, a widespread business depression seriously affected the Harrisons and their many children and grandchildren. Anna's hair was white now, and often she was weary and sick; but she was growing old gracefully. She accepted the situation cheerfully and economized carefully to keep her household going.

Then, quite unexpectedly, General Harrison became a major political figure. America had not forgotten old "Tippecanoe" and his war record, and party leaders needed someone to offset Van Buren's reputed wealth. Delegations came and sampled the plain food served at the North Bend table. They sized up the General and his wife, and went away with favorable reports of their piety, frugality, and patriotism. But Harrison was defeated in the Presidential election that followed.

The politicians, however, were determined. In 1840, at the age of 68, Harrison and Tyler were elected. But this triumph was not without its sad aspects. Harrison's son, Benjamin, died that summer at the age of 33. Anna and her husband, it seemed, had not been able to transmit to their offspring the strength and vitality that marked their own lives. They had brought ten children into the world, and half of them had died. Anna suddenly began to feel old; for the first time in her life she became seriously ill. She wished her husband's friends and political backers would leave him in North Bend, "happy and contented in retirement." In February, 1841, when Harrison left for the inauguration in Washington, she was too ill to accompany him.

Anna Symmes Harrison never saw her husband again. At the inauguration ceremonies, the President caught a cold which developed into pneumonia. He died in Washington on the morning of April 4th, as his wife was starting off to join him at the White House.

For twenty years after Harrison's death, Anna made her home with her son, John, who managed the family farm. As the wife of one President and the grandmother of another, her place in history is secure. She was devoted to her church, her family, and her country. As long as she lived, she was keenly interested in and well-informed on the political trends of the period. In her childhood she had been proud of her father and his role in the Revolutionary War; as an old lady in her eighties she was proud of her grandsons in the ranks of the Union Army. Her memory was remarkable. She did not live to see the close of the Civil War. On February 25, 1864, she slipped away peacefully, in the eighty-ninth year of her age.

Letitia Christian Tyler

FIRST LADY OF THE "FABULOUS FORTIES"

TWO women shared the responsibilities and the political fortunes of John Tyler, tenth President of the United States. Tyler's first love, Letitia, was born on November 12, 1790, at the family estate, Cedar Grove, near Richmond. She was the daughter of Robert Christian, a wealthy Virginia gentleman-planter; and was eighteen when she met John Tyler. Historians agree that she was appealingly lovely in character and appearance.

Letitia was a black-eyed brunette with an aristocratic nose and finely chiseled features. Many an admirer wrote reverently of her "raven locks, olive skin, and dainty, delicate air." She wore her luxuriant black hair combed over her ears in curls; and, in a period when low-necked gowns were the fashion, Letitia's were outstanding for their modest cut. Although she has been described as highly religious, domestic, and gentle, she must have had spirit. For she refused to give up John Tyler, son of the governor of Virginia, even though her family and his held opposite political beliefs. The struggle was long; the engagement lasted nearly five years. Letitia was twenty-three when her parents finally withdrew their objections, and the lovers were married on Tyler's twenty-third birthday, March 29, 1813.

Many years later, one of their sons said his father's courtship "was much more formal than that of today. He was seldom alone with her before marriage, and . . . never mustered up courage enough to kiss his sweetheart's hand until three weeks before the wedding . . . When he visited her . . . he was entertained in the parlor where the members of the family were assembled . . ."

So the resourceful young man, who was full of music and

poetry, wrote flowery sonnets and long impassioned letters to his adored Letitia, insisting he had "nothing to boast but an honest and upright soul, and a heart of purest love." Although he was not as wealthy as Letitia's family, he had as imposing an array of ancestors as she; he was educated at William and Mary College and elected to the Virginia legislature at the age of twenty-one.

The newlyweds started housekeeping at *Mons Sacer,* a modest farm next door to Greenway, the Tyler homestead. Like Abigail Adams, Letitia was a good manager. She superintended the planting of gardens and fruit orchards, set out the roses, and watched over the family budget. She also helped her husband in his professional and political career, for the large Christian family was prominent and influential in Virginia. And, since both of Letitia's parents died shortly after her marriage, the legacy she received and turned over to her husband must have been of great aid to the young lawyer just getting started.

At the age of twenty-six Tyler was sent to Congress for three terms. During this period he acquired his father's Greenway estate. Here, in the old home where her husband was born, life was easier for Letitia. The mansion was well-furnished, and the many outbuildings included a well-stocked dairy, a meathouse, granaries, stables, and servants' quarters. Behind the house the broad acres were planted in wheat, corn, and tobacco, and there were vegetable gardens and quantities of the flowers which Letitia loved.

Here, we can imagine the dark-eyed Letitia in the evenings after the children were asleep, carefully jotting down purchases and sales, receipts and expenditures. Here, in the cool of early morning, she inspected the kitchens and visited the servants' quarters. Here, in the shade of the great willow tree in the garden, she must have loved to sit through the sunny afternoons, teaching her youngsters their ABC's. As the years passed and her husband became more and more important in national affairs, she was content at home, playing her preferred part as a good wife and mother.

When in 1840 William Harrison was elected President with Tyler as Vice President, not much importance was attached to the latter office. Then suddenly, a month after his inauguration, Harrison died, and Williamsburg's inhabitants became proudly conscious that one of their favorite sons had been thrust into the highest office in the land. Since Harrison was the first President to die in office, there was no precedent to suggest whether the Vice President should inherit the power and dignity accorded an elected Chief Executive. At heart, Tyler was a Democrat; now he was the designated head of the Whig party. He surprised his opponents by adopting an independent attitude. Then and there, he set the precedent that the Vice President is the legitimate successor of the President, and that precedent has been followed to this day. Tyler refused to be browbeaten. He became known as the "veto" President; the Cabinet resigned; he faced many diplomatic problems.

Letitia, too, faced problems. She had no desire for social prominence and she was physically unable to take on the duties of First Lady. She was 50, had borne seven children, and had not been well since the birth of the youngest. In 1838, she had suffered a stroke. In 1841, an almost helpless invalid, she accompanied her husband to the White House.

The belle of the Washington season during their first year was their daughter Elizabeth, who was married in the White House in January, 1842. One of Elizabeth's letters, written shortly after her wedding, reveals that her mother was down-stairs on this occasion for the first time since she arrived in Washington.

A few months later, on September 10, 1842, Letitia Tyler died; and, after a White House funeral, she was buried in the Christian family plot in Virginia.

That winter, with the Tyler family in mourning, there was little official entertaining and Letitia, the namesake daughter, presided over her father's household. The President indulged in reading and meditation. The invention of cheaper printing methods made available more books, magazines, and news-papers. It was also the golden age of Bryant, Hawthorne, Irving, Whitman, Longfellow, Thoreau, and many other important thinkers and writers. Thousands of Americans were attending lectures on art, science, letters, and human welfare. Zealous reformers were demanding free schools for both sexes, equality of legal privileges, and the abolition of slavery. Great advances were being made in medical science. Greater ease of communication had been established through Morse's invention of the telegraph. Steamboats and railroads were replacing clipper ships and stagecoaches. The cotton gin, the reaper, and other inventions were quickening in-dustry. It was a period of creative thinking and commercial activity. The President found it difficult to keep up with the times.

During the winter of 1843, society was stirred over the arrival in Washington of Miss Julia Gardiner, celebrated in sonnet and poster as "The Rose of Long Island." At twenty-three, Julia Gardiner must have looked somewhat as Letitia did at her age. Julia had "large gray eyes, raven hair, and the clearest olive complexion." There, however, the similarity ended, for Julia was gay, assured, and sophisticated. She had left a string of broken hearts, it was said, in Saratoga, London, Paris, Rome, and New York.

For twelve generations her father's family had lived on the Gardiner's Island (New York) estate where she was born in July, 1820. Julia and her sisters had been trained from the beginning to become socialites. As children they visited fashionable Saratoga. When Julia was twenty, the family toured Europe. Two years later, when the Gardiners went to Washington for the social season, they stayed at Miss Peyton's fashionable boarding house.

Among the guests at the White House one evening were Mr. Gardiner and his daughters. President Tyler must have been immediately attracted to the vivacious and beautiful Miss Julia, for shortly afterward, in February, 1844, she and her father were his guests on the flagship Princeton for a day's outing on the Potomac. A gun, fired in salute as they passed Mount Vernon, exploded. Among the several prominent men killed in the accident was Julia's father. The story goes that Julia fainted and was borne tenderly down the gangplank in Tyler's arms. In any event, the two were married quietly on the morning of June 26, 1844, in the Church of the Ascension on lower Fifth Avenue. The news astounded the nation, for no one except the President's family even knew he was in New York. This secret wedding of the first President to be married while in office drew many newspaper headlines.

The Tyler children regarded the matter quite seriously. Their father was fifty-four; his bride thirty years younger. During Tyler's presidency and for many years afterward, they made no comment; but, forty years later, Letitia's one surviving son intimated that they were bitterly opposed to the marriage.

Julia Gardiner Tyler

In contrast to the first Mrs. Tyler, Julia loved the gay life of the capital, which became even gayer during her eight months as First Lady. Young and full of high spirits, Julia was fond of extravagant clothes and jewels, and she thrived on the admiration she received. Tyler, infatuated with his "Rose of Long Island," denied her nothing and was accused of living in a style far too lavish for his position.

Criticisms, however, have a way of being tempered by time. Historians generally agree that the second Mrs. Tyler was a gracious, well-educated woman and a highly popular First Lady. She adored her husband and adopted all his political views. When he signed the bill for the annexation of Texas and handed her the pen he had used, she declared proudly that she would always wear "suspended from my neck the immortal gold pen with which the President signed the Annexation Bill."

For seventeen years after the end of Tyler's term, he and his Julia lived happily at their home, Sherwood Forest, on the banks of the James River. There, six of their seven children were born. Apparently, however, Julia continued to be extravagant. Her life in Virginia was enlivened by annual trips north and in 1846, in a letter to his son John, Tyler admitted he was "desperately bare of cash."

When the Civil War came and his state chose the South against the North, Tyler renounced his allegiance to the United States and was appointed a member of the Confederate Provisional Congress. Julia, too, embraced the cause of the secessionists; her husband's state was now her own, and Richmond was her home. It remained her home even after John Tyler's death on January 18, 1862, at the age of seventy-one. She mourned him for the rest of her life. In the 1870's she became a Roman Catholic, and on July 10, 1889, she died in the same hotel where her husband had passed away twenty-seven years earlier.

Julia Gardiner Tyler was always proud of her husband's political record. She would have us remember that Tyler, as President, was without a party or a majority in Congress, a situation which presented difficulties at the start. Yet he negotiated the first treaty between the United States and China, granting Americans the right to live and trade in five ports. He transformed a Post Office Department with a debt of $500,000 into a debt-free organization. He took over our government at the close of a four-year depression and left it—after paying a considerable portion of the national debt—with seven million dollars in the Treasury.

Letitia, the first Mrs. Tyler, was buried on the plantation where she was born. Julia, the second wife, was laid to rest beside her husband in Hollywood Cemetery, Richmond, Virginia. The spot is marked by a $10,000 monument voted by Congress in 1914.

Sarah Childress Polk

FIRST FIRST LADY TO ACT AS SECRETARY
TO THE PRESIDENT

THE nation's capital was deluged by a downpour of rain, and the air was chilly on March 4, 1845. But the stormy weather did not dampen the spirits of Sarah Childress Polk. Proudly she stood beside her husband on the inaugural platform, looking down onto a sea of umbrellas, as she listened to his earnest, clearly spoken words:

> "I do solemnly swear that I will faithfully execute the Office of President of the United States, and will to the best of my ability preserve, protect, and defend the Constitution of the United States."

As he began his inaugural address to the thousands who had gathered there, Sarah's thoughts slipped back over the years which had led to this crowning honor. Ever since their marriage on New Year's Day, 1824, she had shared his ambitions and his hopes as he worked his way from the little law office in Columbia, Tennessee, to a place in the state legislature; then on to Congress, where he served seven consecutive terms; to the Governor's Mansion. As a lawyer, James discussed his first cases with Sarah and listened carefully to her suggestions. Later, when he entered politics, they labored together over his speeches. When James K. Polk was nominated by the National Democratic Convention in 1844, he and Sarah began the most serious work of their lives—the five months' campaign to win the presidential election. At their home in Columbia, the two worked day and night, studying newspapers, cutting and filing clippings, answering letters, and writing to party leaders. By November their task was complete. Now, on March 4th, they stood triumphant in the rain, while Washington resounded with cheer and good wishes for the new Chief Executive and his tall, handsome, brunette First Lady.

It was the first time in the history of the United States that an "unknown" had been elected to the highest office. "Who is this man Polk?" people up and down the Atlantic Coast had asked when the "dark horse" was nominated. In Tennessee, they talked about what a good fighter Polk was; but generally it was thought he didn't stand a chance of winning from Henry Clay. Only Sarah was certain of the outcome, and she communicated her wholehearted faith to her husband.

Sarah Childress (called Sally by Andrew Jackson, whom she addressed affectionately as "Uncle Andrew"), was one of the most intellectual women of her time. She was the daughter of Joel Childress, a successful merchant, and was born near Murfreesboro, Tennessee, on September 4, 1803. When she reached school age she was enrolled in the Moravian Institute at Salem, North Carolina; and in that highly religious atmosphere she was strictly and carefully educated.

Some historians claim that Andrew Jackson, a good friend of young Polk, urged him to marry and suggested that nowhere could he find a sweeter woman or a more intelligent wife than Sally Childress. Whether it was due to Jackson's advice or to the promptings of his own heart, Congressman James Polk married Sally when she was twenty. The next year, she went to Washington with him. Twenty years later she entered the White House as First Lady.

Sarah Polk not only presided over the social affairs of the Executive Mansion with dignity and serenity, but also continued to act as confidential secretary to her husband. She was the first First Lady to be employed officially in that capacity. As they had no children, she was able to devote herself exclusively to the service of her husband; and to the smooth running of White House functions. She took charge of his papers and reminded him of appointments. It is interesting to consider how great an influence this woman wielded over the eleventh President of the United States. Polk relied on Sarah's intelligence. One of her daily chores during their four years in the White House was the careful studying of the nation's most important newspapers and the clipping of items which, in her judgment, were important for her husband to read. She also chose certain books and magazine articles, thus saving the President's time. This is clear evidence of the influence of a woman in the White House.

Gas pipes were installed in the White House in 1848, and great was the enthusiasm for this new means of illumination. Mrs. Polk, however, insisted on keeping the reception hall as it was, "with its elegant chandelier for the use of candles." On the first reception night on which the gas lights were in use, the company was suddenly left in darkness. But, as Mrs. Polk was fond of relating in later years, there was "one room still lustrous with many points of light—the reception room where the wax candles were shedding their soft radiance."

Some writers of the period said Sarah Polk had a dignity and charm strongly reminiscent of Dolley Madison. But a careful study of the temperaments of these two women indicates that Sarah was more frugal and imposed greater restrictions on her public than did the popular Dolley. Sarah banned alcohol, card playing, and dancing in the White House during her stay there; although she held two state receptions each week, gave many state dinners, and arranged frequent musicals and informal parties. Also, when Congress was in session, she instituted Saturday morning receptions for senators and congressmen. This gave her an opportunity to make friends for her husband. Sarah was a good listener and had an excellent memory. She had lived long enough in Washington to have a good grasp of affairs of state. Doubtless she was able to get the reactions and opinions of many important public men and talk them over with her husband. President Polk himself said: "None but Sarah knew so intimately my private affairs."

Her chief concern, toward the close of his term, was his failing health. He had taken office at fifty, and was one of our youngest Presidents; but instead of delegating many tasks to others, he insisted upon burdening himself with all problems, however trivial. Perhaps that was due to his conscientious desire to do his utmost for America. His integrity, like Sarah's, was irreproachable; no corrupting influence ever touched either of them. Both were firm believers in States' rights. As governor of Tennessee, and in later years, Polk brought all his influence to bear in strengthening State government; and he was alarmed lest the Federal government should gain too much control. There were other worries, too. A controversy raged as to the southwestern boundary of Texas. Texans claimed it was the Rio Grande; Mexico insisted it was the Rio Nueces. President Polk ordered American troops under General Zachary Taylor to hold the disputed territory, and when they were attacked by Mexican forces, he declared that was sufficient reason for starting war. Congress supported him in this; and while General Taylor pressed southward into Mexico, Americans on the Pacific coast raised the Stars and Stripes in California. Vast new territories came into our possession when peace was made with Mexico. Polk also compromised with the British in Oregon Territory, and the forty-ninth parallel became the permanent boundary.

During the Polks' stay in the White House, there was a wave of prosperity in the United States. Gold was discovered in California and settlers flocked west. The old controversy over slavery flared up again. Since Polk was a Southerner and a slave-owner, he was thought to be working for the South rather than for the entire nation. He had little chance of being re-elected. Also, he neither wanted nor sought a second term.

Sarah was relieved when his administration ended. More and more, in those last months, she saw his health failing. But he was full of plans. They made their trip to Nashville by way of New Orleans, being feted in all the towns and villages along the way. After a brief rest, they wanted to take a European tour. That dream, however, was never realized. Soon after they were settled in the fine new house they had bought in Nashville, Polk sickened; and on June 15, 1849, just a few months after he and Sarah had left Washington, he died.

Sarah Polk was only forty-five when her husband passed away. She was fine-looking, well-to-do, and brilliant, but though she lived on for more than forty years, she never re-married. Instead, she plunged into the management of her cotton-raising factory, which she later sold at a nice profit. Exactly what prompted her to sell a successful business is not known, but Sarah Polk was a shrewd business woman. She kept herself well-informed on the affairs of the nation. The date of the sale was 1860. Perhaps she realized that, with the growing unrest between the North and the South, it might be wise to dispose of property which she might not be able to control.

When the Civil War did come, it affected her but little. She remained in her home in Nashville all the while the fighting went on. She entertained Confederate generals, and when Nashville fell into the hands of the North, she was equally hospitable to ranking Union officers. Both sides had such respect and admiration for the ex-First Lady that her property was not harmed in any way. Years later, she said: "When it came to actual conflict, and the lives of people with whom I always lived, and whose ways were my ways, my *sympathies* were with them; but my sympathies did not involve my principles. I have always belonged, and now belong, to the whole country."

Mrs. Polk was always devoutly religious. During their stay in Washington, neither she nor her husband even went to a theatre. Each Sunday found them in church, and even the most important dignitaries were not received in the White House on the Sabbath. It has been said that the aging Dolley Madison did much to "humanize" the strait-laced Polks. But Sarah had a strong personality of her own and iron-clad convictions. As the years passed she became almost a religious fanatic.

Her husband was buried in her own dooryard, and there she built for his remains a temple of Tennessee marble which became a shrine for visitors to the region. Dressed in mourning, with a black crepe bandeau around her hair, the widow of James K. Polk received these visitors graciously, conducting them through the rooms of the house, where his books still lined the walls of his study and his writings and his pens still lay on the table. Sarah would have nothing touched, nothing changed. Her home became a memorial to her husband; every picture he had ever had taken was displayed. Every document and letter, including his private diary, was carefully preserved.

She never left those precious mementos, except to attend church; and she would permit no hand but hers to dust them. Sarah Polk presided over the memorial until she died in August, 1891, in her 88th year.

An outstanding figure of the nineteenth century, she was the first First Lady to be politically minded, and the first to act as secretary to her husband during his term of office.

Margaret Mackall Smith Taylor

A GOOD SOLDIER

IF Margaret Smith Taylor, wife of "Old Rough and Ready," had been asked about herself in 1847, after her husband's troops had won an important battle in the war with Mexico, she would have denied any claim to fame. Yet she had every right to declare, as General Zachary Taylor did: "For more than a quarter of a century my house has been the tent, and my home the battlefield." His wife may not have been *on* the field of battle, but she was never far from it. As her children grew old enough to do without her care, she sent them back to "the settlements" to be educated, while she accompanied her husband to nearly every army post from the Great Lakes to Baton Rouge.

Often during the early days of her married life, he cautioned her to watch out for "redskins"; and to keep her powder dry. Margaret smiled reassuringly at his warnings, and kept her pistol handy in the big square pocket of her army coat. She never knew fear until her husband was nominated for the Presidency. From that day until the day of his election, she prayed nightly that his opponent would become President.

A pioneer woman in every sense of the word, Margaret Mackall Smith was born in Calvert County, Maryland, on September 21, 1788. Her father, a major in the Revolutionary War, died when she was twelve. Little seems to be known of her childhood. Her story begins when, with her older sister, Mrs. Samuel Chew, she was living at Harrods Wood Creek, on the Kentucky frontier.

There she first met Lieut. Zachary Taylor, a thickset young Indian fighter, with twinkling gray eyes and dark wavy hair. She was twenty-one and he was twenty-five. It was spring in Kentucky, and, after a whirlwind courtship, they were married on June 21, 1810, in the log-cabin home of Margaret's sister. There is nothing to tell us how the bride looked as she stood beside the young officer on that June day. There are pictures of the children she bore, and of her husband, but there is no known portrait of our twelfth First Lady. We do know, however, that she was a good soldier.

Her introduction to army life came during the Indian wars of the Ohio territory, when Zachary Taylor served under General Harrison. At the beginning of the Tecumseh uprising her first baby, Ann Mackall Taylor, was born. After her husband's successful defense of Fort Knox, he was made a captain. Margaret quickly adapted herself to the conditions of a brawling army post. There, in 1815, a second child was born. They named her Sarah Knox, and always called her Knox to commemorate her father's brilliant defense of the fort.

That the young mother sometimes longed for company is shown by a letter Zachary Taylor wrote to his brother: "Peggy says she is very lonesome and is in hopes you will be as good as your word in paying us the visit you promised. If you come over, Peggy says you must bring her some cotton for 'nitting' which she wants Mother to have spun for her."

Lonesome or not, Margaret Taylor managed. As the children grew old enough, she sent some of them to her husband's people in Kentucky, and others to her own folks in Maryland to get their schooling, while she shared with Zachary the wilderness dangers, the rough garrison life, and the frequent journeys from post to post. No doubt she often longed for a safe home where they could stay put for a while.

After the War of 1812, in which Taylor became a major, the Taylors did settle down on the Bear Grass Creek land which had been Zachary's wedding present from his father. For eleven months Margaret superintended the family washing in the creek, and did her spinning and sewing, her cooking and housework, while Zachary had his wish of "making a crop of corn."

But army men who knew Zachary Taylor's fighting ability would not leave him on a farm. In the spring of 1816, President Madison commissioned him a major in the Third Infantry, and he was sent to Green Bay, Wisconsin. Margaret stayed behind until her third daughter was born. Then she joined her husband in the cold, lonely Green Bay country.

In 1819, the Taylor family was again on the move, going first to Louisville and then to Bayou Sara, where Margaret's sister was then living. At that Louisiana settlement, in July, a fourth baby girl was born and named for her mother. While Zachary went down to New Orleans on military business, swamp fever attacked Margaret, her small daughter Octavia, and the new baby. Octavia and the baby died. Margaret herself was very ill; and losing two of her children within four months seemed almost more than she could bear.

Then, as always, however, her husband was her first concern. Soon they were on the march again, going to one southern post after another. In 1824, another daughter, Mary Elizabeth, was born; and two years later came the birth of an only son, Richard. At this time, Taylor was summoned to Washington to serve on the Militia Board. In 1828, he was placed in command of Fort Snelling, the farthest northwest of all the army posts; and transferred the following year to Fort Crawford, in Michigan territory. Again Margaret Taylor was an army wife, but this time she had her oldest girl, Ann, along with her for company.

Taylor continued to distinguish himself as a soldier. He

fought in the Black Hawk War of 1832; and in the Seminole War of 1837. Margaret, too, did her share in the battles against the Indians. She nursed the sick and the wounded, without the aid of anesthetics and with scanty medical supplies; she wrote their letters, mended their clothes, and encouraged them by her cheerful presence.

In 1838, as Brigadier General, Zachary Taylor was given command of the American troops in Florida; and by the summer of 1841, he was in charge of the First Military Department, which covered the entire southeast. His headquarters were in Baton Rouge, Louisiana, where his old regiment, the First Infantry, was stationed. Here, among old friends, Margaret felt she could have a real home at last. There were many well-equipped and inviting new brick buildings in the officers' quarters from which to choose, but she fell in love at once with a little tumble-down house on the bank of the river, which had been built some forty years earlier when this was a Spanish possession.

With the help of her daughter Betty and some invalided soldiers, Mrs. Taylor converted the old house into a cozy, comfortable dwelling. A pasture was rented for cows, and Taylor soon bought that as well as the old house, for he saw that his wife now had what she had most wanted ever since their marriage—a home.

There, Margaret Taylor knew true contentment. While her husband traveled about the countryside, she tended her cows, house, and vegetable garden; she planted flowers and watched the scows, flatboats, and river steamers as they made their way up the Mississippi to Natchez or down to New Orleans.

In the spring of 1845, when Congress passed the joint resolution for the annexation of Texas, General Taylor was directed to have his troops ready for action on the Texas frontier. No sooner was war declared between the United States and Mexico than "Old Rough and Ready" began to win victory after victory. When he defeated General Santa Anna in the famous battle of Buena Vista (February 22, 1847), the American public hailed him as the hero of the hour. Even before he left Mexico his name had been suggested for the Presidency.

Margaret Taylor was bitterly opposed to this idea, and not without reason. Years before, she had witnessed the trial by fire of another great military hero, Andrew Jackson, when the slander hurled at him and his wife Rachel during the political campaign had brought grief, bitterness, and death. Margaret remembered, too, how another soldier-hero, William Henry Harrison, had found the responsibilities of Chief Executive too heavy to bear and had died a month after his inauguration.

She was getting along in life now; she was sixty. She had borne six children and had lost three of her girls. Knox, her second-born, had died less than three months after her marriage to Jefferson Davis, in 1835.

Zachary, her husband, in his long career in the service of his country, had distinguished himself over and over again as a soldier; she felt he deserved a rest. In the little Episcopal chapel which she had established at Baton Rouge, she prayed that they might be permitted to retire in peace.

Zachary Taylor agreed with his wife; he had no wish for the Presidency. But he knew he would continue to serve his country as long as the people wanted him.

In November, 1848, Taylor was elected the twelfth President of the United States. Margaret prepared to leave the little house beside the Mississippi and set off with her husband for the White House. There, though she appeared at public functions whenever occasion demanded, she left much of of the entertaining to her youngest daughter. Betty was now the wife of Colonel Bliss, who had been Taylor's adjutant during the Mexican War.

A new order of informal hospitality and friendliness began with the new administration. The Taylors had moved into the Executive Mansion on a wave of rejoicing over the winning of the war. America was enthusiastic over its hero-President. Blonde, blue-eyed Betty was a gay and vivacious hostess, and she was highly popular with the Washington social set. But, more and more, Margaret Taylor withdrew to her own suite, which she had furnished to resemble the little cottage at Baton Rouge.

President Taylor undertook to see that the laws passed by Congress were carried out. He soon learned, however, that he would have to do more than that—he would have to quell the rising dissension between North and South and preserve the Union. If "Old Rough and Ready" had lived, it may be that he would have succeeded. But the responsibilities of the Presidency were too great for the man who had fought so well in the field. Sixteen months after his inauguration, Zachary Taylor became ill. Five days later, on July 9, 1850, he lay dead in the White House.

Proudly, in her grief, his wife read the eulogy written by a rising young congressman named Abraham Lincoln:

"It did not happen to General Taylor once in his life to fight a battle on equal terms, or on terms advantageous to himself—and yet he was never beaten and never retreated. In all, the odds were greatly against him; in each, defeat seemed inevitable; and yet in all he triumphed."

Margaret Smith Taylor did not long survive her husband. In 1852, she died in Louisiana at the home of her son, Richard.

Abigail Powers Fillmore

WHO INSTALLED THE FIRST LIBRARY
IN THE WHITE HOUSE

INSIDE the country schoolhouse, the pupils were growing restive. Outside, the dusty roads and flaming autumn woods were bright with sunshine. Overgrown "back-bench" lads in homespun longed to stretch their legs and go hunting for butternuts and chestnuts; beginners and intermediates shuffled their feet; prim little girls in starched white pinafores fidgeted in their seats as they laboriously formed the letters of the alphabet on their slates.

Their teacher glanced at the old Dutch clock on the wall. She was little more than a girl herself. It was easy for her to understand the eagerness of her pupils to put away their books and go streaking out in the crisp October air. But Abigail Powers was not one to shirk her duty. Everybody in the county agreed that she was a good teacher. Even the older boys sat at attention when she spoke. They knew from experience that their pretty, blue-eyed, red-haired schoolmistress, tiny though she was, would tolerate no nonsense.

Only one tall, broad-shouldered lad remained at his desk when Abigail dismissed them for the day. As the children scrambled to put away their books and darted noisily out of the door, he continued to study the large print in the reader before him. Older than the others, grown to manhood at seventeen, Millard Fillmore had set his mind on an education. Whenever he could spare the time from his work as a clothier's apprentice, he struggled with reading, writing, and arithmetic.

As quietly as she could, the teacher banked the fire in the big iron stove. Methodically, she straightened out her books and papers and prepared to lock up. But only when she had put on her bonnet and shawl and jingled the little bunch of keys she carried, did Millard glance in her direction, contrition in his bright, eager eyes.

"Come along!" said Abigail, smiling. "I will help you with the reading this evening."

That offer of help to the determined young student was the keynote of Abigail Powers' entire life. Her name is not outstanding in American history, but this village schoolteacher, only two years older than Millard Fillmore, probably did more than anyone else to direct his footsteps along the path that eventually led to the White House.

Many years later, in a document opened after his death, ex-President Fillmore told a story very much like the foregoing. He had earned his living from the time he was twelve years old, and Abigail's school was the only one he ever attended. He described her as a good teacher—"eight years my sweetheart, twenty-seven my wife."

Abigail, youngest child of Lemuel Powers, a Baptist minister, was born at Stillwater, Saratoga County, New York, in March, 1798, when that region was little more than a wilderness. Her father died when she was very young; the family was poor. The Widow Powers decided to go out to the "new western counties"; she believed her two youngsters, a boy and girl, would get a better start in life there and that money would go further. Probably the mother taught her children from the books her husband had left, for by the time Abigail was sixteen she began to earn her living by teaching school.

Abigail was nineteen when she first met Millard Fillmore. He had come up from farm boy and woodchopper to clothier's apprentice. Free from his apprenticeship for a few months and ambitious to get ahead in the world, he set out for the village school, where he found the little teacher who completely won his heart. Then Abigail was transferred to another school.

Their engagement lasted five years; and, during the last three, young Fillmore could not afford to visit his bride-to-be. But there was never any doubt in the minds of either that they loved each other. In 1826, eight years after their first meeting, they were married and went to live in the little house in Aurora which Millard built with his own hands.

The young bride, during the early years of her married life, cheerfully went about her housekeeping, continued to teach school, and tutored her husband during the evenings. It was most unusual for married women to work in those days. Abigail Powers Fillmore was the first First Lady who worked for a living before marriage and continued to work for a salary after marriage. She did this to relieve her husband of the responsibility of supporting her while he studied law. Thus, in sharing the financial burdens, she became the forerunner of the capable young women of today who work to help their husbands get a better start in life.

Even after their son, Millard Powers Fillmore, was born in 1828, Abigail resumed her teaching job. With her help, Millard Fillmore acquired knowledge, completed his studies, secured clients, and made many friends. It was not until her husband became a successful lawyer that she consented to devote her full time to the managing of a home and family. In 1830, they moved to Buffalo, where there were greater opportunities for his business. In 1832, he was elected to Congress. Also in that year, a second child, Mary Abigail Fillmore, was born.

As Millard Fillmore became more and more well-known in Congress and at home, and as politicians began to recognize his skill in drafting resolutions and defending them,

Abigail stayed most of the time in Buffalo. For the first time in her life she was well-to-do. With two children and a husband to watch over, she might well have decided to take things easy. She was past thirty, and she had worked hard. But Abigail was not one to stand still. She taught herself French, and when she had mastered it so that she could read and translate easily, she took up music. After diligent practice she learned to play the piano; and years later, when she was First Lady, there were many pleasant musical evenings when she and her daughter played and sang duets for their friends.

As the children grew older, Abigail went with her husband to Albany, where they lived in a "quiet, temperance hotel" while he attended sessions of the State legislature. She also accompanied him to Washington for the sessions of Congress. Washington circles were much impressed with handsome, intellectual Mrs. Fillmore. In 1848, Abigail had her first glimpse of the interior of the White House, when she and her husband were invited to dinner by President and Mrs. Polk.

As President Polk's term drew to a close and he refused to consider renomination, the Whig party began to look about for a running mate for General Zachary Taylor; and Millard Fillmore was chosen. Abigail again went to Washington in 1849, this time as the wife of the Vice President. The clothier's apprentice had come a long way!

Sixteen months later, in true success-story style, opportunity again knocked on the door of the poor boy who, at the age of twelve, had been earning his living as a woodchopper. President Zachary Taylor died on July 9, 1850, after serving less than a third of his term; and Millard Fillmore was sworn in as President of the United States.

Abigail, penniless daughter of a Baptist preacher, who had started to earn her living when she was sixteen, was now First Lady—and quite equal to the task, although she was not as strong physically, at fifty-two, as she would have liked to be. Strong, however, in intellect, and strong in her pride in her husband, she entered the White House "a matron of commanding person and beautiful countenance." Success did not change her in the least. Modern and forward-looking in her ideas, she did not confine her social life entirely to the President's house, but went about Washington as freely as she had done in previous years. When the famous Swedish singer, Jenny Lind, arrived in Washington, Abigail Fillmore attended the concert. With her daughter, she also went to public lectures, banquets, art exhibits, and literary meetings.

This daughter, Mary Abigail, was much like her mother. She was graduated from the State Normal School of New York, became a teacher, and taught in a Buffalo public school. She spoke French, German, and Spanish, was proficient in music, and was an amateur sculptor. She continued to teach even after her father became President; and it was only at her mother's urgent request that she went to the White House to help with the duties of hostess.

Mrs. Fillmore, modern though she was, did not forget her religious upbringing. On Sundays, the Executive Mansion was closed to all visitors while the family devoted itself to rest, meditation, and regular attendance at church.

Gas and water pipes were now coming into general use. Mrs. Fillmore, always considerate of the working people who had to carry bath water by hand, had water pipes and a zinc bathtub installed in the White House. She also supervised the purchase of new carpets and new furniture.

But the most important innovation of all was the new White House library. When the First Lady discovered that there wasn't one book in the Executive Mansion, she prevailed upon her husband to get an appropriation from Congress, and while the amount was not large, Mrs. Fillmore enthusiastically went to work. Under her careful supervision, books were chosen which became the nucleus of the first White House library.

The big, cheerful room with its well-filled bookcases was a decided novelty in Washington social life. There was a piano in the library, and there she and Mary Abigail received their friends, informally, for impromptu musicals. They gave small dinners, too, every Saturday evening in the family dining room. And each Thursday evening there were large state dinners in the big Congressional dining room.

Probably Abigail's greatest luxury, however, was provided by friends and admirers of New York state—a handsome, silver-mounted harness for the First Lady's carriage horses. The Fillmores rode grandly through the streets of Washington in a splendid coach behind a liveried coachman.

While Abigail was a competent and charming First Lady, Millard Fillmore was not successful as a President. He made many mistakes in judgment. He had always been outspoken against slavery, but he apparently did not have the courage of his convictions, for he gave his support to what was called the Great Compromise of 1850. This law provided for the hunting down of fugitive slaves in the North, and returning them to their Southern owners; and it made Fillmore highly unpopular with his followers in the North. He served out the term of Zachary Taylor, but he was not nominated to succeed himself.

Fillmore's defeat hurt Abigail, but she cheerfully began making plans to welcome President-elect Franklin Pierce and his wife.

Inauguration day was cold and stormy. Beside her husband, as always, Abigail took part in all the outdoor ceremonies. It was said afterward that she caught a cold while standing with Thackeray and Irving on the windswept portico of the Capitol as the new President took the oath of office and delivered his inaugural address. The Fillmores had planned to go back to Buffalo for a while and then take a trip abroad. But Mrs. Fillmore never saw her old home in Buffalo again; she never left Washington.

Her husband took her to Willard's Hotel and there, in the suite used by Pierce before he entered the White House, Abigail Powers Fillmore died on March 30, 1853. Three days later she was laid to rest at Forest Lawn, in Buffalo, N.Y.

Jane Means Appleton Pierce

RELUCTANT FIRST LADY

OF all the First Ladies in America's history, none ever crossed the threshold of the White House as reluctantly as did Jane Appleton Pierce, wife of our fourteenth President. Mrs. Franklin Pierce was more than unhappy; she was painfully shy. Her nerves had been shattered by recent grief.

A few days before the inauguration of her husband, while the family was returning from Boston to their home in Concord, New Hampshire, the axle of one of the passenger cars broke, and the coach bearing President-elect Pierce, his wife, and their only living son was hurled down a steep embankment. After the crash Mr. Pierce, slightly bruised, succeeded in extricating his wife from the ruins; then he returned to search for the twelve-year-old boy. He soon found the crushed and lifeless body.

Highly sensitive, delicate in mind and body, torn constantly by many anxieties, it is not surprising that Jane Appleton Pierce could not put away her grief and take an active part in the life of her husband. Washington society, in that year of 1853, knew her only as "the shadow in the White House." To gain a better understanding of her temperament, we must go back to her early life and consider her heredity and environment.

She was born Jane Means Appleton at Hampton, New Hampshire, on March 12, 1806. When she was a year old, her father, Rev. Jesse Appleton, became President of Bowdoin College. Dr. Appleton was an unusual person, to say the least. Even among the most pious, he was regarded as a religious fanatic who worked and prayed himself into an early grave. Jane was thirteen when her father died of tuberculosis. The nature of his disease, his erratic temperament, and his death must have left their imprint on the mind of the impressionable little girl.

Mrs. Appleton belonged to a well-to-do family of Amherst, Massachusetts, and to that city she returned with her six children. There Jane received a thorough education, with considerable emphasis, no doubt, on Biblical instruction.

She was twenty when she met the dashing young Frank Pierce, son of a former governor of New Hampshire. Pierce was completing his studies in a Northampton law office, and it wasn't long before the young graduate of Bowdoin discovered, just across the river, the girl who soon became his "dearest Jeanie."

A portrait of her, painted at that time, shows a fragile young woman as delicately beautiful as a cameo. She was small and slender, with large dark eyes under gracefully curving brows. Her black hair, parted in the middle, hung in ringlets over her ears. The Jeanie in the picture is lovely, but here is no frivolous, fun-loving girl. The influence of her pious father is apparent in her severe black bonnet and plain, dark, cloth coat with a high velvet collar.

This carefully reared, completely feminine, wholly good woman must have found young Frank Pierce highly exciting. A friend and college classmate of Nathaniel Hawthorne and Calvin Stowe, he was very much the man of the world. He mixed with politics and politicians and was said to patronize bars. Only one historian, so far as we know, has actually called Franklin Pierce an alcoholic; but it may be his fondness for the glass that cheers was the reason Jane begged him to give up politics.

When she first met him, he was a handsome young beau, with an engaging personality and a lively disposition. He put his Jeanie on a pedestal and worshiped her; no wonder she returned his love! Their engagement, however, lasted six years. There is a hint that Jane's folks did not altogether approve of young Franklin Pierce and some of his worldly companions. It is entirely possible, too, that the strict views of the Appleton family irked the rising young politician. At any rate, Jane was twenty-eight and Frank was thirty-one when they finally were married.

Although her husband was already a Congressman, Mrs. Pierce rarely went to Washington. From the very beginning of their married life, she pleaded with him to give up politics and settle down as a lawyer in the quiet life of New England.

Their first child, a boy, died in infancy; a second boy, Frank Robert, was born in 1840. In April, 1841, a third son was born. He was called Benny by his parents. Perhaps this period, when Jane was busy mothering her two little boys in Concord, was the happiest of her life. Her husband's earnings made it possible for him to gratify her every wish; and he was devoted to her. Yet, Jane Appleton worried over the health of her children and the welfare of her husband. Adoring them all to the point of possessiveness, she was never content when one of them was away from her side.

Finally, she won her battle against politics—at least temporarily. In June, 1842, Senator Pierce, not quite 38 years old, returned home to his law practice. Two years later, their little son, Frank Robert, died at the age of four. Benny became the one remaining child on whom Jane centered her lavish affections.

Though the solicitous wife and mother was successful in keeping her husband out of politics, all her pleading and all her fears were unavailing when war came along. The declaration of war with Mexico found Franklin Pierce eager to serve his country. He enlisted as a private in a company raised in Concord. In the following year he was appointed colonel and later was promoted to brigadier general. He served in Mexico nine months, while his wife and son remained in the house in Concord.

Upon his return to New Hampshire, Franklin Pierce resumed his law practice. In 1848, for his wife's sake, he refused the nomination for Governor. Four years later he was equally emphatic about not wanting the Democratic nomination for the Presidency; nevertheless he was nominated and elected in a sweeping victory. At forty-eight, he was the youngest man (up to that time) to go into the White House as Chief Executive.

Jane, naturally proud of her husband, tried hard to overcome her shyness and put aside her preference for a retiring, sheltered life. Cheerfully, she made preparations to move to Washington; but when Benny was killed just before the inauguration, she was overcome with grief. She was not present at her husband's inauguration on March 4, 1853, and it was several weeks before she felt strong enough to join him in the capital. She was, without doubt, the saddest First Lady ever to enter the White House. Painfully sensitive, Jane was frightened by Washington society; nevertheless, she tried to do her part at public receptions and formal dinners. The public sympathized with her in her bereavement.

The President did not have an easy time in the White House. The question of slavery was keeping the nation in a constant turmoil. In 1854, a brilliant author fanned the rising flame—Harriet Beecher Stowe's *Uncle Tom's Cabin* was stirring a million readers.

Both North and South had supported Pierce in the election. The southern Democrats liked him because he agreed with their views on slavery. He had supported the Kansas-Nebraska Bill, which set apart Kansas and Nebraska and permitted the people who settled there to decide for themselves whether their states should be free or slave. This bill caused considerable argument because, according to the Missouri Compromise of 1820, all territory above the southern boundary of Missouri was declared to be "free soil." But Congress voted to repeal the Missouri Compromise. As soon as this was done, there was a wild scramble. Settlers flocked to Kansas from North and South, one side wanting it to be a free state, the other demanding that it be slave. There, the first blood was shed in a struggle which later was to develop into the proportions of civil war.

Franklin Pierce continued to throw his influence with those who favored slavery. The whole country recognized at once that their President could not be counted upon to remain neutral. As his administration ended, the "northern man with southern principles" grew less popular, and the Whig party broke up. With the shadows of civil war spreading darkly across the land, Pierce retired on March 4, 1857.

Jane Appleton Pierce at this time was so ill she had to be carried from the Executive Mansion. Once back at home in New Hampshire, however, she began to feel better. The following autumn Mr. and Mrs. Pierce sailed for Madeira. They stayed there for six months, then spent another year and a half traveling through Europe.

On December 2, 1863, Jane Appleton Pierce died at Andover, Massachusetts. Her husband lived to see the end of the Civil War, though he took no part in it. On October 8, 1869, he passed away quietly and peacefully in the New Hampshire hills, and was laid to rest beside his wife and children in the cemetery at Concord. He had served his country as President when the entire nation was in a state of extreme unrest. No doubt he was relieved to turn over the reins of government to James Buchanan who, on March 4, 1857, was inaugurated President of a United States that was no longer united.

Civil war was already raging in Kansas; John Brown tried to start an insurrection among the slaves; the southern states were threatening secession. To be President in this emergency took courage and vision; and some historians say that Buchanan had neither. Born near Mercersburg, Pennsylvania, April 23, 1791, at twenty-one he dropped his work as a lawyer and enlisted as a private to fight against the British in the War of 1812. After the war was over, James Buchanan was touched by a tragedy which cast a shadow over his entire life. He fell in love with a young girl named Anne Coleman, daughter of one of the wealthiest men in Lancaster. They became engaged and were ideally happy until, in the summer of 1819, James received a letter from Anne breaking the engagement. Evil gossip, without foundation in truth, had prompted her to write the letter; and, regardless of his entreaties, she refused to be reconciled. A few months later, while visiting relatives in Philadelphia, Anne Coleman died. Although he was to survive her by 44 years, Buchanan's devotion to Anne Coleman remained his only romance—he lived and died a bachelor. When his executors went over his papers, they found a packet of love letters from the sweetheart of his youth. In accordance with his written request, the faded mementos were destroyed without being read.

When he was elected President, he brought with him to the White House his nephew, Colonel Lane, who acted as his private secretary; and his niece, Harriet Lane, who made quite a name for herself as mistress of the Executive Mansion. Left an orphan at the age of 9, Harriet was well provided with money. She sought the guardianship of her Uncle James, and his house became her home. She was a fun-loving little tomboy, a blonde with deep violet eyes. Buchanan sent her to school, first at Charles Town, in what was then Virginia, then to the convent at Georgetown, D.C.

The graceful, poised young woman who was graduated from the convent was a very different person from the hoydenish child of a few years before. She went with her uncle, then our ambassador to England, to the royal court of Queen Victoria, where her beauty created a sensation. When Buchanan became President, she became the official hostess of the White House.

Not since the reign of Dolley Madison had there been a hostess in the White House as popular as the lovely Harriet Lane. At twenty-four, she was beautiful and vivacious. Her charm, her youth, and her gay spirits brought a revival of social life to Washington. While the nation tottered on the brink of civil war, the President's house saw a round of brilliant festivities, climaxed by a visit from the Prince of Wales. All the world praised Harriet Lane for her efficient handling of the duties of First Lady; but no such praise was accorded James Buchanan for discharging his duties as President of the United States.

He kept changing his mind on every important question which came up. First, he declared that no state had a right to break away from the Union; then he stated that the government had no power to prevent secession. He announced it his duty to call out the army and navy to enforce Federal laws, yet he did nothing. As a result of his inability to make decisions, both North and South lost faith in his leadership.

Just before the close of his tragic administration, there were two Presidents in the country. Jefferson Davis, Senator from

Mississippi, announced his state's withdrawal from the Union, and then himself withdrew from the United States Senate. Two weeks later, the newly formed confederacy chose him as its leader.

Abused by both sides, unhappy and bewildered, James Buchanan retired at the close of his term to his home in Pennsylvania, while the nation hailed the simple, homely Abraham Lincoln from Illinois, steadfast in his purpose and determined to preserve the Union at all costs.

In the events which followed the public soon forgot James Buchanan. But there was one who did not forget. Harriet Lane, who never wavered in her loyalty to the uncle who had brought her up through an orphaned childhood, bequeathed one hundred thousand dollars for the erection, in Washington, of a monument to his memory.

Mary Todd Lincoln

MUCH CRITICIZED FIRST LADY

WHEN Mary Todd was one of the most popular young women of New Salem, Illinois, with several suitors competing for her favor, she was asked: "Which man do you intend to marry?" Her answer came quickly: "The one that has the best chance to be President." That remark has since been widely quoted to support the contention that the pretty and willful brunette was highly ambitious. It appears in biographical sketches even more often than another remark she made when she was the middle-aged wife of Abraham Lincoln: "I often laugh and tell Mr. Lincoln that I am determined my next husband shall be rich!"

It is quite probable that Mary was joking on both occasions. No one enjoyed a laugh more than Lincoln himself. "One 'd' is enough for God," he used to tell his friends in Springfield, "but not for the Todds!" And, years later, one evening at the White House when Mrs. Lincoln appeared before him in a magnificent new gown with a sweeping train, his tired eyes twinkled, and he said: "My, our cat has a long tail to-night!"

Perhaps these two people, so sadly mismated, so completely different in character and temperament, realized the need for jesting. Otherwise, their close association, never a happy marriage, might have been unbearable. Some early historians politely omit reference to Mary Todd Lincoln's vagaries and shortcomings, but in recent years she has become the most controversial figure in the long line of First Ladies.

Did she ever love Abraham Lincoln? Did she marry him because of a consuming ambition to preside over the White

House? Did she help or hinder his career? When did she lose her sanity?

These are some of the questions that may never be answered with certainty. Many biographers believe young Mary Todd was deeply in love with the tall, witty Kentuckian; and point out that she refused Stephen A. Douglas, whose prospects at that time seemed far brighter than those of the struggling, poverty-ridden Lincoln. Others insist she was convinced from the beginning that Abraham Lincoln would one day become President of the United States.

There is a third premise that may well be nearer the truth. Mary Todd was radiantly pretty, with clear blue eyes, long dark lashes, brown hair, and a winsome dimpled smile. Her friends made a great fuss over her, and she had more spending money than most of her young associates. From the time she was a child she had been accustomed to having everything she wanted. Lincoln was probably the only young man of her acquaintance who seemed quite indifferent to her charms. He had been deeply in love with his first sweetheart, Ann Rutledge, and would surely have married her had she not died during their engagement. Later, he twice proposed to the tall, handsome Mary Owens, who twice refused him. Lincoln thereupon wrote his friend, Mrs. O. H. Browning:

"I have come to the conclusion never more to think of marrying, and for this reason,—that I can never be satisfied with any one who would be fool enough to have me."

It seems logical to conclude that the impulsive, spoiled, and self-centered Mary Todd, infuriated by Lincoln's indifference, made up her mind to capture his attention. Later, after they were engaged, Lincoln feared the marriage would not be a happy one and begged her to call the whole thing off. Ward Lamon, his biographer, states that he failed to be present at the time first set for the ceremony, though the guests were assembled and the wedding feast was prepared. He became ill, and it was more than a year later, on November 4, 1842, when the two were married. All of which seems to indicate that the marriage of Abraham Lincoln and Mary Todd, when she was nearly twenty-four and he was thirty-three, was based on a determined woman's whim and a kindly man's capitulation to tears and cajolery.

Soon after the wedding, Lincoln wrote to a friend, "Nothing new here, except my marrying, which to me is a matter of profound wonder."

They began life together in poverty, living in a room at the Globe Tavern in Springfield, where Lincoln paid a total of four dollars per week for their lodging and meals. Less than nineteen years later, Lincoln was President and his wife had achieved her highest ambition. Those years between were marked by quarrels, unhappiness, and tragedy; but before the end it is evident that Mary Todd Lincoln grew to love her husband. Meanwhile, Lincoln carried silently and alone the tremendous secret burden of a moody and irresponsible wife.

Mary Todd's life began normally enough on December 13, 1818, in Lexington, Kentucky. Her father was a wealthy lawyer, politician, and businessman. Her mother, Eliza Parker Todd, died when Mary was eight years old, and she was brought up by an aunt. Her sisters said later she was something of a tomboy, though she early displayed a passionate fondness for the sheer embroidered French muslins, bright ribbons, and exquisite laces her father brought her from New Orleans. Like other young girls of well-to-do families, she went to boarding school and then to a fashionable finishing school, both of which she thoroughly enjoyed.

When, at twenty-one, Mary Todd went to live with her sister, Mrs. Edwards (Elizabeth Todd), in Springfield, she was gay, witty, accomplished, and lovely in her hoop-skirted gowns and satin slippers. It was there that Joshua Speed introduced Abraham Lincoln to her; and there, after their stormy courtship, they were married. Her dominating nature began to assert itself at once. She tried to improve Lincoln's manners, change his careless habits, and reform him in the matter of dress. As the years passed, her sharp tongue became sharper. More and more often she was attacked by violent headaches; more and more often she lashed out bitterly against her husband and everybody else who displeased her.

Following the birth of their first child, Robert Todd, the Lincolns lived for a year in a rented house, then they moved into a plain but comfortable dwelling costing $1,500, which was to be the historic Lincoln home.

By the time Lincoln was elected to Congress in 1846, there was already a second baby, Edward Baker. Mary Lincoln was jubilant over her husband's appointment; and she insisted on taking him to Lexington, Kentucky, before they went to Washington, so that she could show him off to relatives and friends.

When, on March 4, 1861, Abraham Lincoln was inaugurated as President, the country already was seething with civil war. His First Lady was either unable to appraise the situation or incapable of caring about the difficult position into which her husband had been thrust. She was jubilant. At last her ambition was realized: her prophecy had been fulfilled.

Even in the White House, Mary Todd Lincoln seemed unable to control her temper. She terrorized and made enemies of the servants. She was jealous to the point of rudeness of any woman who so much as spoke to her husband. Unlike other American women during the Civil War, she took no part in caring for the thousands of wounded, sick, and dying soldiers and sailors who were brought to Washington.

While the President was filled with anguish and worry, and the lines in his sad face grew deeper, she seemed incapable of thinking of anything but her misfortune in having a husband so busy that he could not spend all his time with her, and a Washington society shadowed by the stringencies of war. To counteract these disappointments, she plunged into an orgy of spending which the entire nation criticized openly. She bought lavish costumes, jewels, and laces. She stormed over the untidiness of President Lincoln's appearance, and quarreled bitterly with him when he was late for meals.

When Mrs. Ord, wife of General Ord, rode on her horse beside the President for a few moments while Mrs. Lincoln and Mrs. Grant were in an ambulance just behind them, Mrs. Lincoln raged: "What does this woman mean by riding by the side of the President—and ahead of me? Does she suppose he wants her by the side of him?" Later, before a crowd of army officers and others, she attacked Mrs. Ord with an outburst of insults and epithets until, as Badeau describes the scene: "The poor woman burst into tears and inquired what she had done, but Mrs. Lincoln refused to be appeased, and stormed till she was tired. Later Mrs. Lincoln suggested before all that General Ord should be removed from command . . . he was unfit for his place . . . to say nothing of his wife."

While Mary Todd Lincoln's aberrations became more and more pronounced until finally people began to refer to her as "a sad case," President Lincoln's patience and self-discipline seemed to increase. Undoubtedly he had known for years what the public was just beginning to realize—his wife was mentally ill.

Four boys were born to the Lincolns within ten years; and even those who were most critical of Mary Lincoln's behavior admitted that she was a good, devoted, loving mother. Little Eddy died in 1850, not quite four years old. In 1862, Willie, a delicate, studious, blue-eyed boy of twelve, took cold while out riding on his pony and became fatally ill. The death of her beloved Willie aggravated the emotional instability from which the distracted mother suffered. For days she lay weeping and moaning, afraid of the dark, giving way to hallucinations, while Lincoln, also grief-stricken, put aside his personal feelings and labored day and night to preserve the Union.

It was during this period, while Mrs. Lincoln was struggling with her sorrow and loss, that she made the mistake of inviting to the White House some of her own people, whose sympathies were with the South. The secessionist relatives, it is said, took advantage of Lincoln's hospitality by carrying back medicines through the Union lines on a Presidential pass; and young Tad Lincoln, unrestrained by his mother, made a playmate of the daughter of a Confederate spy who was then imprisoned in Washington.

These incidents were not crimes, but in those turbulent times, as in all wars, people were unduly suspicious and quick to accuse. Mrs. Lincoln was suspected of having sympathies with the South. While this accusation was unjust, it aroused such public reaction against President Lincoln toward the close of his first term that his re-election seemed doubtful.

As the campaign got under way, Mrs. Lincoln's creditors, to whom she owed thousands of dollars, began to pursue her and demand immediate payment. Easy-going, generous, and occupied with more important matters, her husband had no idea that she was deeply in debt. Only Elizabeth Keckley, a colored seamstress who worked in the White House, shared the First Lady's secret. All her life Mary Lincoln had loved display, had wanted to impress people with her social importance. Now, it seemed as if her house of gilded cards might tumble at any moment. She realized that she had few friends in Washington and that even her servants had no loyalty or love for her. Obsessed by these gloomy thoughts, she felt that everyone would be glad to witness her downfall.

Her thoughts must have turned many times to that first reception at the White House, when the crowds were so great that many guests had to step out through the windows, so that those thronging the doors could get in. The President that night had been dressed as usual in plain black broadcloth, and he wore white kid gloves. Mary Lincoln was elegant in rich rose-colored brocaded silk, her wide flounces trimmed elaborately with the finest of point lace. Her jewels were diamonds and pearls, and her blue eyes sparkled with the triumph of success.

There were few brilliant parties in the months and years that followed. She was not as fortunate as other First Ladies in this respect, and, in judging her, it is well to keep this in mind. Mary Todd Lincoln was a lonely woman much of the time. During the summers she wandered from one fashionable resort to another, while the President labored on in the heat of Washington.

Through all those bloodstained months and years of his administration, Lincoln never swerved in carrying out his oath to preserve the Union. On September 22, 1862, he issued the warning that if the states in rebellion did not return to the Union by the following January 1, he would issue a proclamation declaring the slaves in these states to "be forever free."

That warning was ignored, and on New Year's Day, 1863, Abraham Lincoln completed the immortal document on which he had been working for weeks, and signed his name to the Emancipation Proclamation which gave freedom to millions of slaves and assured freedom for untold millions yet unborn.

The war dragged on. But, slowly, the tide was turning. In July, 1863, came the Battle of Gettysburg and the retreat of General Lee's southern forces to the Potomac. The following November, when a soldiers' national cemetery was dedicated at Gettysburg, Abraham Lincoln offered what he modestly referred to as "half a dozen words of consecration." The brief, simple message of the Gettysburg Address is now written indelibly on the minds of all Americans, and is known throughout the civilized world.

In the summer of 1864, with the South facing certain defeat and the entire nation sick of war, there seemed hope for a just peace, and it became clear that Lincoln would be re-elected to office. On March 4, 1865, with fighting still going on, his second inauguration was held. As he rose to speak, a roar of applause filled the air, and a tremendous shout went up from the crowd. Mary Lincoln, in that moment, must have been proud. Her husband had found his place in the hearts of the people. And she must have been thrilled, as the crowds were that day, when Abraham Lincoln uttered those compassionate words which so clearly demonstrated his great humane qualities:

"With malice toward none; with charity for all; with firmness in the right, as God gives us to see the right, let us strive on to finish the work we are in; to bind up the nation's wounds; to care for him who shall have borne the battle, and for his widow and his orphan—to do all which may achieve and cherish a just and lasting peace among ourselves, and with all nations."

The peace for which Lincoln yearned came one month later, on April 9, 1865, when General Robert E. Lee surrendered to General Ulysses S. Grant at Appomattox Court House, Virginia. That night Lincoln's thin, serious face shone with relief and joy. Mrs. Lincoln, too, was jubilant. The people were hailing her husband as the savior of the Union. Outside the White House the crowds were cheering and shouting his name. Now that he had been re-elected, her creditors ceased to torment her. Her son, Tad, was gradually taking her thoughts away from Willie, whom she had lost. At last it seemed as if life would be pleasanter. Her troubled mind was eased.

A few days later she persuaded her husband to go with her to a performance of *Our American Cousin* at Ford's Theatre, to celebrate victory and get some relaxation. The Lincolns were happy that evening, making plans for the years ahead. As they stepped into the President's box on that evening of April 14, 1865, and the band played "Hail To The Chief," Mary Todd Lincoln's heart was light. Here were gaiety, applause, and entertainment. The President bowed; the play began.

John Wilkes Booth, the assassin, quietly opened the door of the box, put a pistol to the President's head, and fired. Early next morning, without regaining consciousness, Lincoln died. They carried him back to the soil of Illinois, back home where he had so often longed to go. But for five weeks his wife was unable to leave the White House. Then, frantically realizing the debts she had to face, she stripped the Executive Mansion of her personal effects, her clothes, jewels, and the many gifts that had been presented to the family, and shipped them in crates to Chicago.

For the next seventeen years, sorrow, sickness, and wild hallucinations were her close companions. The President had left an estate of some forty thousand dollars, and Congress voted Mrs. Lincoln the $22,000 which would have been due her husband had he finished out the balance of his official year. Robert Lincoln, partner in a law firm in Chicago, felt that $60,000 was ample to care for his mother and young Tad. But Mrs. Lincoln was obsessed by the haunting fear of poverty. "Only my darling Tad prevents me from taking my life," she wrote to Elizabeth Keckley.

At an open sale on Broadway, in New York city, she disposed of her jewels, shawls, and laces; and in a letter to her agent she wildly denounced the Republican leaders who refused to grant her a pension. That letter, to the embarrassment of her family, was promptly publicized in *The New York World,* and after that most of the nation's press made bitter attacks on her. When her son Robert and other members of her family confronted her with questions, she told them about her debts.

Accompanied by her son Tad, she lived very quietly in Europe for the next few years, going from one doctor to another, and continuing to write upbraiding letters to Congress, imploring them to give her a pension. Finally, in 1870, she was voted the sum of $3,000 annually. At fifty-two, she could return to the United States.

But still another sorrow was in store for her. Tad, now a fine young man of eighteen, was ill on the steamship which brought them back, and two weeks later he died of typhoid fever. This last grief was the final blow. From then on, Mary Todd Lincoln, tormented by fears of poverty and assassination, lived completely in an illusory world.

In 1875, her only living son, Robert, took legal steps to have her put in a place of safety. On a train returning from Florida she had created a scene, insisting that her coffee had been poisoned; in a Chicago hotel, while partly undressed, she had walked through the hall and tried to enter an elevator. Facing her across the courtroom, her son testified sadly that she had not been normal since his father's death, and was growing more irrational every year. The jury pronounced Mary Lincoln insane. The next day she tried to kill herself, after which she was taken to a private mental hospital at Batavia, Illinois.

Her sister's family worked steadily for her release; and in June, 1876, a second jury voted Mrs. Lincoln sane enough to be given over to her sister's custody. Not long afterwards she again went abroad, spending several winters in a small apartment in Paris where she lived alone. There, during the winter of 1879, she fell and injured her spine. Once again, when she was able to travel, she decided to return home.

That homecoming must have been sad and bewildering to the weary exile. In October, 1880, she arrived from France on the steamer *Amerique;* and, as the vessel eased into the dock, Mrs. Lincoln saw a large and eager crowd on the wharf. Through the dark confusion of her disordered mind, a lucid spark must have kindled memories of other years and other crowds. She forgot that she was a little old lady whose face was wrinkled, whose hair was whitening, and whose plain black cloak was torn. After four years in France, she was coming home! When the gangplank was lowered and the passengers stepped ashore, a cheer rang out and the crowd pressed closer. Mrs. Lincoln, leaning on the arm of a nephew who had met her at Quarantine, walked toward the gate. A policeman touched her on the shoulder and ordered her to stand back, as an elegant coach and four drove up.

Into the carriage stepped Sarah Bernhardt, the famous French actress. After it had driven off, the other passengers from the *Amerique,* Mary Todd Lincoln among them, were permitted to depart. The fanfare had been for the great Bernhardt.

For two years longer, Mary Todd Lincoln lived with her sister in Springfield, remaining in darkness and seclusion in a little upstairs room of the house from which she had been married. On July 16, 1882, she suffered a stroke and died.

On the wedding ring which Abraham Lincoln placed upon her finger when she was young, were engraved these words: "Love is eternal." Certainly he never failed her in devotion, understanding, and compassion.

Shortly after the death of Mary Todd Lincoln, Phebe Hanaford, author and Quaker preacher, wrote:

> "It is a credit to American manhood that the men who have written of Mrs. Lincoln's death have not forgotten that she was the consort, honored and beloved, of the first martyr to their country, and, as such, passing swiftly by her faults, they have laid with reverent hand the bays of kindly honor on her grave."

This gentle philosophy, phrased in the flowery language of the period, is worth remembering today.

Eliza McCardle Johnson

WIFE OF THE PRESIDENT
WHO NEVER WENT TO SCHOOL

ONE sunny Saturday afternoon in September, 1826, two young girls stood on a corner of Greenville, Tennessee's, main street, watching the approach of a tired and dusty horse led by a tired and dusty young man. Eliza McCardle and her friend had watched many caravans of settlers drive through their town and on toward the west, but never had they seen such a scrawny horse and dilapidated wagon. On the seat sat a shabby, middle-aged woman in rusty black, surrounded by a jumble of pots and pans. The wagon was loaded with chairs, tables, washtubs, and household goods of every description. Plodding along on foot, at the head of his ancient nag, was a broad-shouldered, black-haired lad whose tired face was streaked with dirt.

"I wonder who *he* is!" exclaimed Eliza's friend, laughing.

"Don't laugh; that's my beau!" Eliza replied quickly. Her eyes were bright with mischief. She had never seen the young man before, but there was something about his determined jaw and the look in his piercing black eyes that aroused her sympathy. She liked him. As he helped his mother out of the wagon, Eliza could see that he was not a farmer of the "poor white" class. He was not dressed in butternut or homespun, nor did he walk with the clumsy stride of a boy who had straddled furrows all his life. Apparently he had come to the foothills of the Great Smoky Mountains to settle.

Eliza was sixteen and a schoolteacher. She knew where to get information about the lad who set up business in a tiny shop, hung out his sign "A. Johnson, tailor," and went to work with needle and shears to support his mother. The Widow Johnson and her son had come, she learned, from Raleigh,

North Carolina. They weren't "quality"; at the same time they weren't "nobodies."

In a village such as Greenville, with frequent "hoedowns," "socials," and church picnics, it wasn't long before Andrew Johnson and Eliza McCardle became acquainted. Little by little, as they were together more and more often, she found out that his father had died when he was five, that for the next few years his mother had supported him by weaving, and that, as soon as he was old enough, he had been apprenticed to a tailor. He had never been to school, and he was just beginning to learn to read. Night after night he pored over borrowed books.

To Eliza, who was well educated for a young woman of her day, this was a shame. No man could make much of his life unless he had some knowledge of writing, spelling, arithmetic, history, and geography. On every possible occasion, the patient, brown-haired, mountain girl instructed him in these subjects; she told him of the latest political developments in Nashville and Washington; she clipped from newspapers the speeches of prominent men and read them to Andrew as he sat cross-legged on his bench, cutting and sewing in the little two-room shop where his mother and he lived and worked.

She saw at once that Andrew took an interest in political affairs. The serious-minded girl quickened in him a desire to learn more about Tennessee and the rest of the United States. She schooled him in the proper pronunciation and spelling of words, and opened his eyes to the advances that were being made in the scientific world. Through her teachings, Andrew's ambitions were aroused and he began to realize that he would not have to be a tailor all his life.

It was almost inevitable that the two young people, mountain-bred and having so many interests in common, should fall in love. On May 17, 1827, when Eliza was seventeen and Andrew not yet nineteen, they were married by Mordecai Lincoln, a magistrate of Greenville and a kinsman of Abraham Lincoln.

With money he had saved, Andrew bought a small farm for his mother, and he and Eliza lived in the room behind the tailor shop. Every moment she could spare from housekeeping was devoted to teaching her young husband. Patiently she guided his hand as he learned to write; in the evenings, as he basted and stitched, she read to him; and, by the hour, they talked of what was going on in the world.

In that little mountain village, three women watched over and stimulated the hopes and ambitions of Andrew Johnson—his own mother, Eliza's mother, and Eliza herself, who felt sure he would one day become great. For words came easily at his bidding; the young men of the village often dropped into the little shop to listen to his views. He believed Tennessee was a land of promise and, as he advanced in knowledge, and progressed with his reading, he won the liking and admiration of the workingmen of Greenville. When a debating society was organized, he became one of the most active and enthusiastic members. Once each week he walked four miles to and from the meetings. Eliza did not mind staying at home; Andy, she felt confident, was making a career for himself in public life.

A thrifty manager and hard worker at his trade, Andrew soon was able to buy a comfortable house, and gradually he bought other property as well. When he was twenty, Eliza was elated by his election as alderman; and two years later as mayor, both on the workingmen's ticket. Women were becoming increasingly active in public life, but Eliza Johnson seemed quite content to concentrate her energies on her home, making it a place of refuge for her husband when he was tired or perplexed, and looking after her little daughter, Martha, who was born in 1828. Here in the Greenville house, Eliza remained while Andrew Johnson continued his upward climb to state representative, Congressman, governor of Tennessee, Senator, and finally to the office of Vice President. For as much as two years at a time, Eliza did not see her husband. But he was never absent from her thoughts. She was never ambitious for herself; only for him.

When, during March, 1864, while the Civil War raged, President Lincoln appointed Johnson military governor of Tennessee, Eliza agreed wholeheartedly with her husband that for Tennessee to secede from the Union would be the beginning of the end. She approved his plan to permit the white inhabitants of the territories to decide for themselves whether they would have slavery or not. Nor did she change her opinions when her husband was denounced as a traitor to the South and threatened with assassination.

Eliza Johnson's mother had died in 1854; Andrew's mother had died two years later. Eliza's two girls grew up and married. She had few living relatives and was lonely, miserable, and ill while her husband was military governor at Nashville. When the Civil War began and she was in Greenville with other Unionists of East Tennessee, she was abruptly ordered to leave and pass beyond the Confederate lines within thirty-six hours.

She hoped daily to hear from Johnson, but no word came. Accompanied by her children and grandchildren, Eliza attempted to cross the lines, but she was told by Confederate troops who occupied the town of Murfreesboro that she could not pass through. No accommodations were to be had in the crowded, war-torn town.

During this trying journey, they knew they were likely to be arrested for the slightest offense, and they were insulted again and again by the rabble. After days and nights of suffering and anxiety, they finally reached Nashville. Eliza's health was seriously impaired by this journey, and by her grief at the death of her son, an army surgeon, who was thrown from his horse and killed.

Then came the end of the war, the assassination of President Lincoln, and the hurried swearing-in of her husband as President of the United States. By that time, Eliza McCardle Johnson was a confirmed invalid. She did not appear in society or participate in White House activities; but her little grandchildren enjoyed the freedom of the dwelling and grounds. The duties of White House hostess were well handled by her oldest daughter, Martha Patterson, wife of Senator Patterson of Tennessee. Martha's dignity and poise were remarkable: "We are plain people from the mountains of Tennessee," she said, "called here for a short time by a national calamity. I trust too much will not be expected of us." But from Martha Patterson much was received.

When the Johnsons went to the White House, they found that soldiers had tramped over the Brussels carpets, guards had slept on the sofas, and the furniture on the first floor was worn and soiled. Evidences of neglect and destruction were everywhere. When Congress appropriated thirty thousand dollars to refurnish the Executive Mansion, Mrs. Patterson went to work. Each morning she was up at daylight, in a calico dress and a white apron, attending to household duties and renovating the White House. All through a hot summer in Washington, she labored; and when the White House was opened for the winter season, the transformation was admired by all. Those who went there expecting to meet dowdy, Tennessee mountain women, and to see a house overloaded with gaudy trinkets, were disappointed. Instead they found beside the President, in the comfortable Blue Room, young, golden-haired Mary Johnson Stover, dressed in full mourning for her husband who had been killed in the war; and slender, young Martha Johnson Patterson, dressed in soft rich tints, with a flower in her dark hair and a fine lace shawl about her shoulders. The quiet elegance of these "plain people from Tennessee" amazed Washington society, and their gentle manners charmed even those who had come to criticize. Eliza Johnson had two capable daughters in Mrs. Patterson and Mrs. Stover. Their love, encouragement, and loyalty, like that of their mother, comforted and inspired the President in his seemingly endless struggle with the northern abolitionists.

For forty years Eliza Johnson had stood at Andrew Johnson's side as he weathered one storm after another. Now, another storm was at hand. The radicals in the Senate and the "scalawags" in the South were trying to subvert the governments of the southern states. They wanted to humiliate and punish the white citizens who had been in rebellion. The radicals hoped to get half a million Negro votes in the "rebel" states. It would have been easy for Johnson to cast his lot with this group; but, determined to follow Lincoln's noble example of "binding up the nation's wounds," he took the reins of the government, forgiving the states that had seceded and building up a united nation. Andrew Johnson knew that, no matter what happened, he would keep on fighting to preserve and carry out Lincoln's policies.

Then followed the most disgraceful spectacle our country has ever witnessed—the impeachment trial of President Johnson! It was President against Congress; Supreme Court against Senate. No President of the United States had ever been impeached; it was unthinkable. For thirty-eight years, one President after another had used his constitutional powers to remove inefficient or disloyal Cabinet members, yet the radicals maintained that such members should be removed only by and with the advice and consent of the Senate. Andrew Johnson was charged with having committed "high crimes and misdemeanors," but they were not specified.

Eliza Johnson, his partner and helpmeet through obscurity, illiteracy, poverty, political strife, the Civil War, seizure of their property in the South, criticism and persecution by the North, never doubted that the clouds would lift. Men might strip him of office, but they could not rob him of the courage of his convictions and his desire to carry out Lincoln's ideals. Throughout the accusations, the speeches, and the trial, she and her daughters calmly went about their affairs, making no comment and behaving as if there were no rift in the government. And Andrew Johnson stood firm in defying the radicals. His enemies came within a single vote of impeaching him; but it should be remarked here that in later years the Supreme Court of the United States held that Johnson was within his rights in all of his important vetoes and that he was fully justified in dismissing a Cabinet member.

A White House messenger brought Eliza news of the verdict. Tears came to her eyes, but her voice was firm as she said: "I knew he'd be acquitted. I knew it!" But the strain of one political battle after another, followed by the trial with a "packed" jury, shattered Eliza Johnson's health completely.

Andrew Johnson wanted more than acquittal, however. He wanted personal vindication. At the end of his term of office, he took his family back to Tennessee. He had not seen his home since 1861. For the first time in thirty years, he was a private citizen again. Eliza hoped he would retire, but six years later he ran for U.S. Senator and was elected. Thus he became the first President of the United States to return to the Senate. Of the thirty-five Senators who had voted for his impeachment, only thirteen were still in their Senate seats.

The galleries were packed with spectators on the day Andrew Johnson took the oath of office, and as he reached his seat they broke into applause that was long and loud. That pleased Eliza more than anything that had happened in years. But her husband's return to Congress was a brief triumph; he attended only one session. In July, 1875, at the home of his daughter, Mary, he was stricken with apoplexy; two days later he was dead. Six months later, on January 13, 1876, Eliza passed away.

Inscribed on the monument which marks their last resting place are these words: "His Faith in the People Never Wavered." It might also be said of Eliza McCardle: Her faith in Andrew Johnson never wavered!

Julia Dent Grant

FIRST FIRST LADY FROM MISSOURI

MORE than a hundred years after Ulysses S. Grant conducted his quiet courtship, one still finds it difficult to understand why this husky young frontiersman, graduate of the United States Military Academy at West Point, and breaker and trainer of horses, should be too diffident to ask crotchety old Colonel Dent for permission to marry his favorite daughter, Julia. Grant, destined to become the most successful northern general of the Civil War and eighteenth President of the United States, was the clean-living, hard-working son of an Ohio tanner. No one had ever questioned the quality of his moral fiber. Yet, while he had an understanding with Julia Dent when he left with his regiment to serve near the Mexican border, it was not until a year later that he won the Colonel's grudging consent.

Once he had tried by writing a letter; but the Colonel did not even bother to reply. To an officer fighting for his country, this was discouraging, to say the least. But other members of the family were working in his behalf. Julia's older brother was on Grant's side; they had been roommates at West Point. A younger sister thought Lieutenant Grant was completely fascinating; and Mrs. Dent was impressed by Grant's quiet demeanor and deep understanding of political affairs. She freely predicted that the world would yet hear of him. It was true that Jesse R. Grant, father of the prospective bridegroom, was not in the same social category as the Dents, whose ancestral home in Maryland had been in the family since the days of King Charles. But Jesse's son had inherited, somewhere along the line, a certain forcefulness and determination that intrigued Mrs. Dent.

She remembered Lieutenant Grant's first visit to the plantation. He had reported for duty at Jefferson Barracks, St. Louis, and had ridden out to White Haven at the invitation of Fred, Jr. He finally spotted, in the center of a long valley, the rambling, two-story farmhouse with its barns, stables, and slave quarters. The Lieutenant rode up, dismounted, and introduced himself to Colonel Dent. As a classmate of the Colonel's son, Grant was quite welcome. When Julia returned home, she accepted him as another of her brother's friends; and he accepted her as another of Fred's sisters.

Julia Dent at eighteen was a dainty little creature—plump, of medium height, with beautifully rounded arms, brown hair, brown eyes, and a good figure. She was the belle of the family and already had had several affairs of the heart. Fred was not at home, but there were two other brothers and three sisters. At first, Grant went riding with all of them, singly and together. Young people from nearby plantations gathered at White Haven in the evenings to dance and sing; they went often on long rides and picnics in the woods. When visits were paid, Grant was taken along as a friend of the family.

At first, the Lieutenant visited the Dent family once a week, riding out on his favorite saddle horse. Then, following Julia's return from finishing school, he stepped up his visits to twice a week. Sometimes Mrs. Dent asked him to stay all night. His visits increased from two to three a week; from three to four. But it was not until he received orders to accompany his regiment to Louisiana that he realized he was in love with Julia Dent. Julia likewise discovered that she was in love with Grant when he told her about the move southward—the move which might mean war with Mexico.

In the circumstances, there wasn't anything they could do about it. At the time (1844), she was eighteen; he was twenty-two. His army pay was sixty-four dollars a month, and his

chances of promotion were rather slender. The Colonel, as
Julia well knew, had definite ideas about delicately-bred girls
marrying poorly-paid army officers. After her father had refused to answer Grant's letter, he had told her: "You are too
young to marry; and he has nothing to give you."

"I, too, am poor. I haven't anything to give him!" she had
stormed.

Meanwhile Grant, who had hoped to retire from the army
and get a job at West Point as an instructor in mathematics,
saw his dream of love in a cottage vanishing. Encamped in
Louisiana, he waited a year before obtaining a month's leave
to visit White Haven. As it happened, he rode up to the house
as the Colonel was leaving on a trip to Washington. Knowing
a strategic moment when he saw one, Grant then and there
asked Julia's father for permission to marry her. In a hurry
to get away, Colonel Dent gave his consent. One gathers,
however, that Julia already had paved the way for his prompt
decision.

There was no time to be married; war was too imminent.
The young soldier returned to Louisiana, where the largest
army since the days of George Washington was assembled.
Julia had to be content with letters about love and war, with
an occasional pressed leaf or flower. He told her of marches
on which he and his men could see grand mirages in the sky
—ships and islands reflected from the Gulf of Mexico, sixty
miles away. The months passed slowly. Texas became a part
of the United States, and the army sent troops to occupy the
disputed territory. Grant fought in Mexico and was twice
promoted for gallantry. Once, during a battle, he was able
to be of service to Julia's brother. But it was August, 1848, before he was able to take Julia in his arms and ask her to set
the day.

By this time he was a brevet captain. But brevets were merely compliments; they indicated the position an officer was entitled to hold when a vacancy occurred. In the back of his mind was this sobering thought: He would be a mere first lieutenant in the reduced, peace-time army. It might be years before he became a captain. Could he and Julia live on his pay? It was now about a thousand dollars a year, including rations for himself and wife and forage for his horses. Julia believed they could get along all right. If other wives made ends meet, she could do it, too. The Colonel shook his head sadly; he had suffered financial reverses and was in no position to protest. But he could not picture Julia keeping house without the aid of the personal maid who had looked after her since babyhood.

Julia named the day for the wedding: August 22, 1848, at the Dent winter home in St. Louis. Proudly Ulysses S. Grant took his wife on a river steamer to visit his home and meet his father and mother. In Julia he found a warmth of affection he had never known. He told her of his boyhood; and soon she could see that he got his reticence, his patience, and his equable temper from his mother. She liked his reddish-brown hair and his gray-blue eyes; she was most anxious to get settled in their new home at the army post in Detroit.

At Detroit, Julia experienced her first setback in a life that was to be filled with them. The quartermaster job was no longer open, and her husband was transferred to a little village on Lake Ontario. The bleak winter was over before they were able to pull enough strings to bring them back to the pleasant surroundings and comfortable quarters at Detroit. The trading post was growing; already there were twenty thousand people in and around the place.

For the first time in her life, Julia knew what it was like to be without slaves; but she managed. Grant took her to the weekly cotillions, but she could not persuade him to learn to dance; he preferred to drive a trotter at top speed on the ice of the River Rouge. Once, in a boastful mood, he told her that he and a powerful, long-legged horse named York held the Military Academy high-jump record; she could well believe it. His father had said, during the honeymoon visit, that Ulysses had harnessed horses when he was so small that he had to stand on the manger to put the bit in the animal's mouth and mount a half-bushel measure to fasten the collar.

Julia began to drop out of the dances as the winter waned; she was going to have a baby. As spring came, she and her husband would sit on the back porch, looking at the garden and holding hands. Then Julia went home to St. Louis, where the baby was born on May 30, 1850, and named Frederick Dent Grant. The gold rush to California was in full swing, but Grant did not give it a thought. His thoughts were centered on Julia and their son.

He had grown up in an era when every man was supposed to do his share of drinking, especially on such days as Washington's Birthday, the Fourth of July, and the anniversary of the Battle of New Orleans. Now that he had family responsibilities, Grant at twenty-eight decided to settle down. He stopped drinking and joined the Sons of Temperance. For two years the young couple lived their uneventful lives at the army post near Detroit. Then an order arrived, transferring Lieutenant Grant to the Pacific coast area. To think of taking his wife with him on this long and dangerous trip, by way of the Isthmus of Panama, was out of the question; another baby was on the way. Grant went on alone, and Julia took her two-year-old son back to White Haven.

Julia brought Ulysses, Jr., into the world that year, enduring her pain and loneliness as army wives always have done. Her husband was having his difficulties, too. No sooner had the California-bound passengers been brought safely across the Isthmus than cholera broke out on shipboard. More than a hundred men, women, and children—an average of twelve or fifteen a day—died of the scourge. In his letter he gave few details, but, he assured her that he was quite well, sent her "a thousand kisses," and asked her to write often. He also wrote to her on arrival, telling her how California's population had, in two years, increased from twenty thousand white people to more than a quarter of a million. In return, she wrote to him, and as he read her letters, his eyes would fill with tears. Once, when Julia sent him a penciled outline of the new baby's hand, he walked out of his quarters muttering: "I must earn some extra money, somehow, and bring Julia and the children out here."

His letters to Julia, over the next year, told of the many attempts he made to earn an extra dollar. He was stationed at Ft. Vancouver, on the Columbia River, in a damp and gloomy wilderness. How deeply he felt the separation from his wife and youngsters will never be known. But the records show that, in an era when officers drank a good deal, Grant imbibed more than was good for him—more than his new commanding officer thought wise. He warned the Lieutenant.

Grant said nothing of this in his letters to Julia. He told her, instead, of how he had tried to raise onions, potatoes, grain, and corn; of how the river had overflowed its banks and destroyed most of his crop; of how he cut cords and cords of wood, piled it neatly on the banks of the stream, and had to move it to safety as the water rose. He and a partner bought up all the chickens within twenty miles of the fort and shipped them to San Francisco; practically all of the chickens died on the voyage. The same thing happened to a shipment of cattle and hogs.

At last came his transfer to Humboldt, California, and promotion to Captain; but the small increase in pay which the promotion brought him would not enable him to support Julia and the children in this land of gold-seekers and high prices. Junior officers and enlisted men did most of the work of the Quartermaster's office, leaving Captain Grant with more time on his hands than was good for him. With a new commanding officer, a Colonel who had reprimanded him on one occasion at St. Louis, Grant found life more unbearable than ever. He had loaned—or lost—his money. He took no interest in books. And he had not seen his family in two years. Under these conditions, when the commanding officer found him under the influence of liquor and demanded that the Captain resign from the army or stand trial, Grant resigned. He felt that he simply could not let the news of a court-martial reach Julia.

He had little money; he was nearing middle age, with no trade or profession by which to earn a living. From the moment he reached the Pacific coast, everything had gone wrong. His letters to Julia and his father said merely that he had resigned from the army and was coming home. No amount of gold in California, apparently, could tempt him to remain away from his family any longer.

Jesse Grant received him grimly; the old man was deeply humiliated by this sudden move, taken without consulting him, and reflecting upon the honor of the Grant family. His mother, on the other hand, was glad to have him out of the service. Julia welcomed him with open arms. She helped him regain his shattered morale; to wage a battle, successful for a time, against the liquor habit.

Captain Ulysses S. Grant, hero of the battle of Molino del Rey and Chapultepec, on his part, volunteered his services at White Haven. He bound sheaves of wheat in the wake of black, sweating slaves with their swinging cradles. He helped with the plowing and the planting. He helped build a cabin for his family on the sixty acres which Julia had received from her father as a wedding present. He chopped cordwood and hauled it to St. Louis or "swapped" it at a nearby colliery for coal. In 1857, Julia presented him with another baby—a girl whom they named Ellen—and called Nellie.

Julia Dent Grant had drunk deep from the cup of joy; in the next ten years, she drank from the cup of woe. She lost her mother. She saw her husband try, without success, to borrow from his father, at ten per cent. interest, five hundred dollars for implements and seed for the 1857 crop. She saw him put his pride in his pocket and peddle wood to the army post from which he used to ride forth on his own saddle horse to visit her at White Haven. She went through a business depression with him, when corn and oats were not worth hauling to St. Louis and the banks suspended specie payments. She learned, after one Christmas, that he had pawned his gold watch and chain in order that he might buy presents for her and the children. She saw him flinch when he read his father's letter saying that there was no job for his son in the Grant tanning business.

Colonel Dent rented the White Haven plantation to Grant and went to live in St. Louis. Julia was expecting another baby, but she cooked and sewed and kept house as cheerfully as if she were still the carefree daughter of a well-to-do planter. She knew in her heart, however, that her husband was a failure; that was what hurt. For four years they had tried to make a living on her sixty acres; now Grant was a victim of ague and fever. His shoulders drooped. His blue army overcoat was faded and worn. The ambitious youth of the Mexican War had become prematurely bent and careworn at thirty-five. The crowning blow came the following year when, temporarily disabled by illness, Grant was obliged to give up farming. Julia watched the auctioneer sell their goods and stock, and then they moved to White Haven.

Colonel Dent obtained for Grant a job in his nephew's real-estate office in St. Louis. Julia swallowed her pride and advised him to take it. He lived in a cold, poorly-furnished back room; and on Saturdays he walked the twelve miles to White Haven to see his wife and children, and on Sundays he trudged the twelve miles back to St. Louis. But he was as much of a failure as a rent collector and salesman as he had been as a farmer. The older he became, the more swiftly and relentlessly failure seemed to strike. He had resigned from the army under pressure; he had failed at farming; and it was now apparent that he was unfitted for the real-estate business.

Grant looked about for a job. He applied for that of county engineer, but soon found that he did not belong to the right political party. He secured a clerkship in the customhouse but lost the job a month later when the collector died. By this time, his savings were gone; the buyer of his cabin could not pay the fifteen hundred dollar mortgage when it became due, and his financial affairs were in a deplorable condition. He sat down and counted up the years: eleven years in the army; four years at farming; two years at collecting rents and hunting jobs. In the spring he would be thirty-eight—with no prospects at all. He had lost heart, but Julia had not.

In these dark days, Grant made one sacrifice. He set free from slavery his "Negro man, William," although he probably could have sold the slave for a thousand dollars. Half that amount would have helped to solve many of Grant's financial problems; nevertheless, he emancipated the slave. Moreover, he turned all of Julia's slaves back to Colonel Dent. Then he made a last appeal to his father for a job that would pay enough to support him and his family. He got the job. For fifty dollars a month, he was to keep the firm's books and make collections. He loaded his furniture on a river steamer and, with his wife and children, moved to Galena, Illinois, to make a new start in life.

"We will not always be in this condition," Julia had said, back at the plantation. And now her prediction seemed about to come true. President Lincoln declared that there could be no compromise on the slavery question. War became inevitable, and Lincoln issued his call for volunteers. Almost before Grant realized it, he was caught up in the business of recruiting young men, outfitting them, and teaching them the manual of arms. As a graduate of the United States Military Academy, he volunteered his services in Washington, Ohio, Illinois, and Missouri—and was given the "cold shoulder" in each place. When a commission as colonel finally was tendered, Grant was obliged to borrow the money with which to buy his uniform. When next he returned to the leather store of Jesse Grant, he held the rank of general of the army, with a salary of twenty thousand dollars a year.

But in June, 1861, Grant was still a failure; his application for a commission had not even been answered by the War Department. Eight months later he was a major general, with the most brilliant record that had yet been won in the Civil War to his credit. During the war, Julia was as near him as it was safe for her to be. Through four long years of warfare, she never for a moment hindered General Grant in his career. On the contrary, she constantly encouraged him, and relieved him from all anxiety by assuring him that everything was going well at home. He needed someone like Julia to bolster his confidence in himself. He was no longer the beaten man who had walked the streets of St. Louis, looking for work; but he had not forgotten his various failures in business and farming.

Eleven years after he and Julia had auctioned off their grain, stock, and farm implements and disposed of their cabin, they moved into the White House. Neither of them was very much changed. It was a time of speculation and political corruption. Grant took office without previous political experience. He made mistakes—such as trying to run a group of Cabinet members as he would his military staff. Personally, the new President was above suspicion, but he was most unfortunate in his choice of associates—then and afterward. The Vice President was driven into retirement under a cloud; the Speaker of the House was accused of bartering his influence for private gain; the Secretary of War was found to have been receiving a bribe of six thousand dollars a year; the Secretary of the Treasury, after certain irregularities had been uncovered, was permitted by the lenient Grant to resign.

Throughout her eight years as First Lady, Julia Dent Grant gave the greater part of her time to welcoming the public to the White House. As she herself admitted, this was the happiest period of her life. At the end of her husband's second term, they set out on a trip around the world that lasted almost three years. On their return, Grant bought a home in New York city and joined a brokerage firm of which one of his sons was a member. Despite the national prestige which Grant's name gave the firm, it failed within three years, with a loss of about sixteen million dollars. The General lost everything he and his family owned; his wife even sold the house in Washington. So, except for one achievement—the writing of his memoirs—Grant's career ended, as it began, in failure.

The memoirs were written during the last year of Grant's life, when he was desperately in search of funds to provide for his wife and family. His health was failing rapidly, and for a time it seemed that he would not be able to finish the two volumes. With Julia sitting at his bedside, the General wrote his personal history of the Civil War. By the time he reached the last chapter, he was quite weak; and the indomitable old war horse was obliged to dictate the preface.

In the years that followed, the General's memoirs had an almost unprecedented sale, earning for Julia and her children some four hundred and fifty thousand dollars in royalties. But Grant lived only a short time after the writing was finished. He died on July 23, 1885; Julia passed away seventeen years later. In those years, there must have been many times when she sat alone in the twilight, thinking of the old days. She had stood beside her husband through poverty, sorrow, temptation, illness, and defeat; she had stood proudly beside him as First Lady. Even the failure and disgrace that came later did not change Julia Dent Grant; hers was a love story of unwavering faith and constant devotion.

Lucy Ware Webb Hayes

FIRST FIRST LADY WHO WAS GRADUATED
FROM A CHARTERED COLLEGE

LUCY WEBB HAYES smiled as she read the morning paper. What would the press think of next! She had known on March 4, 1877, when her husband was inaugurated nineteenth President of the United States, that there would be little privacy in her life as First Lady. Everything she and President Hayes did, or failed to do, would be the subject of discussion in the news. Now they were calling her "Lemonade Lucy"!

The alliterative expression intrigued Lucy Hayes. Her highly developed sense of humor and her quick intelligence told her that the good-natured lampooning by the newspapers of the day contained no real bitterness. Since neither she nor her husband ever drank alcoholic beverages or served them in their own home, she saw no reason why they should change their convictions or customs during their four years in the White House. President Hayes agreed with this decision; and, as long as he was Chief Executive and she was First Lady, not even light wines were served at official dinners for American citizens. When visiting foreign diplomats were entertained officially at the White House, the decision was left to Mr. Evarts, Secretary of State. At first, Washington society complained loudly, but Mrs. Hayes was so charming, so sweet, and so womanly that members of the Cabinet, Senators, Congressmen, and other important statesmen dutifully sipped lemonade or drank tea at Lucy Hayes' parties, and most of the nation admired her for having the courage of her convictions.

The Women's Christian Temperance Union, supported by thousands of zealous abstainers, was enthusiastic over the First Lady's stand. They banded together, had a full-length portrait of Mrs. Hayes painted by Huntington, framed it elegantly, and presented it for display in the White House. The picture shows Mrs. Hayes dressed in ruby velvet, holding red roses in her hand.

Aside from such epithets as "Lemonade Lucy" and "strait-laced Puritan," there was never any criticism of the attractive wife of Rutherford B. Hayes. One of the most popular of our First Ladies, she frankly admitted her pleasure at presiding over the White House. During her husband's entire term she was happy, healthy, and busy, particularly in watching over the interests of the Chief Executive. Lucy Webb Hayes considered even the smallest details important if they added in the slightest to her husband's popularity and renown.

She represented, as several historians have pointed out, the "new woman" era, and the beginning of the third period of the history of America's First Ladies. The early wives of the Revolutionary period were strong characters who, of necessity, developed high qualities of courage, fortitude, and sacrifice. They rose nobly to every emergency—and there were many emergencies in the days of Martha Washington, Abigail Adams, Dolley Madison, Elizabeth Monroe, and Louisa Johnson Adams. The country was young and struggling; there were common dangers, problems, and hardships. At the end of the administration of John Quincy Adams, the new republic was more firmly established. First Ladies of this second era found time and opportunity to develop their talents as social leaders and White House hostesses. A few, who had no taste for gaiety or whose health could not stand the strain of public life, lived almost wholly apart during their stay in the Executive Mansion.

As the years passed and more educational advantages were available to women, they began to widen their interests and take a more active part in the bettering of social conditions, exerting to a greater degree than ever before their influence for public welfare. In this third era, while still in the background politically, the women of the last half of the nineteenth century were demanding a voice in government and asking for changes in various laws which they had to obey, but which they had no part in framing.

Lucy Webb Hayes was active in this period of reform. She was also hailed by the press as a reformer in dress. At her husband's inauguration she wore heavy black silk with real lace. *The American Register,* in Paris, wrote shortly afterward:

> "The administration of Mrs. Hayes receives quite as much attention as does that of her husband. Her beauty and simplicity have taken the blasé society of Washington by storm. Her dresses, of rich material, are simply made, high at the neck, long at the wrist with fine laces at both, but no jewelry; her hair is neither puffed nor frizzed, but arranged plainly at the back and held in place with a shell comb . . ."

Lucy Ware Webb was born in Chillicothe, then the capital of Ohio, in 1831. She was the daughter of Dr. James Webb. On her mother's side she was descended from the best Puritan blood of New England; her mother's father was one of the first settlers of Chillicothe.

Lucy's father died when she was a little girl, and Mrs. Webb moved to Delaware, Ohio, so that her children could be educated there. Later, Lucy entered Wesleyan Female College in Cincinnati, the nation's first chartered college for young women. She was graduated with highest honors in 1852, a great favorite with the faculty and her classmates.

During one of her school vacations at a nearby summer

resort she met Rutherford Birchard Hayes, a rising lawyer of
Cincinnati. The gray-eyed, brown-haired girl with the wide
smile and remarkably even, white teeth, immediately attracted
Hayes. Lucy was much impressed with the tall young man
with blue eyes and dark hair, who seemed as fond of literature
and poetry as she herself was. Rutherford's mother, Sophie
Hayes, grew very much attached to the religious, well-educated, womanly Lucy, and it has been said she chose Lucy
Webb for her son long before he made up his mind. But it was
Rutherford who wrote to a friend in Delaware, "My friend
James has introduced me to many of our city belles, but I do
not see anyone who makes me forget the natural gaiety and
attractiveness of Miss Lucy."

Two years later, on December 30, 1852, there was a simple
wedding. Life ran along smoothly for the happy young
couple. Both were well educated, actively interested in world
affairs, and fond of literature and the arts. In Cincinnati they
had many opportunities to meet famous actors, lecturers,
musicians, poets, and writers of the mid-nineteenth century,
Ralph Waldo Emerson among them. Rutherford's law practice flourished, and he was greatly helped by his uncle, Sardis
Birchard, a wealthy bachelor who had footed the bills for the
Hayes family ever since the death of Rutherford's father. With
Uncle Sardis, the boy had traveled about the United States. It
was Uncle Sardis who put him through college; who bought
him the house to which he took his bride; who befriended and
advised him on every occasion; and who finally left Hayes
his fortune.

Eight children—seven sons and one daughter—were borne
by Lucy Hayes; three of the boys died in childhood.

When the Civil War began in 1861, Rutherford Hayes was
eager to get into the fight. He believed in the Union cause

and in Abraham Lincoln. He was a bit weary of the routine of his law office; he loved outdoor life and had the soul of an adventurer. So off to war went the young lawyer, in search of excitement and fame. He found both. He was wounded; and in the battle of South Mountain distinguished himself by leading a charge, despite his wounds.

Mrs. Hayes spent two winters in camp with her husband. She helped nurse him back to health, and she worked in hospitals and camps throughout the war. The soldiers of her husband's regiment (including Major William McKinley, who later became President) adored her. On her twenty-fifth wedding anniversary, celebrated while she was First Lady, they presented her with a large silver platter, affectionately inscribed.

Hayes was a reluctant politician. On July 30, 1864, he wrote his Uncle Sardis: "As for the candidacy for Congress, I care nothing about it, neither for the nomination nor for the election . . . " In August of that same year, he wrote while in camp: "Friend Smith: Your favor of the 7th came to hand . . . An officer fit for duty who at this crisis would abandon his post to electioneer for a seat in Congress ought to be scalped. You may feel perfectly sure I shall do no such thing."

By the end of the war, in which Hayes had been engaged for four years, his friends had elected him to Congress. "I intend to quit public life as soon as my term in Congress ends," he said. But, of course, he didn't. Twice elected governor of Ohio, he could have had a third term if he had wanted it. In 1876 he was elected President of the United States. This was a boom period for America—the West was largely settled, a great network of railroads was stretching out across the country. The year of the Hayes election marked the one hundredth anniversary of the signing of the Declaration of Independence, and great celebrations were in progress, including the Centennial Fair at Philadelphia.

Mrs. Hayes, in addition to being a strong advocate of the Women's Christian Temperance Union, was an ardent believer in woman suffrage and in greater opportunities for women everywhere. During her years as First Lady, she was active in the movement to better the living conditions of the underprivileged. Yet she took a feminine delight in the social affairs of the capital; no one enjoyed public receptions, state dinners, and other festivities more than the wife of the President.

While there is no doubt that her intelligence, common sense, and tact were helpful to her husband's career, she seldom used her position to obtain favors. On one occasion, however, feeling strongly that an injustice had been done, Lucy Webb Hayes went to work without hesitation. A postmistress in a Pennsylvania town had been turned out of office because of her strong temperance views. The Congressman who represented the district in which she held office succeeded in having appointed in her place a man who had no use for temperance organizations. A woman friend telegraphed the facts to Mrs. Hayes, and not long afterward the postmistress was reinstated by order of the President. Rutherford Hayes apparently knew whereof he spoke when, on one occasion, he remarked: "Mrs. Hayes may have no influence with Congress, but she has great influence with me."

Mrs. Hayes was actively interested in her husband's efforts to effect Civil Service reform, advance the welfare of the Indians, and rehabilitate the defeated South. But with all their activities, President and Mrs. Hayes had time to devote to their children; and the happiest hour of the day came after dinner each evening when they helped the younger ones, Scott and

Fanny, with their lessons. Mrs. Hayes was exceedingly fond of young people and planned many parties for them. She also brought to the White House the old established custom of egg-rolling on Easter Monday. Dolley Madison had started the entertaining practice during her regime as First Lady years before, and it had been the custom ever since to have the egg-rolling on the grounds of the Capitol. When, during Lucy Hayes' term as First Lady, Congress passed a law closing the Capitol grounds to children on Easter Monday because they were ruining the grass, Mrs. Hayes promptly opened the White House grounds to them. This warmhearted gesture had the enthusiastic approval of the President, as well as that of all the little children of Washington.

On December 30, 1877, in the White House, the President and his Lucy celebrated their silver wedding anniversary. That Sunday afternoon, before a group of close friends, they renewed their vows, with the same preacher reading the lines and the same bridesmaid who had attended Mrs. Hayes twenty-five years before. The First Lady wore her wedding gown of white brocaded satin; and although she had taken on a little weight, her hair was still dark and glossy and, at forty-six, she was still a very handsome woman.

Following the ceremony, the two young Hayes children were baptized. Then, during the evening, everybody gathered around the piano to sing such favorite old songs as "Hold the Fort" and "The Sweet By and By." The following night, New Year's Eve, a large public reception was held to celebrate the silver wedding anniversary.

As the Hayes administration drew to a close, both the President and his wife were ready to go back home. President Hayes had announced, when he took office, that he would serve only one term, and he could not be swerved from that resolution. Although he was not regarded as a brilliant Chief Executive, at the end of his four years in office he had the satisfaction of seeing the United States well on the road to prosperity after the financial panic of the Grant administration. During the Hayes administration a closer approach had been made to real peace and friendship between the North and the South; and, also during this administration, the first commercial telephone exchange was opened.

Back home in Ohio, in 1881, Mr. and Mrs. Hayes continued to devote much time to social welfare, public schools, bettering prison conditions, and aiding veterans of the Civil War.

Always active and healthy, Lucy Webb Hayes at the last was spared a lingering illness. She died suddenly at her home in Fremont, Ohio, on June 25, 1889. A little less than four years later, on January 17, 1893, her husband passed away and was buried with honors at a state funeral attended by eminent public officials and military men.

Their occupancy of the White House was not marked by world-shaking events, great tragedy, or great triumph, but they spent a very enjoyable four years presiding over the affairs of the nation.

Lucretia Rudolph Garfield

ANOTHER FIRST LADY FROM OHIO

WHEN Lucretia Rudolph Garfield looked up from the telegram she had been reading, there were tears in her eyes. "Aren't you glad and proud to hear of your husband's election?" she was asked. "Oh, yes," she answered. "But it is a terrible responsibility to come to him and to me."

Those who saw her standing there that November day in 1880, in the pleasant parlor of their Ohio home, with a cheerful fire glowing on the hearth, were sure that James A. Garfield and his wife were equal to any responsibility. Yet their stay in the White House was so short and so overshadowed by tragedy that it is impossible to form an idea of what they might have accomplished. For both possessed high integrity and both had the advantage of an excellent education.

Lucretia Rudolph was born in 1832 near Garrettsville, in northeastern Ohio. She was a shy, serious child with brown eyes and light brown hair. Her father, Zebulon Rudolph, was a farmer, and one of the founders of Hiram College; her mother was a daughter of Elijah Mason, of Lebanon, Connecticut.

Lucretia's family was in a far better position to bring up a child than were the parents of little Jim Garfield, of Orange, Cuyahoga County, Ohio. The boy was born in a log cabin on November 19, 1831. Before he was two years old his father died, leaving a widow with two sons, two daughters and a small, partially cleared, debt-laden farm. When Jim was twelve, he worked in the fields from sunrise to sunset; later he got a job on the Erie Canal, driving along the canal path the horses that pulled the heavy barges. Lean years and struggles followed; but Garfield worked, studied, and saved his money. He worked his way through Hiram College, serving as a janitor until somebody discovered that he could teach English literature just as efficiently as he tended fires and swept walks.

It was at Hiram that Lucretia met the husky, broad-shouldered young man with merry blue eyes and red-blond hair. She and big Jim Garfield shared a love of books. Both were fitting themselves to teach. Literature, mathematics, the classics, Latin, and Greek filled their busy days at college. In the evenings, when the students gathered around the piano, Lucretia listened quietly, a dreamy expression in her soft brown eyes, while golden-voiced Jim led in singing "Don't You Remember Sweet Alice, Ben Bolt?" and "Blue Juniata." Lucretia lost her heart to the young man almost at once, but it was four years before Jim Garfield realized he was in love with the quiet, studious girl he always called "Crete." And it wasn't until he was ready to leave Hiram that they made their plans for the future. He was entering Williams College, in Massachusetts. When he completed his course they would be married. Meanwhile, Lucretia went to Cleveland to teach in the public schools.

Their engagement was a long one; it wasn't until November 11, 1858, when Lucretia was twenty-six and Jim was nearing his twenty-seventh birthday, that they were married. They settled down in a little cottage on the campus of Hiram College, where Garfield taught Greek and Latin. At the end of a year he became President of the college. The young couple had very little money in those days, but they were ideally happy. Hiram was like home to both of them, and for more than two years they lived much as they had in their student days, engrossed in books and college life.

In 1859, James Garfield was elected to the Ohio state Senate. In 1861, in response to President Lincoln's call for volunteers, Garfield went to war as a colonel of the Forty-Second Regiment, Ohio Volunteers. Over and over Lucretia read his letters from the field, as she cared for their little daughter, Molly, and for Jim Garfield's aging mother who had come to live with her. Both he and Lucretia wanted to own a home of their own, and Lucretia economized carefully while he was away. She put most of her savings into a small house, which she bought for eight hundred dollars. Garfield found his little family comfortably settled when he returned home. Later they were to own far larger and more pretentious homes in Ohio and Washington, but it is doubtful whether any house they ever lived in gave them more pleasure than the one Lucretia managed to buy while her young husband was away at war.

Back in civil life, Garfield advanced steadily in his political career. He was elected a representative in 1862, and was reelected every two years after that until 1879, when he was elected to the U. S. Senate. He never took his seat there, however, for much to his own surprise he was nominated for the Presidency by the Republican Convention of 1880.

Lucretia, meanwhile, kept busy in her own sphere, helping to prepare her four sons for college and her daughter for high school.

Lucretia must have been an exceptionally good mother, for her self-discipline and emotional control were remarkable. Ten years before she went to the White House, during a summer when she and her children were at their home in Mentor, Ohio, Mrs. Garfield wrote her husband a letter which vividly pictures the character of the woman who was to become First Lady:

"I am glad to tell you," [she wrote,] "that out of all the toil and disappointments of the summer just ended, I have risen up to a victory; that silence of thought since you have been away has won for my spirit a triumph. I read something like this the other day: 'There is no healthy thought without labor, and thought makes the labor happy.' Perhaps this is the way I have been able to climb higher. It came to me one morning when I was making bread. I said to myself: Here I am compelled by an inevitable necessity to make our bread this summer. Why not consider it a pleasant occupation, and make it so by trying to see what perfect bread I can make? It seemed like an inspiration, and the whole of life grew brighter. . . . The wrongly educated woman thinks her duties a disgrace, and frets under them or shrinks [from] them if she can. She sees man triumphantly pursuing his vocation, and thinks it is the kind of work he does which makes him grand and regnant; whereas it is not the kind of work at all, but the way in which he does it."

Lucretia, of course, never dreamed that her husband would one day become President. She was as surprised as he was when, at the Republican convention in 1880, his name was brought up. A group of politicians called Stalwarts were determined to bring Ulysses S. Grant back to the White House for a third term. Other leaders, opposed to a third term for any President, supported James G. Blaine or John Sherman. Ballot after ballot was taken without reaching a conclusion. Then somebody mentioned the name of James A. Garfield!

On the next roll call there was a stampede to him. In November, he was elected the twentieth President of the United States.

All that summer before his election Lucretia worked by his side at their home in Mentor. Telegraph linemen ran a special wire into the shed which Garfield made into an office. Lawnfield, their farm, became a little city of reporters, political leaders, and friends from every part of Ohio. Lucretia fed them, entertained them, and often put them up overnight; meanwhile her husband gave out interviews and worked at his correspondence.

When the telegram announcing her husband's election was received, Lucretia was exhausted. She had followed every phase of the bitterly fought campaign, and she knew the years to come would not be easy. She and her husband had left private life behind; now they were the servants of the people.

A few days after the inauguration, Lucretia opened the White House for official entertainment. The slender, simply dressed First Lady, who wore few, if any, jewels, was gracious, poised, unaffected, and ready for any emergency. And there were many emergencies for her to meet.

President Garfield's administration began under difficult circumstances. His own party was not united in his support, and there was still much bitterness over the unexpected happenings at the convention. When Garfield appointed James G. Blaine as Secretary of State and made William Robertson collector of the port of New York, the Stalwarts, angry because they had not been consulted, turned completely against the President.

Lucretia must have worried over all these developments. She was forty-nine; her husband was nearly fifty. They had come a long way since their Hiram College days. Now, as always, they faced their problems together, trying to decide how best to handle the disagreements and disappointments of politicians.

But all these troubles were forgotten in the events which followed. Less than four months after his inauguration, in the railroad station at Washington, the President was shot by Charles J. Guiteau. With a shout of triumph, the crazed assassin screamed: "I am a Stalwart! Arthur is now President!" Then he fired again before he could be seized.

At Elberon, New Jersey, where her husband had planned to join her for a vacation at the seashore, Lucretia Garfield received the news quietly and hurried back to the White House. Bravely and silently she watched the efforts of the doctors to save his life, and through the heartbreaking weeks that followed she nursed him day and night. In constant pain, but conscious much of the time, James Garfield begged to be taken away from the summer heat of Washington. He was taken to Elberon, where Lucretia continued the fight for his life.

All over the nation, people were eager to help. Many were disturbed by the thought that Garfield might be worried about what would happen to his family if he died. Mr. Cyrus W. Field of New York proposed that a fund of two hundred and fifty thousand dollars be raised for Mrs. Garfield and the children. He started the fund with a generous subscription, and the amount received by the Garfield family eventually reached nearly three hundred and fifty thousand dollars.

Despite all efforts, President James A. Garfield died at Elberon on September 19, 1881, a little more than six months after he was inaugurated. A special train carried the body to Washington, and there it lay in state in the rotunda of the Capitol for two days. On September 24, Garfield's remains were taken to Cleveland, where he was buried in Lake View Cemetery.

Lucretia survived her husband by many years, and in those years she watched with love and pride the steady progress of their children. She saw her son, James, become Secretary of the Interior in 1907. Harry became President of Williams College. Irvin M. was a Boston lawyer, and Abram G. an architect in Cleveland. Mary, the only daughter, became Mrs. Stanley-Brown.

Lucretia Rudolph Garfield died in her eighty-sixth year. When she went to the White House she was asked for some particulars of her life, for publication. Her reply was: "I have done nothing that can be written about. Wait until I have, and then it will be time enough to write."

Perhaps no words better describe the wife of our twentieth President than those her husband jotted down in his diary, shortly after his inauguration:

"C. [Crete] grows up to every new emergency with fine tact and faultless taste."

Ellen Lewis Herndon Arthur

WHO NEVER REACHED THE WHITE HOUSE

E
LLEN HERNDON ARTHUR
would have been a very proud woman if she had lived to see
her husband become President of the United States. And she
would have been deeply moved, as he was, when on September 19, 1881, he received news of the death of President Garfield. At the suggestion of Congress, Chester A. Arthur took
the oath of office at once in his New York city home on Lexington Avenue, where his wife had died a year and a half before, leaving two children.

The *Chicago News,* after Arthur became President, carried
this item:

> "Mrs. Arthur's room in her beautiful New York
> Mansion in which she died has never been disturbed,
> her needle is still threaded and sticking in a bit of
> delicate embroidery in her work-basket undisturbed;
> nor will her husband allow any one to change the
> room in any of its furniture arrangements. There is
> the little rocker beside the standard work-basket,
> and the little negligee crocheted slippers. There
> stands her desk, with the ink dried on her pearl-
> handled pen, which she had hastily put aside from
> some interruption, never to use again on earth. Her
> favored books are placed in a tiny case, with a marker
> in one of them, just as she left it. On the table are
> placed each morning by the order of the President,
> a bunch of her favorite flowers. Even her favorite
> perfumes are in the toilet bottles at her dressing case
> and in the wardrobe hang her dresses. The room is
> bright and sunny, her former maid keeping it neat

. . . and attending the canaries in the window, and tending the flowers. . . . This room is a place where the President takes much comfort in reading and meditation . . ."

There are other mentions of the President's wife in the press of the period, but we have no portrait of her from this or other sources. Ellen Arthur, from all accounts, would have made an efficient and gracious First Lady. She had long been recognized in New York society as an aristocratic and talented woman, famous for her philanthropic work. A native of the South, she was impulsive, affectionate, warmhearted and generous. She was born in 1837 at Culpeper Court House, Virginia, the daughter of Commander William L. Herndon, a naval hero who went down with his ship. His heroism was commemorated in a monument at Annapolis, and a gold medal was voted by Congress to his widow.

Most of Ellen Herndon's girlhood was spent in Fredericksburg, Virginia, and in Washington. She was visiting relatives in New York when she met tall, handsome Chester Alan Arthur; and on October 29, 1859, when she was twenty-two and he was twenty-nine, they were married.

Long before that the young lawyer, born in Vermont the son of a Baptist minister, had attracted attention as a leader. He entered law in 1853, and shortly afterward created somewhat of a sensation with his first big case. Prior to 1855, Negroes were not permitted to ride with white passengers in the street cars of New York city. A colored girl, thinking she might not be noticed, boarded a Fourth Avenue car but was discovered and put off.

The law firm of Culver, Parker, and Arthur decided to make a test case of it. Chester Arthur, the junior partner, appeared as counsel for Lizzie Jennings, won her case in the State Supreme Court, and obtained damages for her. Even more important, the right of Negroes to ride in public conveyances was never again challenged within the jurisdiction of New York state.

When Chester Arthur and Ellen Herndon were married, he had a good law practice and a recognized position in the affairs of his political party. During the Civil War he attained the rank of general. Though he was not a war hero, he had charge of the important task of outfitting, training, and forwarding all the troops from the state of New York.

In 1871 he was appointed collector of the Port of New York. This appointment carried with it considerable authority and the collector often used his power, as was then the custom, to reward members of his political party with good jobs. When Hayes became President in 1877, he was determined that the New York customhouse should cease to be the great political force it was, and he removed Arthur from office. But apparently his reputation suffered little injury, for in 1880, he was nominated for the Vice Presidency on the Republican ticket with James A. Garfield.

Mrs. Arthur did not live to share with him the triumph of the election. Gifted with a beautiful contralto voice which had been carefully trained, she was always much in demand to sing at concerts for charity. After such an appearance one wintry night, she took cold. Three days later, on January 12, 1880, she died of pneumonia.

Her place as mistress of the White House was taken by President Arthur's sister, Mrs. John McElroy, who with her two daughters, his own little daughter Nellie, and his son, Alan, composed the White House family. Mrs. McElroy, a quiet and gentle woman, entered upon her duties with such a desire to please that she soon won the admiration of Washington society. But it was the President whose charm of manner and generous hospitality gave distinction to all gatherings at the Executive Mansion.

The first city man in a long procession of rural or small-town men, President Arthur was described as "the best dressed man to sit in the chair since Washington." Tall, handsome, and graceful, with dignified but easy courtesy, he became highly popular; and he was always so faultlessly dressed that the newspapers referred to him as the "Dude President." He drove the most luxurious turnout ever owned by any Chief Executive—a dark green landau and spirited bays with monogrammed blankets.

Extravagant in his tastes, and well able to gratify them, President Arthur declared on his arrival at Washington that the White House was unfit to live in. Under the direction of Louis Comfort Tiffany, Arthur had it completely done over, while he conducted official business from the home of a friend on Capitol Hill. When Congress reassembled in December, 1881, it found that a transformation had taken place. Washington society crowded into the renovated White House, delighted with its bright and cheerful appearance.

Mrs. McElroy was a busy hostess, for President Arthur liked to entertain, and his receptions and dinners were accompanied by the luxuries of the period. Flowers from the White House conservatories banked the walls of the Red Room, from the thick crimson velvet carpet to the ceiling. The Green Room was magnificent in Nile green satin furnishings and gilt-sprayed walls. In the big oval Blue Room, where the President received his guests, roses, ferns and potted plants were used lavishly, while the blazing lights from ornate chandeliers added brilliance to the scene, and long refreshment tables loaded with delicacies were reminiscent of the fabulous days of Dolley Madison.

At dinner parties, the banquet table of the state dining room sparkled with silver, crystal, satin damask, gilded candlesticks, and flowers—while orchids and white camellias were at each place as corsages for the elegant ladies in velvets, brocades, and laces. To the White House during President Arthur's administration came the famous and the gifted, among them the golden voiced Adelina Patti, who sang there on Washington's Birthday in 1883.

President Arthur was something more than a good host. The man who had been removed from the office of Collector of the Port of New York, accused of ethics none too high in the discharge of his duties, became a different man when faced with the responsibilities of the Presidency. If his party expected that he would continue to be influenced by the spoils system, it was sadly mistaken. As President, he announced he would be guided by the policies of his predecessor. Following words with action, he began an attack on the spoils system in 1883 by signing the Civil Service Reform Act. He also vetoed a Chinese exclusion bill which would have violated a treaty with China; and later vetoed a rivers and harbors bill which carried extravagant and wasteful appropriations.

While he was not a brilliant statesman, President Arthur soon won the admiration and respect of the American people by his integrity and ability. And though he must have had many opportunities among the fashionable and beautiful ladies of Washington to select a second wife, Chester Alan Arthur remained faithful to the memory of his Ellen as long as he lived. Like President Andrew Jackson, his wife's picture was the last thing he saw at night before he went to sleep; and each morning before he left his room in the White House, he paused to look at that picture and to place fresh flowers before it. To St. John's church, which he attended each Sunday while he was President, he gave a stained glass window, installed in memory of Ellen Herndon Arthur, which visitors in the nation's capital may see to this day.

When his term of office neared its close, he refused to have any part in campaigning for another four years in the White House. In March, 1885, after attending the inauguration of the new President, Grover Cleveland, he returned to his home in New York city, where, in accordance with his instructions, his wife's room was still cared for and kept as it always had been when Ellen Arthur was living. Chester Alan Arthur was then fifty-four years old. Less than two years later, on November 18, 1886, he died suddenly of apoplexy, and was buried beside his First Lady in the family cemetery at Albany, New York.

Frances Folsom Cleveland

FIRST FIRST LADY
TO BE MARRIED AT THE WHITE HOUSE

WHEN the steamer *Noordland* from Antwerp arrived in New York in May, 1886, crowds waiting on the dock stared curiously at tall, slender young Frances Folsom and her mother. For they were met by Colonel Lamont, then Secretary to the President of the United States.

A few days later when President Grover Cleveland arrived in Manhattan to assist in the observance of Memorial Day, everybody knew that romance was in the air, for he called at once upon the Folsoms at their hotel. The previous winter they had been guests at the White House. Miss Rose Cleveland, sister of the bachelor President, who was acting as the White House hostess, welcomed them warmly and introduced Frances at receptions as "my little school girl." The little school girl was then twenty-one and as pretty as a picture, with soft brown hair, flashing dark eyes, a dimpled smile, and a faultless profile.

Now, returning from a short trip abroad, she seemed more captivating than ever. Matchmaking mothers with marriageable daughters began to realize that theirs was a lost cause. The news spread quickly, and soon the entire nation buzzed with pleasant excitement. For the first time in history the marriage of a President was to take place in the White House! All over the country people forgot affairs of state and political differences in anticipation of wedding bells and orange blossoms. A few people said it was too bad that there was such a difference in the ages of the engaged couple. Grover Cleveland, they said, was old enough to be her father. It was true he was forty-nine and she was only twenty-one, but generally everybody agreed that it would be a happy marriage—and it was.

Both Frances and the President wanted a simple, informal wedding. Together they wrapped and addressed boxes of wedding cake to be sent with their autographs to a selected few, and the President himself wrote cordial notes of invitation to the fewer than forty invited guests, explaining that it would be a very quiet affair.

On June 2, 1886, the President attended to his public duties as usual. Frances and her mother arrived in Washington that morning and were met by Miss Cleveland. At seven in the evening, Frances Folsom stood in the Blue Room of the Executive Mansion beneath a huge wedding bell of white roses to take the vows that would make her the wife of the man who had been her father's law partner. In her bridal gown of corded white satin banded with orange blossoms, a sheer tulle bridal veil partially covering her hair and falling over her shoulders, the young woman was radiant and completely self-possessed. Except for the setting, the Marine Band, and the quantities of flowers which decorated the White House, the wedding might have been a small home affair anywhere in the United States. There were the usual kisses and congratulations, and probably Mrs. Folsom cried a little, as mothers almost always do on such occasions. Then a supper was served, and shortly afterward the bride and groom started off for a short honeymoon.

Looking back over the years, Frances could scarcely remember a time when she had not been completely devoted to honest, genial Grover Cleveland. She was born in Buffalo, New York, on July 21, 1864, and most of her childhood memories included "Uncle Cleve," who brought her dolls and toys, held her on his knee, and called her "Frank." As her father's close friend and partner, Grover Cleveland seemed like one of the family. When Frances was eleven, her father was thrown from his carriage and instantly killed; and Cleveland, as administrator of the estate and the little girl's guardian, continued to be important in her life. Unmarried and without a family or home of his own, the young lawyer took no part in the social life of Buffalo, and spent most of his spare time at the Folsom home.

Frances was seventeen when her hero, Uncle Cleve, was elected mayor of Buffalo, and she was delighted because she knew about the corrupt government of her city, and she was sure he would restore integrity and honesty. She was not disappointed. In the single year Grover Cleveland served as mayor, he saved Buffalo nearly a million dollars on city contracts and broke up the most determined and corrupt aldermanic ring it had ever known. Before the year was out, the people of New York state elected him Governor, and Frances beamed with increased pride.

Now a student at Wells College, she talked often with her classmates about her wonderful Uncle Cleve, and the other girls were as thrilled as she was each week when long white boxes of roses and other flowers arrived for her, bearing the card of the Governor. At official affairs in Albany, Frances and her mother often sat in his box, and the young girl knew that, no matter how busy he was, Grover Cleveland would find time to watch over her and advise her. Long years of mutual respect, admiration and affection existed between the two, and Uncle Cleve and Mrs. Folsom saw to it that Frances was brought up sensibly.

As First Lady, young and inexperienced Frances Cleveland had no exalted ideas about her position and she made no effort to be a social leader. She was gracious, cordial, and considerate to everybody and presided over state affairs with a dignity and poise that surprised her elders. "Three thousand handshakes in two hours—three thousand smiles," remarked a friend as she saw Mrs. Cleveland greet the last guest at a White House reception. These receptions were held three times each week. The mansion was opened to the public on Wednesdays, Fridays, and Saturdays, and the crowds eager to see the bride were so great that military aides often had to step in and halt the long lines so that she might have a moment to sit down and rest.

Her husband, too, had many duties. Sometimes he worked far into the night. Frances did not complain, for she soon realized the necessity for long hours. Most of the party leaders, she learned, disliked the President because he was not easy to manage. He was stubborn (as she well knew), blunt, and unwilling to provide jobs for the politicians of his party.

The youthful First Lady, a product of the Victorian age when women were generally looked upon as fragile flowers who must be shielded from worldly cares, took an active interest in all that was going on. A competent housekeeper was engaged to keep domestic matters running smoothly, and Mrs. Cleveland cheerfully entertained all visitors and personally planned social affairs.

When the time came, following the election of 1888, for Cleveland to turn over the government to Benjamin Harrison, Frances went happily about her final duties. She saw to it that a luncheon was prepared for the new First Lady, with flowers on the table. Then Mrs. Cleveland said good-by to the White House staff, calling each by name, and they wept to see her go.

During the next four years the Clevelands had leisure, for the first time since their marriage, to enjoy themselves completely. They spent their summer vacations on Cape Cod, where they fished, swam, and wandered along miles of sandy shore. During the winters, Grover Cleveland practiced law. It was during this interlude that Ruth, the first child, was born. Their second child, Esther, was to have the distinction of being the first child of a President to be born in the White House.

At the end of Benjamin Harrison's administration, the people again turned to Grover Cleveland. As he was the only President to be called back as Chief Executive after an interval of four years, Frances Cleveland was the only First Lady to return to the White House after retiring to private life. To her and to the official staff it was a happy reunion. She slipped easily back into her place, and it seemed almost as if she had never been away.

After the second daughter was born, in 1892, Mrs. Cleveland did less social entertaining. With two little girls to look after, much of her time and thought were occupied with them. The President bought a country house so that his family could get out of Washington during the hot summer weather, and he often joined them for weekends. But Mrs. Cleveland, though she followed political affairs less closely than she did during her husband's first administration, knew that he was having a hard battle to uphold the gold standard. A sullen Congress, an unfriendly South, and a fiercely hostile West hampered her husband, and there was widespread unemployment and unrest.

Battles over the currency and the tariff, and other domestic controversies helped to divide the Democratic party, and Frances was much relieved when the second term came to a close. The Clevelands had given eight years of their lives to public service. It seemed good to be able to settle down to private life and the friendly informality of Princeton, New Jersey, where they made their new home.

There were three more children born to the Clevelands in Princeton, of whom all but one survived their father. The former President died eleven years after his retirement, on June 24, 1908.

Frances Folsom Cleveland was still an attractive woman. Five years later she married Professor Thomas J. Preston, Jr., of Princeton University. But until her death on October 29, 1947, at the age of eighty-three, people all over the nation continued to remember her, not as Mrs. Preston, but as Frances Cleveland, a charming and much-beloved First Lady.

Caroline Lavinia Scott Harrison

A HIGHLY DOMESTIC FIRST LADY

HIGH life below stairs ended when Caroline Scott Harrison came to the White House in 1889. Regardless of the indignation of old servants of the Executive Mansion, and the derisive comments of the newspapers, the new First Lady invaded the kitchen, determined to replace carelessness and extravagance with neatness and thrift. She renovated the White House from the attic to cellar, tossed out the useless accumulations of years, and established system and order.

Each new incumbent, since the days of Dolley Madison and Eliza Monroe, had made innovations of one sort or another. Sarah Childress Polk had candle light replaced by gaslight; Mrs. Fillmore is said to have had the first bathtub installed; she also started the first library. Mrs. Hayes was responsible for greatly enlarging the White House conservatories. President Arthur, a widower, said the mansion was "unfit to live in" and engaged Louis Comfort Tiffany to redecorate; but nothing like the thoroughness of Mrs. Benjamin Harrison had been seen at the Executive Mansion for many a long year. Her predecessor, youthful Frances Folsom Cleveland, had been content to engage a "competent housekeeper"; the experienced Mrs. Harrison gave personal attention to every detail of the management of the President's house and had at least three plans for enlarging it.

"We are here for four years"; she told reporters. "I do not look beyond that, as many things may occur in that time, but I am very anxious to see the family of the President provided for properly, and while I am here I hope to be able to get the present building put into good condition. Very few people understand to what straits the President's family has been put at times for lack of accommodations. Really there are only five sleeping apartments and there is no feeling of privacy."

Perhaps one of the reasons for Mrs. Harrison's concern was the size of her own family. At one time there were in the White House, besides the President and herself, their son and his wife, their daughter and her husband, a group of grandchildren, Mrs. Harrison's aged father, and a niece.

Mrs. Harrison did not succeed in getting any major additions to the building, but Congress did appropriate thirty-five thousand dollars to have the old house fixed up, and the First Lady used it carefully and with excellent results. She also found time to create the decorative design for a set of White House china, and to paint china plates for herself and her friends. And, while cleaning out the old closets, she became interested in arranging the White House collection of the china of past Presidents—a collection which has since come to have great historic value and interest.

In addition to her self-imposed domestic duties and her social obligations, she found time for needlework, orchid culture, and literature.

Caroline Lavinia Scott was born in Oxford, Ohio, in 1832. There, when she was nineteen, she met her future husband. Young Benjamin Harrison, grandson of the ninth President of the United States, spent his early years on his father's farm at North Bend, Ohio. As a boy, he had to hustle out of bed before daylight to milk cows, feed stock, plant corn and potatoes, and rake hay. He studied his lessons by a tallow candle; and, despite his many chores, he walked two miles to school and usually had time for a game of "bull-pen" before the bell rang.

At the little country school he learned enough to enter Farmer's College near Cincinnati. From there he went to Miami University at Oxford, Ohio, where he was graduated at eighteen. It is said he left Farmer's College because he had become "enamored of an interesting young lady whose father, Dr. Scott, had established a school for young ladies at Oxford." At any rate, he won the heart of Caroline Lavinia, and they were married on October 20, 1853.

Benjamin was twenty then; his bride was twenty-one. They had no money, and he had no job; but they were healthy and happy, and they had plenty of faith in the future and in their ability to get along. They decided upon Indianapolis as their future home. A lot in Cincinnati had been left to Benjamin by a relative. It must have been a good piece of property, for he was able to borrow eight hundred dollars on it. With this capital, all they had in the world, the young couple went to Indianapolis in March, 1854. There, they lived in a boarding house while Benjamin found desk-room in an office and hung out his shingle as a practicing lawyer. Until he could get clients, the young bridegroom knew he would have to earn money somehow, so he secured a job as a court crier. For this he received two dollars and fifty cents a day, and many years later he said it was the first money he made at the law.

The birth of their first child, Russell, that same year, made it necessary for the Harrisons to find some kind of a home. It was a one-story wooden building, with three rooms and a shed which could be used as a summer kitchen. Caroline managed as economically as she could, doing all her own work; but money was scarce and the future President often went to a druggist friend to borrow five dollars for household expenses.

As the years passed, Harrison's law practice increased, and at the time the Civil War began, he was beginning to earn a fair living. Coming from a long line of patriots, he saw no alternative to serving his country, so he hung the Stars and Stripes in his office window, recruited a company, and went off to war. His military career was impressive. Again and again he was cited for bravery, and before the end of the conflict he was made a brigadier general by brevet.

In one of the many affectionate letters he wrote his wife during that period Harrison told her: "If my ambition is to soar to any more after I come home, you will have to give it wings." How far he was to climb in service to his country, neither of them dreamed then; but it is certain his wife helped him in many ways. At the close of the war, he resumed his law practice in Indianapolis. He was poor and in debt, but soon he was again well established. In 1881 he became a senator.

During his six years in the U. S. Senate, Mrs. Harrison was very popular in Washington, entertaining many callers, engaging in charity work, and following closely her husband's progress in politics. By 1889, when Harrison became President, she was well equipped to take over the duties of First Lady. A tall and queenly figure, she was extremely attractive in middle age, with softly waved white hair, large expressive eyes, and a serene and lovely face. Her poise was broken only in private, when she often was reduced to tears over the attacks of the press on her husband.

President Harrison was anything but a good mixer, and his manner was brusque and forbidding. The newspapers called him the "human iceberg" and "kid-glove Harrison."

Also, he suffered by comparison with his famous grandfather, President William Henry Harrison. The caption "Grandfather's Hat" became a byword, and cartoons frequently pictured Benjamin as a little man wearing a hat several sizes too large for him. Harrison was small in stature, and he was highly sensitive. He was determined to prove that he could be a good President without leaning on the borrowed fame of his grandfather. His misfortune was that, while he inspired respect, he lacked the warm, human qualities to call forth the love and devotion of the public. Caroline Harrison must have realized this, for she was a charming hostess, constantly exerting herself to make friends for her husband. She was greatly disturbed when he decided to run for re-election. She knew he did not want a second term, but he was so enraged by the attacks of the opposition that he would not give up. No Harrison, he declared, had ever run away from a fight, and the coming campaign was going to be a fight. Stubbornly, Harrison went into that fight, but he was defeated. Once again Grover Cleveland was elected, the only President to return to office after four years in private life.

Mrs. Harrison, however, did not live to see her husband's defeat. Early in the spring of 1892, she had had an attack which developed into serious lung trouble. That summer her family, hoping that the mountain air would restore her health, took her to the Adirondacks. But she grew steadily worse and was brought back to Washington the following autumn. On October 24, 1892, she died in the White House; and, after services in the East Room, her remains were taken to her old home in Indianapolis, where she was buried.

Ida Saxton McKinley

WIFE OF THE THIRD MARTYRED PRESIDENT

THE small gilt clock on the mantel struck three, but Ida Saxton McKinley needed no reminder. A frail little figure, she stood in the window of her hotel room staring eagerly across the street at another window, where a tall, broad-shouldered man was waving a large white handkerchief. With her own lacy handkerchief she returned his greeting. Then, with scarcely a glance for the busy city of Columbus, she returned to her comfortable chair, leaning heavily on a cane.

She was ill and solitary, but in her heart there was happiness and contentment, for her husband, then governor of Ohio, had remembered. Each morning as he entered the State House grounds he turned, lifted his hat, and bowed to her. Each afternoon at three, no matter how busy he was or how many callers were in his office, he went to the window and waved.

He seldom returned to their hotel in the evening without a bunch of his wife's favorite roses, and every hour he could spare from his duties was spent in her company. The story of Ida and William McKinley is a love story that lasted for thirty years, and it is all the more touching and pathetic because she was an invalid.

As a child, Ida Saxton was healthy and happy and full of laughter. She was born in Canton, Ohio, on June 8, 1847, the daughter of a leading banker; and everybody said she inherited her mother's bright and cheerful disposition. At the age of sixteen, Ida was graduated from a seminary in Media, Pennsylvania, and later, with her sister, she was taken on a trip to Europe.

It was fun seeing the sights of Paris and Berlin, but she was glad to get back home to stroll through the familiar streets of Canton, where she knew most of the people in town. Young, attractive, and carefree, Ida was surrounded by beaux; but her father, though he was president of the bank and would leave his daughter a sizable fortune, had some firm convictions about her immediate future. He believed girls as well as boys should have a practical business education that would equip them to earn their own living.

So, not long after her return from abroad, young Miss Saxton, neat and prim in dark wool skirt and starched white blouse, with her hair arranged smoothly, found herself seated in a clerk's chair ready to begin her first day's work. Morning after morning she arrived promptly at her desk, puzzling over the maze of figures before her, and wondering whether she would ever learn anything about the banking business. But she was bright and quick, working at a steady job was something of a novelty, and it was not long before she earned her promotion to the position of cashier. For three years she was assistant to her father.

Then to Canton came young and handsome William McKinley, a veteran of the Civil War whose courage under fire had won him a commission and a letter of praise signed by Abraham Lincoln himself. McKinley, like so many young men who later became President, decided to study law. Two years after his return from the war, he gained admittance to the bar, and hung out his shingle in Canton, Ohio.

He had no political ambitions at the time. He wanted to become a good lawyer; and, shortly after he met young Ida Saxton, he wanted to marry her. It was definitely a case of love at first sight; and, though at first he was doubtful whether this attractive young lady who was so popular would ever look at him, he won out after an ardent courtship. After he had been elected prosecuting attorney of Stark County, they were married—on January 25, 1871.

They lived in a boarding house for a while, then began housekeeping in a comfortable little house in Canton, where their first child, a daughter, was born. She lived to be only three years old. That was Ida McKinley's first sorrow, and there were other crushing blows to follow. A second child, also a daughter, died in babyhood. The loss of her two children and the death of her mother during the first five years of her married life changed Ida McKinley from an active healthy young woman into an invalid subject to frequent fainting spells.

But sorrow did not change her sunny disposition. As her husband advanced in public life and traveled about Ohio making political speeches, she went with him. And always he got her settled in comfortable quarters, and arranged his programs so as to spend as much time with her as possible. All the time he was governor, she lived contentedly in the hotel opposite the State House, busy with her knitting or embroidery, and often entertaining friends in her cheerful sitting room with its bouquets of fresh flowers and its sunny windows.

She almost never mentioned the nervous disorder that afflicted her. Those who knew her personally said she seemed to be utterly forgetful of self and showed great thoughtfulness for others. She was able to walk only with the help of a cane and supported by the arm of her husband, but she never lost touch with McKinley's activities, and even took an interest in the tariff, since that was his specialty.

William McKinley served two terms as governor of Ohio, and Ida McKinley was not surprised when he was nominated for the Presidency over his Democratic opponent. She was not surprised either at the story his friend, Mark Hanna, must have told her about her husband's integrity.

Hanna, McKinley's campaign manager, said one day: "You can get both New York's and Pennsylvania's delegates, but there are certain conditions. . . . They want a promise that you will appoint Tom Platt Secretary of the Treasury."

McKinley's answer was characteristic. "There are some things in this world that come too high," he said. "If I can not be President without promising to make Tom Platt Secretary of the Treasurer, I will never be President."

McKinley never compromised with his conscience. Maybe that is one of the reasons why he was elected President. He and his wife went to the White House in 1897, and there he continued to watch over her with a solicitude which touched the heart of the nation. At official dinners, he seated his wife at his right, where he could look after her if she had one of her periodic attacks. When they received in the drawing room, he stood close beside her chair, resting one hand on her shoulder. Much to his regret, there was one custom he could not change. White House etiquette called for serving the President first at dinner; that had been so ever since George Washington's time. But to McKinley the custom seemed a discourtesy to the woman who was always uppermost in his tender thoughts.

For her sake, life at the Executive Mansion was made as quiet and simple as possible. Mrs. McKinley left most of the official duties of hostess to her relatives and to her husband's nieces. When there were no official dinners scheduled, the McKinleys had what they still referred to as "supper" in their own private dining room. After the meal he liked to sit near her, reading the evening papers, while Mrs. McKinley was constantly busy crocheting and knitting for charity. While she was in the White House, she knitted some thirty-five hundred pairs of slippers, which brought large sums when sold at church fairs and bazaars.

During her four and a half years in Washington, Mrs. McKinley was an observer of one of the greatest transition periods in the history of the nation. She helped her husband plan the celebration of Centennial Day, December 12, 1900, the one hundredth anniversary of the opening of the White House in the days when Abigail Adams was presiding as First Lady. McKinley, however, will probably be remembered in history as the President who successfully conducted a war with Spain (after doing everything in his power to prevent it).

When her husband was elected for a second term, Ida McKinley was happy for him. There was little unemployment, the tariff had dropped out of sight as a bone of contention, gold had been discovered in Alaska, prospects for building the Panama Canal were growing brighter, and the United States had acquired Hawaii and the Philippines. The nation was prosperous.

Mrs. McKinley's health seemed to improve a little during that time. She was happy and cheerful as usual when her husband accepted an invitation to visit the Pan-American Exposition at Buffalo. Together the President and his wife journeyed from Canton, Ohio, where they had been enjoying their summer vacation. They stopped to see the sights at Niagara Falls, then went to the home of friends in Buffalo. On the afternoon of September 6, 1901, while Mrs. McKinley rested, the President held a public reception at the Temple of Music, shaking hands with a long line of visitors. When he offered his hand in greeting to a slender young man, two shots rang out.

As the President fell to the floor, he pointed to Czolgosz,

the assassin, who had already been seized by onlookers, and said: "Don't let them hurt him." Then he whispered to his secretary: "My wife—be careful how you tell her—oh, be careful!"

But all the care and gentleness in the world couldn't soften the blow for Ida McKinley when, several hours later, she learned of the shooting. The President died on September 14. His wife accompanied the body to Washington where it lay in state in the rotunda of the Capitol; then on to Canton, Ohio, her home. Throughout the long journeys, in the last coach of the special train, the frail little figure in black kept tender watch over her beloved dead.

Mrs. McKinley was almost always ill after that. Less than six years later, on May 26, 1907, she died, and was laid to rest in Canton beside her husband and their two little girls.

Edith Kermit Carow Roosevelt

"HAPPY DAYS OF A HAPPY LIFE"

THOSE happy days of a happy life began in Norwich, Connecticut, where Edith Kermit Carow was born on August 16, 1861. Her parents, Charles and Gertrude Tyler Carow, came from a long line of sturdy Americans. They were socially prominent, wealthy, and well educated; and little Edith had a cloudless, carefree childhood. With the rest of the children in the family, she was gently reared and trained early in those principles which have made America great—love of God and love of country.

Edith's grandfather offered a prize to any of the youngsters who would recite the Book of Proverbs to him. The tall, spare, dignified old gentleman longed to put the staff of the wisdom of the world in the hands of his clan; and, though none qualified for the prize, he felt that he had accomplished his purpose. For the children turned the pages of their Bibles oftener and doubtless learned many lessons which were valuable to them in later life.

On the nursery wall, side by side in their round frames, hung lithograph portraits of George and Martha Washington. Edith was encouraged to blow kisses to "George and Martha," and that youthful feeling of intimate friendship with them was something she always remembered. Once, when she herself was First Lady, she journeyed on horseback with her boys to Mount Vernon, and came upon the house away from the river, under the trees and up a quiet road, along the route Washington would have taken.

"Almost his presence met us, [she wrote] . . . the man who loved his horses, his fields, and the same

countless trivial pleasures and cares that fill our lives
—the dear friend of my childhood days.

"I don't know why some places have a curiously
penetrating atmosphere of sentiment—but in fact
this seems true, and Wakefield, where Washington
was born, is such a place. I have felt it in the spring,
when the blue cloud of grape hyacinths almost hid
the grass; and again in the late fall afternoon when
I took my children on a pious pilgrimage. Even
writing about it brings back some happy days of a
happy life."

Those thoughtful lines, so gracefully expressed, give a
clearer picture of the character and temperament of the wife
of Theodore Roosevelt, twenty-sixth President of the United
States, than all the thousands of words written by historians.
Edith Kermit Carow had a keen sense of awareness, a love of
beauty, and a literary flair. She was well fitted for the role she
was to occupy in the life of the dynamic Rough Rider hero.

Edith and Theodore met in early childhood. Their families
moved in the same circles. They were often together, both in
New York city, where they lived near each other, and on
Long Island where they spent many happy summers, rowing,
sailing, and swimming. He was three years older than she,
and the little girl was rather impressed by the frail bespecta-
cled lad with light brown hair, nearsighted blue eyes, and a
dogged determination to be an athlete. When at sixteen his
family bundled him off to Algiers, and later to Dresden,
the boy and girl exchanged letters regularly. Later, when
Theodore attended Harvard, he was proud to show off the
beautiful and charming young Edith to his classmates at teas
and dances. Then, for a time, the paths of the two young

people separated. During his college days Theodore fell in love with Alice Hathaway Lee, of Boston, and they were married a few months after his graduation. For three years they were blissfully happy; then, following the birth of their daughter Alice, the young mother died on February 14, 1884. Theodore knew double sorrow on that St. Valentine's Day; for death came not only to his wife but to his mother.

At twenty-six, Roosevelt was already well started upon a career. Although he had no worries about the need for earning a living, a lazy life never appealed to him. Before he was twenty-three he was the author of a naval history of the War of 1812—the first of some thirty books he wrote as the years went by. He was twenty-three when he took his seat at Albany as the youngest member of the State Assembly, where he was re-elected and served also during 1883 and 1884. Crushed by loneliness and sorrow at the loss of his wife and his mother, and always a lover of the outdoors, he turned to ranch life in the Dakotas. Soon he was again writing letters to his old friend, Edith Carow, who was touring abroad. He traveled all the way to London to marry her on December 2, 1886. After a long honeymoon, visiting all their favorite haunts, they returned home to settle down happily in the big many-chimneyed house at Sagamore Hill, with its meadows and woodland, where they could look out upon the familiar waters of Oyster Bay and Long Island Sound.

Later, as their children came along, Theodore and Edith Roosevelt shared with their youngsters—Ted, Kermit, Ethel, Archie and Quentin—the happy adventures of field and countryside. A closely knit and carefree family, they went on cross-country hikes, had picnics on the shore, and sailed and swam in the bay. The children, like their father, loved flowers and pets. Into the nursery they brought rabbits, squirrels, guinea pigs, snakes, field mice, and birds with broken wings. Ponies and dogs were their almost constant companions, and their gentle mother, who was companion to all their small joys and triumphs, never complained about the variety of strange creatures in the big, rambling old house.

When in 1901, after the assassination of President McKinley, Vice President Theodore Roosevelt was suddenly thrust into the office of Chief Executive, life for the lively and energetic Roosevelt family went on much as usual. Ted and Kermit, the older boys, were away at school at Groton then; but Ethel, Archie, and Quentin were transferred with their dogs, rabbits, snakes, stilts, kites, and other treasures to Washington, and moved into the former cabinet room on the third floor of the White House, which Edith Roosevelt had fitted up as a playroom and nursery. The beloved ponies were officially installed in the stables, but it was no uncommon sight during the Theodore Roosevelt administration to see young Archie, assisted by Mr. Ike Hoover, White House usher, smuggling his pony into the elevator to take him up to the playroom!

Edith and Theodore Roosevelt were young and full of compelling charm. When he was tired, she made him rest; when the responsibilities of government weighed him down, she cheered him. He depended upon her; once he told a friend: "Whenever I go against her judgment I regret it."

Working late and strenuously each evening, he would hear just as surely as half-past ten o'clock came, the gentle tapping of her slippered foot on the floor above, reminding him that it was bedtime. "Edie, my darling!" he would call out, "give me just ten minutes more!" But she was firm.

Distinguished visitors from all over the world lunched and dined informally with the Roosevelts, and they were always welcomed into the heart of family life. Even the baby in his high chair sat at the table with diplomats, artists, writers, and statesmen. Everybody was interested in the fascinating Roosevelts. Alice, the first White House debutante since President Grant's daughter, was the idol of the nation. Ted was a rough-and-tumble schoolboy with spectacles; Kermit, Ethel, Archie and baby Quentin were like any other girls and boys. They had friends from all walks of life who came to play with them at the White House; and, while they were encouraged to have a wide number of interests and activities, they were never pampered.

Though the President and his First Lady naturally had many duties and social obligations, they were never too busy to spend hours each day with their youngsters. To conserve time, Mrs. Roosevelt engaged a social secretary—the first to be employed in the Executive Mansion. An efficient manager and a skilled hostess, Mrs. Roosevelt hired caterers to serve state dinners, which left her free to supervise other important details. At the request of the President, Congress appropriated money for White House renovations. A new structure was also built to house the executive office. Under Edith Roosevelt's capable management, hospitality at the White House was bountiful; and, even with all the formal entertainments, family life for herself, her husband, and the children went on as happily and informally as before.

Busy with her brood, her social duties, and many other activities, Edith Roosevelt made no attempt to inject herself into politics. That was her husband's domain, and one which he thoroughly enjoyed. He was energetic, full of firm convictions, and he was only forty-two—years younger than any President the country had ever had. The nation loved him, cheered him, and wondered what he would do next. He had proved, in the Spanish-American War, that he was a fighter. Within three years he had become a war hero, the governor of New York state, the Vice President, and now he was the Chief Executive. He was democratic, eager, friendly, a smasher of rackets, and he got things done. He fought vice and crime; he favored imposing income and inheritance taxes; he worked for forest conservation and western irrigation. He proposed the Pure Food Law and government inspection of meat. He dispatched a fleet of battleships around the world to demonstrate our naval strength; he went to Panama to inspect the progress of the new canal; and in 1906 he won the Nobel Peace Prize for persuading Russia and Japan to end the war they were waging.

One of the most popular Presidents the nation has ever had, Theodore Roosevelt easily won election after he had completed the term for which McKinley had been elected to serve. He received a popular vote three times greater than any candidate had ever received. His wife and children were as happy about his victory as he was. They thoroughly enjoyed their life in Washington. When, in 1906, young Alice Roosevelt was married to Nicholas Longworth, there was a wedding at the White House such as it had never seen before. There were a thousand guests, and every detail of the attendant festivities was followed eagerly through the press by people all over the nation.

The Theodore Roosevelts probably could have remained in the White House for an additional four years, had not the President made it clear, when he was elected in 1904, that he would not run again. On March 4, 1909, he gave his blessing to the new President, William Howard Taft, and took his wife and children back home.

Within a few weeks, Roosevelt was off to Africa on an expedition. After an absence of fifteen months he returned, and later organized the Progressive party, which nominated him in 1912. President Taft was the Republican nominee; but both Taft and Roosevelt lost out. Aided by the split in the Republican party, Woodrow Wilson, the Democratic candidate, was elected.

When World War I came, Roosevelt tried to get into it, although he was in his fifty-ninth year, but no place was found for him. His wife and he saw their four sons go off to war, and they lost their youngest, Quentin, who was a fighter pilot.

On Monday, January 6, 1919, Theodore Roosevelt died at his home in Oyster Bay and was laid to rest in the village cemetery as he had wished.

Edith Roosevelt was bereft; but she was to live on twenty-nine years without her husband. With her children settled in life and having homes and interests of their own, she embarked on what she later called "The Odyssey of a Grandmother" and found in far places the peace and serenity which her spirit needed.

In the account of her many travels during her years of widowhood she observed:

> "Women who marry pass their best and happiest years in giving life and fostering it, meeting and facing the problems of the next generation and helping the universe to move, and those born with the wander-foot are sometimes a bit irked by the weight of the always beloved shackles. Then the birds fly, the nest is empty, and at the feet of the knitters in the sun lies the wide world."

Into that wide world went Edith Kermit Roosevelt in 1919. She went to Paris first and to the grave of her son in war-shattered France; then to the sunshine and warmth of Italy; and back home on an Italian ship carrying American troops. The year 1920 found her in South America, in a little hotel where she sat in the deep shade, and looked on the beauty of the mountain Corcovado. That same year, full of aches and pains, she crawled aboard a little ship bound for Grenada, and Port-of-Spain, with its white surf dashing high on golden beaches. Then followed long days of peace and sunshine in a primitive little boat, paddled by natives up to the Kaieteur Falls in Demerara, British Guiana.

Far places still beckoned, and in 1921 she was again in Paris, spending long happy days alone, wandering through the streets, browsing among the bookstalls along the Seine. Although planes were not as reliable then as they are now, Grandmother Roosevelt flew from Paris to London, where she left for Capetown on a little ship which stopped at every island on the way.

A trip around the world with her son Kermit was the holiday she enjoyed in 1924; and the following year she was reveling in the color, beauty, and fragrance of Malta and Sicily. But it wasn't until after she had made a trip through the jungles of South and Central America, to satisfy her longing to see the great falls of the Iguassu and the mighty Mayan ruins at Uxmal, that she was content to return home to Oyster Bay. "All my journeys begin and end with the ocean, as much of the ocean as may be," she said. "I have 'salt water around my heart' as the Breton saying goes."

It was 1927, and the famous Odyssey of a famous woman was over. She was back in the countryside she had loved since her girlhood. Nearby were the homes of her children. Kermit lived at Cove Neck; Theodore, junior, at Sagamore Hill. Ethel was there at Oyster Bay, too, with her husband, Dr.

Richard Derby. Archie's home was at Cold Spring Harbor.

On Sagamore Hill, beside the bay where she had so often gone voyaging in a small boat piloted by the young Theodore who was to become President, Edith Roosevelt read, embroidered, knitted, and wrote the history of her mother's New England family.[1]

In the final lines of her "Odyssey of a Grandmother," [2] she disclosed the same searching philosophy which had governed all her years:

> "Now wanderings are done, for the old nurseries
> are once again full of children, the fields and woods
> are the setting of their games. The Lilliputians have
> bound Gulliver, and the cords held in small hands
> are strong. The fire of life sinks for one generation,
> but it flames high for another."

Edith Kermit Carow Roosevelt passed away on September 30, 1948, at the age of eighty-seven. In a long, useful, and active career, she had, in the words of her own favorite quotation, "warmed both hands before the fire of life."

[1] *American Backlogs: the History of Gertrude Tyler and Her Family, from 1680 to 1860,* with Kermit Roosevelt (Charles Scribner's Sons, New York, 1928.)

[2] "The Odyssey of a Grandmother" appears in the book *Cleared for Strange Ports,* by Mrs. Theodore Roosevelt, Sr., Mrs. Kermit Roosevelt, Richard Derby, and Kermit Roosevelt (Charles Scribner's Sons, New York, 1927.)

Helen Herron Taft

WHO ESTABLISHED WASHINGTON'S
FAMOUS CHERRY BLOSSOMS

H

ELEN HERRON TAFT stared
ruefully from the second floor bedroom windows early on the
morning of March 4, 1909. No day could possibly be worse for
her husband's inauguration. The blizzard of the night before
had increased in violence. Snow lay deep upon the White
House grounds and the wind swept around the corner of the
building. The loud crackling noise which had awakened her
was the snapping of twigs and branches, creaking with the
weight of the ice that encased them.

At the invitation of President Theodore Roosevelt, she and
Mr. Taft had arrived at the White House on March 3. It was
Roosevelt's way of giving a warm welcome in advance to the
good friend who was to succeed him.

Both men seemed happy and carefree as they met in the
great lower hall on Inauguration morning.

"Well, Will," chuckled the President, "the storm will soon
be over. It isn't a regular storm; it's nature's echo of Senator
Rainer's denunciations of me. As soon as I am out where I can
do no further damage to the Constitution, it will cease!"

"You're wrong," said Will Taft. "It is *my* storm. I always
said it would be a cold day when I got to be President of the
United States!"

Despite her worries over the weather, Mrs. Taft laughed at
his reply. She knew he had never wanted to be President; his
life-long dream was to become Chief Justice of the United
States.

As the storm continued, the inaugural ceremonies were
held indoors, in the Senate Chamber at the Capitol. Wearing
a purple satin suit and a small hat trimmed with gold lace and
a high, white aigrette, Mrs. Taft joined her children who were

already in the gallery eagerly awaiting the proceedings. Robert and Helen were awed by the importance of the occasion, but Charlie, who was only eleven, brought along his copy of *Treasure Island,* with which he intended to while away the time in case his father's speech should prove too long! It was a tribute to Taft's eloquence that the book by Robert Louis Stevenson was not opened that day.

Since Theodore Roosevelt broke a precedent by not riding back to the White House with the new President, Mrs. Taft decided she too would break one. She seated herself beside her husband in the official coach and four. Fortunately the weather had cleared and the sun was shining as they drove slowly through the streets, waving and smiling to the cheering crowds. For the first time in America's history, a President's wife shared the honor of the return drive to the Executive Mansion. Later she confessed the ride was, for her, the outstanding event of the day, even more exciting than the Inaugural Ball that evening, when she was radiant in white satin with a train yards long.

Mrs. Taft was not a stranger to her new home. When she was seventeen she spent a week at the White House as the guest of Lucy Webb Hayes. Years later, while William H. Taft was Secretary of War, his wife appeared with him at many state dinners and receptions, and she attended Mrs. Theodore Roosevelt's "parlor cabinet" each week. Mrs. Roosevelt called the wives of Cabinet members together for these meetings to keep down rivalries among them, to decree social standing, and make social events run more smoothly. With these contacts and associations, Helen Taft was well schooled in her duties when she became First Lady.

Helen Herron was born in 1861, in Cincinnati, Ohio. Her father was at one time a law partner of Rutherford B. Hayes and had twice declined appointments to the bench because the salary was not enough to support his large family. Helen's girlhood days were spent sedately at a private school for girls; and, when she wasn't studying languages and literature, she spent hours practicing on the family piano. Later she became an accomplished musician, and was the founder of the Cincinnati Orchestra.

She and Will Taft met at a bobsled party one bright moonlit evening when she was eighteen, and after that they were often together. They took part in amateur theatricals and went to dances, parties, and plays. Deciding she was perhaps too frivolous, Nellie Herron launched a "salon" for literary and economic discussions, and for a time she taught school.

But on June 19, 1886, the pert, dark-eyed, dark-haired young lady with the slightly turned-up nose was married to big, broad-shouldered, genial Will Taft; and they sailed away on a wedding trip. They saw the sights of London and the cathedral towns; wandered over the Scottish heath; bought Delft plates in Holland; and went to the opera in Paris. They were gone just one hundred days and the trip cost just one thousand dollars. They began the year of 1887 under their own roof and, though the new house was mortgaged, the struggling young law reporter and his bride were happier than ever before. Their first child, Robert, was born there in 1889. Then, when Taft was made Solicitor General, they lived for two exciting years in the nation's capital, where a second baby, Helen, came along in 1891. On Sunday afternoons the Tafts climbed into their surrey with their little ones and rode out to the Old Soldiers' Home, which was the fashionable drive in those days.

They were back in Cincinnati in 1892 when President Harrison appointed Will Taft a judge of the Circuit Court, and it was during that period, with two little children to look after, that Helen Taft organized and managed the Cincinnati Orchestra Association. Their last child, Charles, was born in 1897.

When Charlie was a little over two, his father returned from a quick trip to Washington and said casually to his wife: "President McKinley wants me to go to the Philippine Islands. Want to go?"

"Yes, of course!" she answered promptly. So, with Robert, ten; Helen, eight; and baby Charlie, the Tafts started out blithely for an unknown land ten thousand miles away! The Philippine Islands had been under Spanish domination for three centuries—until the Spanish-American War. Taft knew no more about the Filipinos than the average citizen does; but he was in favor of giving them political independence as soon as they were ready for it. He set eagerly to work at his job of establishing a civil government for the islands.

Both during his years as governor general of the Philippines and throughout his political career, Nellie Taft was an important factor in the life of William H. Taft. Before her youngest son was eight years old, she had accompanied her husband twice around the world. As the "first lady" of the first governor of the Philippines, she held out the hand of friendship to the Filipinos. She used wisdom and diplomacy in furthering Taft's efforts, and made the natives understand that she and her husband were there only to help them. They came, two thousand strong, to Mrs. Taft's garden parties at the Malacañan Palace; they brought gifts for the whole family.

When Taft was finally recalled to Washington by President Theodore Roosevelt, the entire population of Manila staged a giant protest parade, carrying placards: "We Want Taft." Big-bodied, big-hearted genial Will Taft had won their confidence by giving them schools, roads, and courts of justice. He taught them the principles of democracy, and protected their interests. For them he sacrificed the big chance for which he had been waiting—the chance to become Chief Justice of the United States Supreme Court—an appointment Roosevelt urged him to accept and which he refused only because he felt his work in the Philippines was not completed.

Taft made a special trip to Rome and, in a personal interview with the Pope, arranged for a transfer of Philippine lands owned by the church. For years, the natives and the priests had been quarreling over those lands. Taft persuaded the church to sell them to the United States; and Congress voted more than seven million dollars to pay for them. Mrs. Taft went right along with her husband on that trip, and when the Pope learned she could speak French he talked with her for half an hour in that language.

Unofficially, Nellie Taft fought as earnestly as her husband to protect the rights of the Filipinos. Years later, when President Roosevelt was thinking about a successor to himself in the Presidency, he mentioned the matter to Taft, then his Secretary of War. "I see something hanging over your head," said President Roosevelt, his eyes twinkling, "but I can't tell whether it is the Presidency or the Chief Justiceship."

"Make it the Presidency!" said Mrs. Taft.

"Make it the Chief Justiceship," urged Will Taft. Then he added, with a smile: "As my wife is the politician and she will be able to meet all . . . issues, perhaps we can keep a stiff upper lip."

But even though his wife undoubtedly had keen discernment in political matters, William H. Taft was an able and industrious man in any capacity. As Secretary of War, he supervised the construction of the Panama Canal, taking Mrs.

Taft with him to look over the situation. Together they traveled around the world on a mission of peace and diplomacy; and, while they were settling affairs in Cuba, Mrs. Taft reigned as "first lady" for a brief, crowded three days in the palace at Havana.

When Taft came into office as President on the tail end of the blizzard, Mrs. Taft was ready to carry her share of White House burdens. She put Negro footmen in blue livery at the White House door, engaged a competent woman as housekeeper to replace the man steward who had been in charge, organized a small dancing class because her husband was an excellent dancer and they both liked the exercise, presided at most state functions, and entertained her friends. She still had leisure to sit with her husband on balmy spring evenings on the south portico, enjoying the fragrance of Andrew Jackson's magnolia tree, watching the play of lights on the White House lawn, and listening to favorite phonograph records. Many of the great artists who made those recordings, including Madame Ernestine Schumann-Heink, were guests at the White House during the Taft administration.

Mrs. Taft, who had kept a garden in Manila, thoroughly enjoyed the luxury of being able to order as many roses as she liked from the White House greenhouses. She used them lavishly, along with ferns and palms, for special occasions.

Young Helen Taft attended many entertainments during the winter of 1909 whenever she was home from college. When her mother suffered a slight stroke, from which she recovered remarkably, the namesake daughter acted as White House hostess. Early in the winter of 1910, Mrs. Taft gave two parties to introduce Helen to society—an afternoon "at home" and a ball in the East Room.

The most important occasion of all for President and Mrs.

Taft, however, was the celebration of their silver wedding anniversary. Twenty-five years married, they had spent all but a single year in public service. Some four or five thousand invited guests came to the night garden party. The White House grounds were a blaze of lights; the great fountain sparkled with every color of the rainbow; while the gleam of powerful searchlights shone steadily on the flag waving in the breeze atop the Executive Mansion.

But for President Taft, life in Washington was more serious than parties and celebrations. His four years in the White House were far from happy. He lost many friends by the removal from office of men appointed by Theodore Roosevelt. Always honest and sincere, Taft did not hesitate to replace those whom he considered inefficient. During his administration he recommended the levying of income taxes, urged Congress to set up a national budget, fought monopolies and trusts, and lowered the scale on import duties. His enemies opposed a second term, calling him too conservative.

Mrs. Taft naturally wanted her husband to be re-elected, but being fully aware of bitter opposition, she felt he was fighting for a lost cause. Long in advance of the election of Woodrow Wilson she had packed up all personal possessions and was ready to move.

William H. Taft was much too active to consider retiring. He became a professor of law at Yale University, joined President Woodrow Wilson in opposing America's entry into World War I; and at its close, favored the League of Nations for world peace. On the death of Chief Justice White in 1921, President Harding appointed Mr. Taft as Chief Justice of the United States. One of the happiest moments of Mrs. Taft's life came when she heard the news of this appointment; it was the goal he had been dreaming of all through his career. He presided over the Supreme Court for nine years, and died on March 8, 1930.

Mrs. Taft survived her husband by many years, and lived to see the full flowering of her favorite project, started when she was First Lady in the White House. During her stay in the Philippines, she had loved Manila and its Luneta, an oval drive with a bandstand at either end, where everybody greeted everybody else in the cool of the evening. And she was determined, if possible, to convert Potomac Park into a glorified Luneta where all Washington could meet in the late afternoon, listen to band concerts, and enjoy the beauty of the scene and the river-cooled air. She also planned for a Japanese cherry-blossom season. Through her efforts, some three thousand cherry trees were secured as a gift from the mayor of Tokyo and were planted around the Tidal Basin. Bandstands were erected and the Marine Band gave concerts twice a week.

When President and Mrs. Taft, "in a small landaulette motor-car" (something of a novelty in those days), attended the first concert, Potomac Park was packed with people. Ten thousand visitors crowded the lawns and paths, and the drive was filled with vehicles of every description. Everybody had a wonderful time, and there was the same exchange of friendly greetings that had always made the Luneta such a pleasant meeting place. The famous cherry trees were tiny then and not yet blooming, but for many years in later life Mrs. Taft was able to enjoy their fragrance and beauty.

Helen Herron Taft died in 1943, at the age of eighty-two, but her beloved cherry trees live on and each spring, with their cloud of pink and white blossoms, they give pleasure to thousands of visitors from all parts of the United States.

Ellen Louisa Axson Wilson

FIRST LADY OF THE WORLD WAR I ERA

MRS. WOODROW WILSON
drew her three daughters to a south window overlooking the
Ellipse and the Washington Monument. "Isn't it lovely, children!" she exclaimed, and from that moment they all knew
they were going to like living in the White House. Ellie Lou
Wilson, who had moved many times during her married
life, seemed to be able to create a feeling of home in each new
place. And always, as she looked about with discerning brown
eyes, she found a beautiful view.

When she had leisure, which wasn't often, she skillfully
wielded a pencil or brush and put what she saw on canvas or
paper. She enjoyed sketching and painting, and when she first
met Thomas Woodrow Wilson she was well on the way to
making art her career. For the studious young man with
the lantern-jawed face and serious gray eyes, Ellie Lou put
away her dream of becoming a famous painter. Then, and for
the rest of her life, Wilson and his career, comfort, and well-
being came before everything else. To her, he was a god. Ike
Hoover, White House chief usher, said of Mrs. Wilson and
her daughters: "They pampered him and petted him and
looked up to him as their lord and master."

Ellen Louisa Axson was born in Rome, Georgia, in 1860. As
the daughter of a Presbyterian minister, she was brought up
in a highly religious atmosphere. Ellie Lou, with her soft
southern drawl and winsome ways, was a pretty child. She
had large velvety brown eyes and shining chestnut hair which,
as a little girl, she wore in long dangling braids. That was how
she looked when young "Tommy" Wilson arrived in town to
visit his cousin Jessie, Ellie Lou's best friend.

"Tommy," who rode around on a brand new bicycle, was

four years older than Ellie Lou and he paid no attention whatever to the child in pigtails. But it was quite another story one summer several years later. The minister's daughter, pouring tea at a lawn party, caught his eye at once. Her smooth white hands handled the teacups deftly, and she moved with a serenity and poise that somehow rested him and put him at ease. In a white muslin dress with a fichu knotted at her breast, her bright hair piled high on her head, Ellie Lou was slender and womanly. She wore white stockings and little black-strapped slippers, and looked as though she had stepped straight out of a Jane Austen novel.

As for the young Princeton graduate, Jessie was almost apologetic when she begged Ellie Lou to be nice to him. Wilson was shy and awkward in the presence of girls. He didn't dance, and he had no talent for the small talk, flattery, and attentions which most young ladies expected. Ellie Lou, however, was herself completely unworldly. She had been educated at Shorter College, and she shared with the diffident young man a very serious outlook on life and its responsibilities.

In September, 1883, a few months after their second meeting, they became engaged, although they could make no plans for an immediate marriage. Ellie Lou had set her heart on going to New York to study portrait painting; Woodrow wanted to complete a course in political economy at Johns Hopkins University before looking about for a teaching job.

During the next year or two, Ellen Axson attended the Art Students League in New York city, while, in Baltimore, Woodrow Wilson (who had dropped the "Thomas" and kept the maiden surname of his mother) worked for his doctorate. As soon as he received the degree, Ellen put aside her own ambitions. They were married on June 24, 1885, at the home of the bride's grandfather in Savannah, and that autumn they went north to Pennsylvania, where young Dr. Wilson began his career as a teacher at Bryn Mawr College.

Then and there, Ellen Wilson began a job of her own, which undoubtedly helped her husband to advance steadily. He was reserved, sensitive, and absorbed in study. Her warm-hearted nature, her slow southern voice, and her generous hospitality did much to win friends for him. During those first years of her marriage she took lessons twice a week in a Philadelphia cooking school. She sewed beautifully and designed all her own clothes. And when, in 1890, they went to Princeton, where he became Professor of Jurisprudence and of Political Economy, it was Ellen who brought out the best in his nature and surrounded him with a happy home life. Being naturally artistic, she made their home attractive and livable, whether it was on the college campus or in various other places that came with her husband's different positions. By the time Woodrow Wilson became President of Princeton University, Ellen was the mother of three little girls, and they lived in a big house where relatives were constantly coming to visit and students, professors, and others dropped in at all hours.

Ellen also entertained Wilson's many women friends now and then. He regarded friendship between a man and a woman in the same way that he regarded friendship between two men. He enjoyed the society of brilliant, intellectual women—women of wit and gaiety, women who were good listeners, women of all ages. Often he laughingly said: "I am submerged in petticoats!" He was referring then to his wife, his daughters, and an assortment of visiting cousins, aunts, and nieces. But he delighted in being surrounded by them, as well as by other women, married and single, whose companionship stimulated him. It is fortunate that Ellen Wilson didn't have an ounce of jealousy in her makeup. She realized that her husband's friendships were intellectual only.

When Wilson became President of the United States, his wife adapted herself easily to the new setting, giving their apartments in the White House a cheerful, homelike atmosphere. As First Lady she was a gracious hostess. With her three daughters, she made the mansion the center of interest for young people all over the nation. Her garden parties were delightfully informal, with their tea, hot biscuits, preserves, baked Virginia ham, and little cakes dusted with powdered sugar. The garden itself was dear to her heart. She directed the planting of rose trees and many other shrubs and plants which gave increased beauty to the White House grounds.

The Wilsons found themselves in a gay social whirl during their first year in Washington. They went to the Executive Mansion in March, 1913. In November of the same year, their daughter, Jessie, was married in the East Room; the following May, Eleanor took her vows in the Blue Room.

With two of her girls married, Mrs. Wilson turned eagerly to her painting once more. She was happily oblivious of the political turmoil going on around her; the White House was managed by a capable housekeeper; and the First Lady had more leisure than she could remember since the first year of her marriage.

In the summer of 1914, Ellen Wilson became ill. When she realized her condition was desperate, only one thing worried her. "Promise me that you will take care of Woodrow," she begged her physician, Dr. Cary T. Grayson. When the doctor promised, a grateful smile lighted her thin face, and she seemed resigned to whatever might happen. On August 6th, she died without knowing that a war had begun in Europe; a war in which her husband was destined to become a world figure.

President Wilson was a lost and lonely man. He was in his fifty-ninth year, and he was desolate without a companion in the midst of heavy cares, great responsibilities, and difficult decisions. Always dependent for encouragement upon women, it is not surprising that he was attracted when he first made the acquaintance of Edith Bolling Galt, daughter of a Virginia judge and widow of Norman Galt, Washington jeweler.

Mrs. Galt was forty-two at that time and a handsome woman. Above medium height, she had dark hair, expressive eyes, a patrician nose, and a deep cleft in her chin. She was born in Wytheville,[1] Virginia, on October 15, 1872, a lineal descendant in the ninth generation of Pocahontas and John Rolfe. Before the Civil War the family had been wealthy and owned many slaves. Later, with everything swept away, they were poverty-stricken.

Until the summer before she was thirteen, Edith Bolling had never been out of the little town where she was born, and she had not been to school. Grandmother Bolling taught her to read and write and instructed her in French. On her fifteenth birthday, the young girl went off to boarding school in Abingdon; the following year she was sent to Powell's School in Richmond. It was during a winter in Washington that she met Norman Galt, who was several years older than she. After a close friendship of four years, the two were married; and the nation's capital became home to the girl from Virginia. Following her husband's death in 1908, Edith Galt put every cent she could spare into his jewelry business until

[1] Pronounced *With*-ville.

it was free and clear of debt. By the time she met President Wilson, she was a successful business woman with an established income and a small house of her own.

In that house, on December 18, 1915, she and Woodrow Wilson were married. Because both disliked publicity, it was a small, quiet wedding. The bride wore black velvet with a large picture hat of black beaver. The plain wedding band which the groom placed on her finger was made from a gold nugget—a gift of the people of California.

There were those who criticized the President for remarrying only a little more than a year after his first wife died. But all that was soon forgotten in the larger events that followed. In 1916 he was re-elected. On April 6, 1917, the United States declared war on Germany and Woodrow Wilson's cares and worries increased. Since the beginning of the conflict abroad in 1914, pressure had been brought upon him to bring America into the fighting. But Woodrow Wilson hated war. He could not be persuaded to forsake neutrality until he was convinced the United States could no longer maintain an honorable peace.

During the war Edith Bolling Wilson volunteered her services to the Red Cross and geared the White House to the stringencies that faced the nation. There were wheatless days, meatless days, and regulations for the saving of food, fuel, wool, and other necessities. With manpower needed for war, help was scarce. Sheep were secured to crop the White House lawn. When they were sheared, the wool was auctioned off. Patriotism ran high, and the wool brought nearly $100,000, which was turned over to the Red Cross.

Social life was negligible then, and Mrs. Wilson often sat with her husband until far into the night, decoding cables from Europe and coding his replies. Efficient, intelligent, and untiring, she shared his burdens and perplexities. Margaret Wilson, the unmarried daughter, made two long and profitable concert tours and gave her earnings as a singer to the Red Cross. Wilson's second marriage had the complete approval of his daughters.

Edith Wilson's days were full to overflowing. She did relief work, prepared bandages for the hospitals, and handled reams of correspondence from frantic fathers and mothers whose sons were missing in action. She was a cheerful companion for the President when he was tired and discouraged.

Two months after the signing of the Armistice on November 11, 1918, the President and Mrs. Wilson sailed for Europe. This marked the first time a Chief Executive had gone abroad during his term of office, and Mrs. Wilson was the first First Lady to leave the country while she was mistress of the White House. The people of Europe regarded Woodrow Wilson as an inspired leader. He declared that permanent peace must be established throughout the world, and he went to Paris to draw up a peace treaty between the Allies and our late enemies.

There were interminable delays while the various delegates wrangled over the terms to be imposed upon Germany. While they waited, the Wilsons were royally entertained at Buckingham Palace in London; they visited the crowned heads of Italy and Belgium. In France the crowds threw flowers into the Presidential carriage and shouted their admiration of America's First Lady.

After signing the treaty of Versailles, President Wilson returned home. Edith Wilson watched her husband anxiously. He had put his whole soul into working out a just peace and establishing the League of Nations. Several times, during his speeches abroad, she saw him close to the breaking point. She

Edith Bolling Wilson

nursed him through a siege of influenza and watched with concern the hostile attitude which some members of Congress took toward the League.

When the Senate refused to ratify the treaty of Versailles, and long debates were held as to whether the United States should join the League of Nations, Mrs. Wilson knew that her husband would never rest until he had done his utmost to carry the project through. Against her protests and those of his physician and friends, President Wilson started on a trip across the continent in the hope of arousing public opinion so that the Senate would be compelled to go along with him and ratify the treaty.

This effort was too much for Woodrow Wilson, in his weakened condition. Following a speech at Pueblo, Colorado, in September, 1919, he collapsed. His wife, at his side as always, began the most unusual job ever held by any woman—that of carrying on for the Chief Executive of the United States. At her command, the special train sped back to Washington. Both she and Doctor Grayson realized that President Wilson was a very sick man. They realized, too, the importance of keeping from the nation and the world the news that he had suffered a stroke shortly after his return from the western trip, and was partially paralyzed. The White House gates were shut, and sentries were posted at them. A brief statement was issued announcing simply that the President was ill.

In the emergency, Edith Wilson became nurse, companion, and executive secretary. She received government officials, discussed routine business over the teacups, and carried messages of importance to her husband's bedside. Only essential matters were brought to the President's attention, and his wife made notes of the letters she would write later in the day to carry out his wishes. All state papers were submitted to her.

If she felt doubtful as to the effect they might have on the sick man, she consulted Dr. Grayson. If he thought President Wilson was strong enough to pass judgment upon them, they were read to him. If not, they were passed upon by members of the Cabinet in whom Edith Wilson had confidence.

By Christmas, 1919, the President was able to sit up for a few hours each day. His wife read to him, talked, or just sat quietly beside him, holding his hand. During those months many rumors were spread, about both Woodrow Wilson and the First Lady. The myth that persisted longest was that he was insane, although actually his mind was as clear and keen as it always had been. Mrs. Wilson, they said, was running the government; she, of course, had no such idea. Her whole aim was to help the man she loved, to make things easier for him. She was thankful that his term in the White House would soon come to an end.

Washington had long been home to her, and she began looking for a comfortable house. When she found one she liked on S Street, she gave her husband such an enthusiastic report that he bought it as a gift to her. It was in that house that Woodrow Wilson died on February 3, 1924, still clinging to his idealistic dreams of world peace and fraternity, still crushed in spirit because the Senate had repudiated his efforts at Versailles.

Edith Bolling Wilson shared his beliefs and his ideals. For several years after her husband's death she made an annual pilgrimage to Geneva, Switzerland, home of the League of Nations. In 1931 she went to Poland to see the unveiling of a statue of Woodrow Wilson which Paderewski, statesman and pianist, presented to his Polish countrymen.

As First Lady, Edith Bolling Wilson had thrust upon her by the illness of the President a situation unique in America's history. She proved more than equal to the emergency, and she served her husband and the nation with loyalty and skill.

On December 28, 1961, Mrs. Wilson died at her beautiful town house on S Street in Washington, D.C., which became her home when she and President Wilson left the White House more than forty years earlier. She was eighty-nine years old.

Florence Kling Harding

POLITICALLY MINDED FIRST LADY

FLORENCE KLING HARDING,
keen-minded and ambitious, coveted the Presidency for her
husband far more than he did. She has been widely credited
with getting him into the White House. Certainly, once imbued with the idea, she worked as hard as any Ohio politician
on his behalf. In fact, she was much more active than Warren
Harding during the fight for the Presidential nomination in
1920.

She accompanied him to Chicago for the convention and,
while he refused to enter into the political battle, Mrs. Harding appeared regularly each morning at the Coliseum, seated
herself in a box, watched the faces of the delegates, and missed
no word of the speeches and arguments. Most of the crowds
that filled the convention hall visibly suffered through those
hot, sultry June days, but the well-groomed, completely poised
woman from Marion, Ohio, seemed not to notice the tempera-
ture. Not a wisp of her perfectly marcelled gray hair was out
of place; not a muscle of her set face revealed any emotion.

From early childhood she had been carefully trained by
her father, Amos Kling, a Marion banker. He had wanted a
boy, and he brought her up as he would have brought up a
son. She was born on August 15, 1860, and throughout her
school days she and her father were constant companions.
When she had completed a course at the Cincinnati Conser-
vatory of Music, she returned home to keep house for him,
and for a time, taught music. Even after she married Henry
De Wolfe, father and daughter continued the close association
they had always enjoyed. It wasn't until she met young Warren Harding that there was a rift between them.

Her first marriage had ended in divorce, and Mr. Kling

was bitterly opposed to her second marriage, the main reason being that Harding was a good five years her junior and was considered by many to be a small-town playboy. Harding had tried reading law, selling insurance, and working as a reporter on a newspaper. He lost his job on the paper because his employer said he spent too much time at Republican headquarters in political talk. At nineteen, he and two of his friends managed to get together enough money to buy the bankrupt *Star*, a local weekly.

In 1891, Florence Kling De Wolfe, without the permission of her father, married husky, handsome Warren G. Harding, and it was she who did more than anyone else to make the *Star* the highly successful daily newspaper it later became. Not long after their marriage, she offered to lend a hand on the paper: "I went down there," she told reporters many years later, "intending to help out for a few days—and remained fourteen years."

Florence Harding was a moving force on the *Star,* just as she was a moving force in her husband's career. She was shrewd and keen, with the mind of a man; and, though she had neither beauty nor charm, she was completely devoted to her genial, pleasure-loving young husband, who was such a good mixer and engaging talker.

She was determined, first of all, to get the *Star* on a better financial basis, and acquainted herself with every phase of the business. After she took charge of the circulation department, the weekly soon became a daily. Year after year she started out each morning on her bicycle, acting as advertising solicitor, reporter, editorial writer, and circulation manager. And year after year she returned home each night to cook dinner and do the housework.

Warren Harding, spurred on by her example, did his

share. He liked getting out among the people and picking up news, and with his amiable disposition it was easy for him to make friends with men in all walks of life. He had worked for the Republican party before he was old enough to vote; it was natural that he should get into politics. He had, however, no great ambition for high office. Without his wife's persistence, he probably would have been completely happy in a newspaper career. As the *Star* prospered under the firm hand of Florence Harding, and the town of Marion grew, Editor Harding became a leading citizen. Ohio politicians did not overlook the handsome, magnetic newspaperman who had such a host of friends and who talked so well. He was sent to the Ohio Senate, and he was sent to the United States Senate in 1915.

In 1920, when they decided to groom Harding for the White House, politicians enlisted the aid of Mrs. Harding to help keep him in the fight for the nomination. After he was chosen as the Presidential candidate, he conducted a dignified campaign. He did not leave his own front porch in Marion, but made speeches which were sent by news associations out over the country. Harding received delegations that called at his home and Mrs. Harding remained at his side, extending a gracious welcome to one and all. In November, 1920, Warren G. Harding was elected.

After the inaugural ceremonies were over, the White House took on new gaiety. On inauguration night, at the direction of the new First Lady, everything was thrown wide open. Even the window shades were left up, and crowds swarming through the White House grounds stared into the brightly lighted windows. It was "the people's house," Mrs. Harding insisted; why shouldn't they be permitted to see it? This action and the warm, friendly smile of the new President had a favorable effect on the country. The hearts of the people were also touched by his establishing in the White House a dog named Laddie Boy. The Hardings had no children.

For four long years the gates of the White House had been locked and guarded by sentries. America, after the stringencies of war and the lofty ideals of Woodrow Wilson, was ready to relax with the easy-going Harding, who simply wanted what he called "a return to normalcy."

The Hardings were an impressive looking couple. She was almost sixty-one, and her husband was fifty-five on Inauguration Day, 1921. Florence Harding's hair had long been gray and it was always meticulously waved and dressed. Her clothes were modish and in good taste. Harding himself, with his charming smile, was one of the handsomest Presidents America has ever had. He was more than six feet tall, broad of shoulder, and majestic in his bearing.

Mrs. Harding's inauguration present from her husband was a diamond sunburst which she wore on a black velvet band about her neck. Harding and his most intimate friends always referred to her as "the Duchess." She adored her husband, and all her ambitions toward the Presidency were for him, rather than for her own satisfaction.

Once in the White House, she threw herself into the tremendous political and social job of First Lady with energy, entertaining with dignity and seeing to it that the spotlight centered on her husband in his honored position as the leader of the nation. The nation, for its part, was quite willing to applaud him, even though from the beginning, Harding used his high office to put his Ohio friends and relatives into positions of importance, regardless of their ability.

The war had been over for two years; the Prohibition Amendment (the Eighteenth) was entering its second year, and bootleggers and rumrunners were openly defying the law, as were some of the citizens. The Harding era marked the day of the "flapper" and new freedom for women. It was the beginning of a revolution in manners and morals. Women, having won the right to vote in 1920, were emancipated. With automobiles, radio, movies, and other diversions, they were less content to stick to their housekeeping. Their work was considerably lightened, too, with the advent of electric washing machines and electric irons, ready-made clothing, vacuum cleaners, and smaller houses. Having a telephone within easy reach, they were less apt to spend long hours at marketing. Cooking was simplified by an increasing amount of canned foods and the great number of bake shops.

More and more American women became career-conscious (Mrs. Harding among them), and married women as well as unmarried ones were getting into the business world.

In the days of Martha Washington, Abigail Adams, and Dolley Madison, entertaining at the White House meant that the cooks in the kitchen had to spend much time preparing every variety of delicacy served at state dinners, teas, and receptions. When Florence Harding was First Lady, a staff at the White House handled all details, and caterers could be called in to take care of planning, ordering, cooking, and serving. But the First Ladies of colonial times entertained comparatively small groups at dinner parties, and even at public receptions were never called upon to receive the thousands which thronged the White House after the turn of the twentieth century.

While the social amenities were smoothly taken care of by Mrs. Harding, it was soon apparent that the public was losing faith in the President. His administration was sharply criticized during his years in office, and in later years. He was largely dependent, when confronted by questions of policy, upon friends and subordinates whose brains worked more quickly than his own; and he seemed unable to realize that some of them were completely lacking in ethics. The graft and corruption that went on during his administration aroused the indignation of the public. And, while people generally trusted the President, they blamed him for refusing to recognize the betrayal of trust by those he continued to retain in offices of responsibility.

With considerable scandal, rumors, and gossip beginning to circulate about conditions in the nation's capital, as well as certain derelictions in his private life, it is not surprising that President Harding was losing his popularity among upright American citizens. Yet, with all his faults, there was a warmth and kindness about him that endeared him to the people. Perhaps because he was aware of his own human frailty, he was always ready to forgive others who made mistakes.

If Florence Harding was aware of the situation, she made no sign. She accompanied her husband at all public functions. Whenever he made an address, she was at his side. She was with him at the dedication of the Lincoln Memorial; with him when, on behalf of the women of America, he presented Madame Marie Curie with a gram of radium, that rare element of which she was codiscoverer. Mrs. Harding was with her husband at the burial of the Unknown Soldier in Arlington, on Armistice Day, 1921.

And when, through friends who had betrayed him, his honor began to be questioned and he began to try to think of a way out of his difficulties, she was there by his side. Together, they started in the summer of 1923 for a tour of Alaska and the Pacific coast. She knew, on that journey, that her husband was a weary and worried man. He could not rest or sleep.

They visited cities on the west coast, and Harding was the first President to visit Alaska. When he reached Seattle, on the homeward trip, he became ill with what his doctor called ptomaine poisoning. Arriving in San Francisco he contracted pneumonia, and the nation watched the newspaper reports with concern. Then, just as he appeared to be getting well, he died suddenly on the evening of August 2, 1923, while his wife sat reading to him.

Whatever his faults or shortcomings, the whole nation mourned him sincerely. His widow, on the funeral train that carried his body back to Washington, must have wished that he could see the thousands of men, women, and children gathered all along the route eastward to pay their respects to his memory.

Making one final effort to protect that memory and to prevent the general public from knowing the extent of graft and dishonesty perpetrated by his friends in office during his administration, Mrs. Harding destroyed every private paper she could lay her hands on. Then she went back to her old home in Marion, Ohio.

A little more than a year later, on November 21, 1924, she, too, passed away and was buried beside her husband at the foot of the great monument which the Harding Memorial Association raised in his honor. How much or how little she knew of the derelictions of Warren G. Harding, and how she reacted emotionally, will probably never be known. Books concerning the scandal and rumor of his regime were written in the years following his death. But the innermost personality of our twenty-ninth President remains clouded in mystery, as does the personality of his First Lady. They lived in an amazing and difficult era, and played their parts in the drama of life according to their own interpretations.

Grace Anna Goodhue Coolidge

FIRST FIRST LADY FROM VERMONT

THE White House grounds swarmed with happy children, wild with the exuberance of April. With sudden, incredible speed and agility they pursued the brightly-colored Easter eggs rolling down the terraces. Next to Christmas, Easter Monday was the most exciting day in all the year for the little boys and girls of Washington, D.C. Carefully pressed knee pants and starchy white dresses became grass-stained; hair-ribbons and little boys' caps dotted the lawn as starry-eyed youngsters competed for prizes, their noisy shouts and young laughter mingling with the spirited music of the Marine Band.

Among them, looking very pretty in her gay spring dress, strolled a pleasant-faced woman, carrying in her arms a pet baby raccoon. Though fashion decreed short bobbed hair and knee-length skirts in that year of 1926, Grace Goodhue Coolidge ignored these extreme styles, and she did not seem out of place with her thick, glossy black braids wound about her head, and long, full skirts blowing in the breeze. The children crowded around her with shrieks of delight as they saw the little raccoon. The First Lady smiled warmly. Having raised two boys of her own, and being gifted with an understanding heart, she knew very well how to make friends with children.

In fact, Mrs. Coolidge had an instinctive gift for making friends with everybody, young and old. According to Chief Usher Ike Hoover, members of the household at the White House said that she was "ninety per cent of the Coolidge administration." From the moment she arrived in Washington, her graciousness and simplicity won added support for her shy, silent husband who never used two words when one would do.

But, although Calvin Coolidge was often described as a sour-faced, tight-lipped Vermonter, small in stature and un-imposing in appearance, the nation welcomed his administration. He had what Americans have always wanted most in a Chief Executive: uncompromising honesty, sincerity of purpose, and a determination to operate the government without waste or extravagance.

After the scandals of the Harding regime, the coming of the Coolidges to the White House was like a clean, fresh breath of air from their own New England hills.

Calvin Coolidge's ancestors came to this country around 1630. Most of them were farmers—respectable, virtuous, and thrifty. Calvin was born on July 4, 1872, in the little town of Plymouth, Vermont.

Grace Anna Goodhue was also a Vermonter. Almost seven years younger than Coolidge, she was born in Burlington on January 3, 1879. As a child, she was content with simple toys. She played with a doll dressed by her mother, and rocked the doll to sleep in a small wooden cradle fashioned by her father. When friends dropped in from neighboring farms to visit, young Grace listened raptly to the talk of the grownups and looked up into their faces, her big hazel eyes alight with animation. She loved people. Many years later, when she was First Lady and was discussing with a friend how little time she had at the White House for reading, she said: "People are my books."

Grace Goodhue was graduated from the University of Vermont in 1902, and her consuming interest in people soon led her into work which required patience and sympathy. Dr. Caroline A. Yale, a friend of the Goodhue family, was principal of a school in Northampton, Massachusetts, for children who were hard of hearing. As Grace learned more and more about their needs, she decided to take part in the good work. She went to Northampton and, for three years, taught at the Clarke School for the Deaf.

During the winter of 1904–1905, she met another Vermonter who had gone to Northampton after his graduation from Amherst College. Calvin Coolidge was thirty-two then, and Grace Goodhue was the only girl who had ever attracted him. Shy, studious, and retiring Cal knew from the moment they met that he wanted her for his wife.

They were married on October 4, 1905, at Grace's home in Burlington, and after a week of honeymooning in Montreal, lived for a few weeks in a Northampton hotel while they went house-hunting. They chose a modest little home, renting half of a double house, and there they started housekeeping. In that small dwelling on Massasoit Street their two sons, John and Calvin, junior, were born. Bringing up these children was largely the responsibility of Mrs. Coolidge, for when the Massachusetts state legislature was in session, their father, a member of the lower House, lived in Boston and came home only for weekends.

As state senator and later as lieutenant governor, his salary was small, and his young wife had to manage her household with rigid economy. When the Coolidges started life together in Northampton, the Norwood Hotel was about to close. With true New England thrift, Grace Coolidge bought a quantity of equipment from its stock. For many years, her sheets, pillowcases, table linen, and even her plated silver bore the mark "Norwood Hotel."

Even when Calvin Coolidge was elected governor of Massachusetts, their unpretentious way of living did not change. There was no executive mansion provided by the state for its chief executive, and Boston saw little of the governor's lady.

She was far too busy, still in the home of her bridal days, keeping house, sewing, cooking, and getting John and young Calvin off to school. The governor lived in the Adams House (which has since been torn down) in Boston. Each Saturday he climbed into a day coach for a weekend with his family in Northampton.

Summer was the time they all liked best, for that meant rest and relaxation up in their beloved Vermont hills. There John and Calvin, junior, helped Grandfather Coolidge with the farm chores, while Governor Coolidge, in an ancient, faded blue smock and a wide-brimmed straw hat, chopped wood, pitched hay, and milked cows, just as he had done in his boyhood. Even after he became Vice President of the United States and moved his family to Washington, he returned each summer to the house where he was born. Both Calvin and Grace Coolidge were bound by strong ties to that little village of Plymouth, with its six or seven farmhouses, the church, the cemetery, the blacksmith shop, the general store, and the post office.

There, just past midnight on August 3, 1923, the Coolidges were roused from sleep by a momentous message. Calvin's father, who was a poor sleeper, heard a loud knock on the door. Lighting a kerosene lamp, he went to see who could be wanting to come in at that "ungodly hour." Then he climbed the narrow stairs again and called: "Calvin!" The old man's voice may have trembled slightly, for he was the bearer of heart-stirring news. His son had just become President of the United States!

Mrs. Coolidge received the news calmly, as did her husband. He read the telegram slowly in the dim light, washed in the old-fashioned china bowl, dressed quickly in a dark suit with a black tie, and knelt in his bedroom to pray. He then wrote a letter in longhand to Mrs. Harding and sent a typewritten statement to the press, with a reassuring message to the people of the United States.

Shortly before three in the morning, "Colonel" Coolidge, who was a notary public, faced his son across a big, square, mahogany table [1] which held two oil lamps and the family Bible. By the glow of the lamps, a brief but solemn ritual was performed. For the first time in history, a father administered the oath of the highest office in the land to his son and was the first to address him as "Mr. President."

Installed in the White House, the new Chief Executive and his wife were the same kindly, unaffected people they had always been. Mrs. Coolidge found pleasure in her new responsibilities and took great pride in the historic home of the Presidents. While she was First Lady, she found time to crochet a spread for the huge four-poster bed that had been Abraham Lincoln's. It was her gift to the White House.

Always an early riser, Mrs. Coolidge usually was up long before eight o'clock. As she sat in her dressing-room, brushing her long dark hair, two canaries sang in the sunny windows and two dogs lay on a rug nearby. Promptly at nine each morning, she began her work. With the large, shaggy, white dog, Prudence Prim, who followed her about everywhere, Mrs. Coolidge went happily to what she called her "sky parlor." In this glass-enclosed sunroom above the south portico, she blithely tackled large stacks of mail—sorting out personal

[1] This table is usually described by reporters and historians as "marble-topped." Mrs. Coolidge, who was present at the swearing-in ceremony, states that although there is a marble-topped table in the old Coolidge house in Plymouth, a larger table which she believes to be mahogany was the one used when Calvin Coolidge took the oath of office. (Letter to the authors, dated March 12, 1953.)

letters, invitations, requests for photographs and donations.

Grace Coolidge sang and whistled at her work, or turned on the radio to catch the latest news or a bit of music. Just before noon, she slipped out for a short, quick walk around the White House grounds before receiving the onrush of visitors which usually began about lunch time. As the months passed, she became noticeably prettier; she seemed to thrive on the exacting social responsibilities of a First Lady. Everybody loved her; everybody wanted to be photographed with her; all America wanted to shake her hand. Willingly she accepted the fact that she belonged to the public; and, as often as possible, she relieved her busy husband of the burden of meeting the thousands who came to see the White House.

As for the President himself, cartoonists of the day pictured him as a dour, pinchpenny little man whose face never relaxed into a smile. It is true that, as President, he insisted upon economy. In three years he reduced the national debt by two billion dollars! He recommended no major changes in foreign policy, and he was satisfied to see the nation enter a period of peace and prosperity greater than it had ever enjoyed before. No blame was attached to him for the graft and waste that went on during the administration of his predecessor. The people trusted implicitly in the honesty of Calvin Coolidge, and as soon as he took office he went to work to clean up an unsavory situation. Integrity—or as he termed it, "moral fibre"—was what he preached and practiced; and America was delighted. In 1924, he was elected President in his own right by a large majority.

Mrs. Coolidge often smiled at a singular weakness of her husband—where she was concerned. Though a close, thrifty New Englander, he was extravagant in the matter of her clothes. He loved vivid colors and big hats loaded with fancy trimmings. Whenever a dress, a coat, or a hat in a shop window caught his eye, he had it sent to the White House on approval. He adored his wife and objected when she wore any costume a second time at state functions. Sometimes Mrs. Coolidge approved his choice, but often the brightly colored dresses and overtrimmed hats were quietly returned. She had excellent taste, and she never affected the tight, knee-length skirts that were in vogue when she was First Lady. At one state reception, she wore a most becoming gown of heavy white brocaded satin with a long court train.

Early in the summer of 1924, a great tragedy occurred which touched the hearts of people across the nation. The younger son, Calvin Coolidge, Jr., developed a blister on his foot while playing tennis with his brother John. A few days later the trouble had spread so alarmingly that an operation was necessary. On July 7th, the sixteen-year-old boy died at Walter Reed Hospital. From all over the country, thousands of letters poured in from parents who knew the anguish of losing a child, and from other parents who realized how they might feel if a son or a daughter were suddenly taken from them.

After services in the East Room of the White House, the body of Calvin Coolidge, Jr., was laid to rest in the family plot at Plymouth, Vermont. If Mrs. Coolidge smiled less often and less brightly after the ordeal was over, she was still a cheerful, busy woman whose private sorrow was not permitted to interfere with her duties as First Lady.

But social life in the nation's capital is a burden that even the healthiest and most energetic are apt to find wearing. President Coolidge, though he said little, thought deeply. Without consulting his wife, he made a decision. Summoning reporters one morning, exactly four years after he had taken office upon the death of Harding, Coolidge handed out neatly typed slips of paper which contained these few words: "I do not choose to run for President in 1928." Consideration for his wife was the major reason for that decision, and no amount of persuasion could change his mind.

Mrs. Coolidge did not hear about his now-famous statement until several hours after he received the press; then the news reached her through a friend who was surprised that she did not know about it. But it was no surprise to Grace Coolidge that her husband had not confided in her. All through his years of public life, he kept his political affairs to himself, regarding them as entirely separate from his home life. Mrs. Coolidge knew only what she read in the papers or heard on the radio, and she was completely satisfied with the arrangement.

After five years and seven months in the White House, the Coolidges were eager to return to private life in their beloved New England. The President ended his administration with the country prosperous and the government on a balanced budget. His final message to Congress was a warning against rash spending.

Following advice with example, he and Mrs. Coolidge went back to their plain little house on Massasoit Street, in Northampton, where they lived as simply as they had when they went there as bride and groom. But they were no longer unknown citizens. For greater privacy, they later bought a place with grounds around it, called The Beeches. There Calvin Coolidge wrote his autobiography and a syndicated column for the newspapers. Mrs. Coolidge pursued her quiet way, looked after her family, did some writing of poetry, and continued her interest in the Clarke School for the Deaf.

Those were contented years for the Coolidges, who still

journeyed each summer to the Vermont hills. Calvin Coolidge spent the last summer of his life in the old house where he was born. The following winter, on January 5, 1933, he died suddenly and painlessly of a heart attack at Northampton, Massachusetts.

After her husband's death, Mrs. Coolidge sold The Beeches and built a new house, not far from the old house on Massasoit Street where she first started housekeeping as a bride.

There Mrs. Coolidge settled down cheerfully, surrounded by a wide circle of friends and relatives. Her two granddaughters helped her to keep a youthful, lively viewpoint, and she had leisure for the activities she missed when she was a busy hostess at the Executive Mansion. There were picnics, parties and family reunions, and carefree summers at the old homestead in Vermont. Mrs. Coolidge also continued her active interest in handicapped boys and girls and in the Clarke School for the Deaf, where she had been a teacher before her marriage.

On July 8, 1957, after an illness of many months, Grace Coolidge died in her Northampton home at the age of seventy-eight, and was laid to rest beside her husband and their son, Calvin, Jr., in the family plot at Plymouth, Vermont.

President Coolidge, tight-lipped and seldom given to pretty speeches, once paid tribute to his wife for "bearing with my infirmities and brightening my life with her graces." Grace Coolidge, with her understanding heart and her great gift for making friends, brightened the lives of many people in all walks of life. Perhaps that is one of the reasons why she will always be remembered as a lovable and gracious First Lady.

Lou Henry Hoover

FIRST FIRST LADY FROM IOWA

LOU HENRY was the only girl in the geology class. She joined the men on their first excursion afield under the professor's scientific eye, in search of specimens, rock formations, and so forth. The other Stanford University students were not too keen about having a girl along, and were picturing in their minds what a bother it would be to help her over fences and across streams. When they arrived at a barred gate, she solved their problem by putting a hand on the top rail and vaulting lightly over!

At least one of her fellow students was tremendously impressed. The next Friday evening Herbert Hoover put on his best suit and called on Lou Henry at her dormitory.

She was nineteen at the time and slim and supple as a reed. Herbert Hoover felt it his duty to aid the young lady "in her studies, both in the laboratory and in the field." Many years later in his *Memoirs* he admitted that this call to duty was stimulated by Lou Henry's frank blue eyes and broad grin.

Born in Waterloo, Iowa, on March 29, 1874, the infant at once won her father's heart. He had hoped his baby would be a boy. When it turned out otherwise, his disappointment was not too great, for his little girl early developed his own love of the great outdoors. As a child she rode like a Comanche Indian, wasn't afraid of snakes, and was completely at home in field and forest. He took her on fishing trips, taught her to make a campfire, pitch a tent, find her way about in the woods, make biscuits, and clean and fry mountain trout. They camped and hiked in the hills, slept in the open under the high, bright stars, and enjoyed together the miracle of sunrise and the music of bird song.

Lou Henry's education began in the public schools of Iowa

and California, then she went to normal school at San Jose. About this time, when her home was in Monterey, the young girl attended a lecture on geology by a Stanford professor. The exciting picture he drew of the bones of the earth fired her with ambition to become a geologist. At Stanford, she found that hazel-eyed, broad-shouldered Herbert Hoover was the prize student in that department. When he was graduated a year later, the two began a correspondence.

Lou Henry at Stanford read and reread Hoover's letters, telling her how he had gone to work as a common laborer in a Nevada mine before he secured an engineering job with a San Francisco mining firm. He came down to see her several times. Then they became engaged. But, being sensible young people, they agreed that Hoover must earn more money and she must get her diploma before they could be married.

By the time Lou Henry was graduated from Stanford, Herbert Hoover was well established on the staff of a London concern, which sent him to the gold fields of far-off Australia. His reputation as a mining engineer became international. When the head of the Chinese Bureau of Mines offered him a position as director general of mines, the young engineer sent off two cables, one accepting the job in China; the other to Lou Henry of Monterey, California.

She smiled as she read the brief message: "Will you marry me?" Her cabled reply went off at once, and it was even more brief: "Yes."

They were married on February 11, 1899, and sailed for the Orient a few hours later. In the years that followed, the Hoovers journeyed to every continent and to almost every country. To the amazement of the foreign colonies in Tientsin and Peking, the young bride went along with her husband on his trips into the interior of China. Regardless of talk about bandits, hardships, and fever, she traveled where he did, sharing his interest in geology and mining, eagerly awaiting each new adventure.

The Hoovers were in Tientsin during the Boxer Rebellion, when 25,000 Chinese marched upon the city, sworn to "kill all the foreign devils" in China and to confiscate their property. Food was scarce and water scant in the partly walled-in foreign settlement. Shells burst in the streets; bullets smashed into walls. Lou Hoover took charge of rationing dwindling food supplies while her husband, at the head of a thousand terrified Christian Chinese, threw up a barricade of sacked grain, sugar, and rice along the exposed side of the town.

With a staff of two doctors and one trained nurse, Lou Hoover tended the wounded. Calm and self-reliant, she reported for duty on her bicycle each morning, and she soon learned to ride close to the walls of buildings and avoid stray bullets. Mrs. Hoover didn't see much of her husband during the next three weeks. Eventually they were relieved by British, American, Russian, and Japanese forces. But Mrs. Hoover refused to leave the city for a place of safety because some of her patients could not be moved.

Snipers still fired into the settlement; and Cossack soldiers of the relief forces were making off with food, bundles of blankets, silverware, and all sorts of loot. Since the war was nearly over, the Cossacks doubtless wanted to take home a few souvenirs. But they reckoned without the American lady, whose blue eyes flashed as she ordered: "Put those things down—*quick!*" The Cossacks could not understand her words, but her meaning was quite clear. Sheepishly, they surrendered their bundles and made off. She found her home a shambles. Every bureau, closet, and cupboard had been ransacked. Apparently the marauders found no use for her typewriter; they left it on the table. But before leaving, they poured into it a jar of strawberry jam!

One day near the end of the siege, Mrs. Hoover was sitting in her room playing a game of solitaire, when an enemy shell plowed through the wall and exploded at the bottom of the stairs. When rescuers dashed in, they found her amid a shower of dust from the riddled plaster—still playing solitaire!

When her husband was offered a junior partnership in his London firm, he was as happy as she was to get out of China. The Hoovers arrived in England in November, 1901; and, though his work would take him to all parts of the world, they decided to get a house. Of all their temporary homes, perhaps the old Red House near Kensington Gardens was closest to their hearts. They lined the walls with their large collection of books, brought out the treasures they had picked up on their travels, and planted a garden behind the house.

Wherever they went, Lou Hoover rented a place and set up housekeeping as casually and efficiently as she did everything else. She was a good camper and a good comrade. With her husband she traveled all over the globe—to Poland, Russia, Egypt, Burma, Japan, Mongolia, Manchuria, New Zealand, Australia, the Hawaiian Islands, Germany, Canada, Korea. There was scarcely a spot on earth that the Hoovers did not visit at one time or another. Their headquarters, however, remained in London, where Herbert junior was born in 1903. Five weeks later, taking along a nurse for the baby, the family started for Australia. Allan Henry was born in 1907.

As often as possible, usually once a year, Mrs. Hoover returned to California for a brief vacation.

Herbert Hoover was forty years old, and a millionaire when World War I broke out. He and his family were summering at the Savoy Hotel in London. Hundreds of Americans fled from the continent to London, and tried frantically to get back to the United States. But only gold would buy staterooms home—and nobody had gold. Caught by the wave of conflict, they were unable even to cash travelers' checks.

Hoover was the unanimous choice to head a relief committee and Lou Hoover joined her executive ability with his. While he called meetings of American residents in London, Mrs. Hoover called similar meetings of American women in the city. Their hotel supplied them with free office space, and soon they were, as Hoover expresses it in his *Memoirs,* "on top of their job."

Hoover had his engineers gather all the gold and currency his firm had on hand and take it to the consul general. There it was loaned in small amounts to stranded American tourists. With a staff of five hundred volunteers, the Hoovers cared for women and children, set up committees in the principal continental cities, arranged temporary lodgings in London, and engaged American and other neutral ships for transportation.

During the next six weeks the Hoover committees aided some 120,000 stranded people and loaned them more than a million and a half dollars, which, with the small exception of about three hundred dollars, was later repaid. Then Mrs. Hoover took her two boys back to school in California, while her husband organized a great campaign on behalf of the starving Belgians, innocent victims of the war.

Once her two boys were placed in capable hands in California, Lou Hoover lost no time in rejoining her husband in London. Then she defied the waters of the North Sea, planted with deadly mines, and went with him on his second trip to Brussels. There she engaged in every sort of relief work and was one of the organizers of the American Woman's Hospital.

In 1917, when the United States entered the conflict and Hoover was recalled by President Wilson to act as U.S. Food Administrator, Lou Hoover brought her boys to Washington and rented a house. Settling her family comfortably in new quarters was by that time a routine job with her, and she was enthusiastic over her husband's opportunity to serve the country. He had worked abroad since the first week in August, 1914, without pay; and he stipulated, in accepting his appointment as Food Administrator, that he was to work without salary. Lou Hoover liked that arrangement; it seemed the fair and patriotic thing to do. Soon the master slogan which she coined—"Food Will Win the War"—went out all over the country. And when the war was won, the energetic Hoovers had another big job on their hands. Following the armistice Hoover was appointed, on behalf of some twenty-two governments, to bring about the economic rehabilitation of Europe.

In 1921 Hoover was named Secretary of Commerce in the Harding Cabinet; four years later President Coolidge reappointed him to that post. Accepting the Harding offer was not an easy decision to make. Hoover had to choose between a partnership in a mining firm, which would bring him comparative freedom and considerable wealth, and a career in public affairs which would surely be punctuated with thorns and brickbats. Lou Hoover and he talked things over and they decided against the mining partnership.

Determined that her husband should have a comfortable home in Washington, Mrs. Hoover bought a colonial house on S Street, with an acre of gardens and old oak trees. "For the fifth time in our twenty-two years of married life," wrote Hoover, "she ran a different house, with her usual good taste and economy." She even permitted her younger son to bring in a couple of turtles, though she uttered a quiet "No" when he wanted to put two young alligators in one of the bathtubs.

During the eight years they lived on S Street, Mrs. Hoover kept open house. Scarcely a meal went by without guests. They even came to breakfast. During this period Mrs. Hoover was elected president of the Girl Scouts. Since she never lent her name to any organization without taking an active part in its work, she spent a large part of her time in leading the national Girl Scout movement. She directed classes, went with Scout groups on bird walks and camping trips, and was active in councils and at rallies. During her regime, more than two million dollars was raised and membership was increased from 100,000 to almost a million girls. She donated a little house for their headquarters in Washington and often took a dozen girls out on hikes.

As the wife of a Cabinet member, Lou Hoover also had many social duties, and no one entertained more often or more hospitably than the slender blue-eyed woman whose hair at this time was silvery white. Her family was smaller now. The owner of the turtles and alligators had grown up and entered Stanford University, and his older brother had gotten married.

On March 4, 1929, thirty years after their marriage, President and Mrs. Hoover moved into the White House—and entertained eighteen hundred guests at an elaborate luncheon. The new First Lady was beautifully dressed in dark, plum-colored velvet, with a hat to match. Natural, vital, and smiling, she moved among her guests, enjoying this new adventure as much as she always enjoyed every experience in her busy life.

As First Lady, she continued to drive her own car about Washington and Virginia. If she felt like inviting a Girl Scout and an Associate Justice of the Supreme Court to the same

White House dinner, she did so—for the simple reason that she liked them both. Though her husband was a millionaire, even at formal affairs she never wore jewels. She never wore high-heeled shoes, either, which might hamper her free, swinging stride. She spoke five languages, pored over books on economics and sociology before going to bed, could carve a turkey, draw plans for a house, and preside over a New Year reception for four thousand guests.

During her stay in the White House she superintended the erection and furnishing of several log cabins at her husband's summer camp in the Blue Ridge Mountains. At the end of his term, President Hoover presented the buildings, equipment, and land to the Shenandoah National Park for the use of the White House, the Boy Scouts, and the Girl Scouts.

Mrs. Hoover had avoided public appearances and at times had even refused to grant interviews. But that was before she became First Lady. To relieve the President as much as possible, she received delegations, directed assemblies, appeared at college commencements, christened new ships, and made speeches.

But with all she did to help her husband, she could not stop the rising tide of dissatisfaction that swept over the country during his administration. One October day in 1929 the American stock market collapsed and vast fortunes were swept away overnight. Soon the depression was in full swing, and conditions were no better abroad. Hoover did everything he could to provide employment and relief for the people, but in 1932 when he ran for re-election he was defeated.

At last the Hoovers could enjoy a little leisure in the spot they loved best, the permanent home Lou Hoover had designed years before. The white stucco building stood on the crest of San Juan hill in Palo Alto. Tall cypress trees and flowering vines grew within the garden walls. There was an outdoor fireplace for camping-out meals and a swimming pool which sparkled in the California sunshine. Out beyond the hills were the coastal cities and the broad Pacific.

Mrs. Hoover died on January 7, 1944, in her seventy-first year, leaving her husband to carry on the great humanitarian work they had shared during their happy, busy years together.

Anna Eleanor Roosevelt

INTERNATIONALLY FAMOUS FIRST LADY

IN a small office nineteen floors above
the hurrying crowds on Park Avenue, a tall gray-haired
woman sat before a flat-topped desk. Her capable hands rested
quietly in her lap. In her frilled white blouse, black circular
skirt, and low-heeled shoes, she might have been any one of
countless poised, efficient women who work for a living in
New York city. Staring thoughtfully into space, her vividly
blue eyes serious, she replied to a question:

"I don't think I've ever done anything of great importance."

The speaker was Anna Eleanor Roosevelt, United States
Representative in the General Assembly of the United Nations, and Chairman of the Human Rights Commission. Her
statement was highly characteristic; humility and reserve were
her outstanding traits. When the discussion turned specifi-
cally to the role women have played in influencing history, she
added slowly: "Perhaps, applying to women, one thing is that
I have been able through my work . . . to help all other
women to go on having more and more representation in
government and world affairs."

The emergence of Eleanor Roosevelt from a painfully shy,
awkward little girl with protruding teeth and poor posture
into a self-possessed public speaker of international repute is
one of the most fascinating of all the stories of America's
First Ladies.

Her earliest recollections point to an unhappy, frustrated
childhood. It was not easy for the little girl of seven to hear
her mother describe her to friends as a "funny child," or to
be called "granny" by her elders because she was so old-
fashioned. They did not mean to be cruel, but young Eleanor
spent many anguished hours hiding from strangers and

brooding over the fact that, in a family famous for its good looks and social graces, she somehow did not "belong."

Her father, Elliott Roosevelt, was the younger brother of Theodore Roosevelt, twenty-sixth President of the United States. They were descended from a long line of distinguished ancestors, the first of whom arrived in America from Amsterdam about the middle of the seventeenth century. Eleanor's mother, the beautiful Anna Hall, stemmed from an equally impressive family tree. She was related to the Clarksons, the De Peysters, and the Livingstons. Robert R. Livingston became famous in America's history as one of the members of the committee appointed to draw up the Declaration of Independence.

Into this background of aristocracy and wealth Anna Eleanor Roosevelt was born on October 11, 1884, in the brownstone Roosevelt house in New York city. Since her mother, for whom she was named, was always called Anna, it was soon decided, to avoid confusion, to call the new baby Eleanor. When she was eight, her mother died. Two years later she lost her father. From then on, with her two little brothers, Eleanor was brought up by Grandmother Hall, who put her on such a strict allowance until she was twenty-one that the girl learned, as she herself often said later, "to do with what I had."

There were many other lessons for the quiet, introspective child to learn. Her girlhood was one long, continual struggle for self-improvement. There were braces to straighten her round shoulders and braces to straighten her wayward teeth. There were hours of ballet instruction and practice which Grandma Hall hoped might give the long-legged, clumsy little girl balance and poise. Governesses and tutors kept her busy studying lessons, including French and music; and they, with Grandma Hall, disciplined her constantly to improve her self-confidence and manners. When she was sent to school in England at the age of fifteen, aware that she was completely without beauty or charm, she was almost convinced that there was no use trying to be like other children of her age. But the courageous spirit of Eleanor Roosevelt, which was later developed by circumstances to such a high degree, came to the fore. During the years that followed she put herself through the severest self-discipline in an effort to overcome her timidity and gain self-respect. At Allenswood, the girl's school in England, she won her first victory, working stubbornly at field hockey until she made the team. Long after she had become an international figure, she said: ". . . that was one of the proudest moments of my life."

In those difficult years of girlhood in a strange land, Eleanor Roosevelt was helped greatly by Mlle. Souvestre, the wise and understanding French woman who was headmistress of Allenswood. With Mlle. Souvestre, the shy girl traveled in France, Germany, and Italy, learning to shoulder responsibility, to discover the adventure in living, and trying to understand the problems and reactions of others. In the companionship of the older woman, Eleanor came to realize that, if she could forget herself and take a genuine interest in those around her, she could lead a useful, happy life. Thus, her innate kindness and eager desire to be helpful were developed. And, as her horizon widened and her interests and activities grew, a measure of self-confidence began to assert itself.

Back in New York at the age of eighteen, much of her old shyness returned. Grandmother Hall felt it was time for Eleanor to take an active part in social life; but dances, dinners, and parties appalled her. And one of her aunts did not help when she remarked bluntly that Eleanor probably would never have the beaux the rest of the women in the family had had, because she was the ugly duckling.

There were some, however, who appreciated the plain girl with the sweet, shy smile and soft brown hair. Among them was handsome young Franklin Roosevelt, a distant cousin who was in his senior year at Harvard. When Eleanor was nineteen they became engaged, and on March 17, 1905, they were married. The date was chosen because Uncle Theodore, then President, was to be in New York on the seventeenth to review the St. Patrick's Day Parade on Fifth Avenue. Even on her wedding day, Eleanor Roosevelt was not the center of attraction. But she willingly conceded the spotlight to the jovial and popular "Rough Rider" President, who gave her in marriage.

The first years of her married life were years of difficult adjustment for Eleanor. She knew little about running a household and rearing children. Again her lack of self-confidence annoyed her, while Franklin's mother, more than willing to assume responsibility and look after her adored son, took almost complete charge. Once more, as in her childhood, Eleanor brooded over the fact that she did not seem to be useful.

In 1910, however, when Franklin D. Roosevelt was twenty-eight and she was twenty-five, she proved that she had plenty of initiative and began what was to be her lifework. When her husband was elected state senator, and the family moved to Albany, Eleanor Roosevelt found herself in new surroundings, with new interests and new responsibilities. She became completely absorbed in her young husband's career, entertained his political associates, attended sessions of the state legislature, listened carefully, and learned her first lessons in

politics. After three years in the state capital, she was well prepared for her duties in the nation's capital when her husband
was appointed Assistant Secretary of the Navy.

When the United States entered World War I in 1917,
Eleanor Roosevelt, now an experienced Washington hostess,
became an untiring war worker. As wife of the Assistant Secretary, she still had social obligations; as the mother of five
children, she had many domestic responsibilities. But she
spent most of her time and energy in war work. Many hours
of each day were devoted to Red Cross activities. Several days
each week she cooked and served meals in a canteen in the
railroad yards; she visited hospitals; engaged in all sorts of
public welfare projects. She had considerable executive ability, and wherever she saw conditions which she felt needed
changing she reported direct to the government officials concerned. During the war year of 1918, she kept busy from
early morning until midnight and was back on her volunteer
job again the following morning.

In 1920, when her husband was nominated on the Democratic ticket for Vice President of the United States, she accompanied him on a campaign tour and became actively interested in politics. After the election, in which the Democrats were defeated, she joined the state board of the League of
Women Voters. Her duties in the League called for the study
of various bills brought up before Congress, and through this
work she learned to analyze important issues affecting the
affairs of the nation.

Then, in the summer of 1921, while on vacation at Campo-
bello, her husband, at thirty-nine, was suddenly stricken with
infantile paralysis. Eleanor Roosevelt brought him back to
New York on a stretcher, and he spent the next month in the
hospital. His hands and arms, as well as his legs, were par-

tially paralyzed at first. Gradually he regained the use of his arms and hands; but his legs remained useless. Then and there Franklin D. Roosevelt began the fight of his life—for his life. Three people—his wife, his mother, and his secretary, Louis Howe—fought beside him every step of the way. The foremost of these was Eleanor Roosevelt. Knowing that the greatest incentive to his recovery would be a renewal of interest in public affairs, she joined the Women's Trade Union as an associate member, concentrating her efforts on improving conditions for working women. At the suggestion of Louis Howe, she also became active in the women's division of the State Democratic Committee. Probably the most harrowing part of these activities was the need for making public speeches. She was so nervous that she could scarcely hold the papers in her trembling hands, and her voice, under such stress, rose to a high and unnatural pitch. Eleanor Roosevelt always dreaded making speeches, and said frankly: "I suppose inwardly I'm still shy and dislike talking and appearing in public. I don't think anyone ever gets over that, really, but I might say I can now control my feelings and hide my inward shyness so that outwardly I appear calm and unafraid."

With her husband crippled and unable to share actively in the life of their children, she became both father and mother to them in this respect. She had never learned to swim in childhood, but in order to encourage them, she went to the Young Women's Christian Association and mastered swimming. Then, though she hated automobiles and was afraid to run one, she learned to drive. When Franklin D. Roosevelt became governor of New York in 1928, she was launched on such a busy career of public service and of helping her husband and running her household that she had to budget every moment of her time. In order to furnish work for jobless men in the neighborhood, she established the Val Kill furniture factory on the Roosevelt farm near Hyde Park.

In New York, as vice-principal of the Todhunter School, she taught classes in civics, continued her political work, and was active in various welfare programs of the state. Every Sunday evening she planned meals for the week to come, then took a train for New York city to be ready for her Monday morning classes. All day Tuesday and on Wednesday morning she devoted herself to teaching and keeping appointments. Wednesday noon she was back on the train for Albany again, using the three-hour ride for marking class papers and planning the study schedule for the following week. Arriving back home, she entertained officially in Albany at the Governor's Mansion, and drove with her husband to hospitals, asylums, and other public institutions. Since he was unable to get around easily, she herself toured the buildings, studying minutely how they were run, paying strict attention to sanitary conditions, food served, and other details so that she could report her exact findings to her husband.

As First Lady of the White House, Eleanor Roosevelt led an even busier life. As ears and eyes for her husband, she traveled all over the country, and often abroad, flying or driving off at a moment's notice, studying conditions, addressing Campfire Girls, Girl Scouts, and many other organizations, and returning to give careful reports to the President.

During the first year of his administration, she traveled 38,000 miles; in the second, 42,000 miles; in the third, 35,000. After that the reporters admitted they had lost count. No woman ever took up her duties as First Lady with such a groundwork of political experience as did Eleanor Roosevelt. She worked with the women's division of the Democratic State Committee in New York for six years; she worked in political campaigns for Alfred E. Smith and for her husband. She toured the country making campaign speeches long before going to the White House. As First Lady, she broke all traditions, not only by traveling around the country on missions of interest to her husband, but by pursuing an active career of her own. Despite her mother-in-law's objections to her earning money, she made public appearances, talked over the radio, went on planned, paid lecture tours, wrote for newspapers and magazines, ran a syndicated column, "My Day," and later signed a contract for a page in a woman's magazine under the title, "If You Ask Me."

At the White House, Mrs. Roosevelt organized her household affairs so well that they needed little supervision on her part. She rode over Boulder Dam and Norris Dam in a "bucket"; she flew around the globe. Yet she still found time to have afternoon tea with her husband when she was at home, and to give him lengthy reports on what she had seen and heard in her travels.

During World War II, her interest in our fighting men led her to visit England, when she saw the work of the British women in the war and visited American troops abroad. In 1943 she made a flying trip to the Pacific, wearing the uniform of the Red Cross; in the spring of 1944 she toured the Caribbean and South American bases. Wherever she went she talked with the men and women in our armed forces, and she brought back to her husband in Washington a clear picture of what was going on.

Because of these trips, and because in other ways she did not conform to the traditions followed by other First Ladies, she became the center of a storm of criticism. Hideous caricatures of her constantly appeared in hostile newspapers, and countless jokes were made about her propensity for traveling.

She herself enjoyed some of the jokes, particularly one which originated in her own family circle. One day during the war, when she was scheduled to visit a prison in Baltimore, she had to leave the White House very early in the morning, long before her husband was awake, so she did not say good-bye to him. On his way to the office later, President Roosevelt called to Miss Thompson, whom they always called "Tommy," and asked where his wife was.

"She's in prison, Mr. President!" Tommy said.

"I'm not surprised," said Franklin D. Roosevelt, "but what for?"

Though her husband never told her she was a good reporter, and many of her trips in the early days were her own idea, Eleanor Roosevelt realized that he would not question her so closely if he were not interested. And though she modestly disclaimed having had any great influence with the President, she admitted that she argued with him on many occasions, giving her views on important matters—which seemed opposite to his views. Later, she would hear him supporting her views and using her arguments in talking with various Cabinet members.

On one occasion, the President did give her special credit. After her speech at the 1940 Democratic Convention, when (largely through her efforts) Henry A. Wallace was nominated for Vice President, her husband remarked that she had said "just the right thing."

From the moment she entered the White House as First Lady in 1933, Eleanor Roosevelt, like her husband, broke precedents. "Unconsciously," she wrote, "I did many things that shocked the ushers, especially Ike Hoover. My first act was to insist on running the elevator myself without waiting for one of the doormen to run it for me." She also started moving the furniture around, to the horror of the household staff. She insisted upon driving her own car, and would have neither chauffeur nor Secret Service agent around to hamper her movements. Since the country was in the grip of the worst depression it had ever known, and people were losing their jobs on every hand, Eleanor Roosevelt decided to help the women newspaper reporters of Washington; for if they did not find something new to write about, she reasoned, their managing editors would soon dispense with their services. She therefore became the first First Lady to hold weekly press conferences. She received the women in the Red Room, and said later: "I could feel the disapproval of the ushers as I went in, with fear and trembling." But in she went, nevertheless, often in riding clothes when there was not time to change.

Though caring little for appearance, Eleanor Roosevelt could and did dress magnificently when occasion demanded. At the first diplomatic reception of her husband's administration, she looked every inch a First Lady. Her thick, glossy brown hair was waved and caught in a knot low at the back of her head. Tall and queenly in a long, flowing gown of white shot with silver, and a diamond necklace about her neck, she glittered from head to foot as she stood in the Blue Room beside the President.

In the summer of 1938, there was an influx of royal visitors. In May, the Roosevelts entertained Denmark's Crown Prince and Princess. A few weeks later, the Crown Prince and Princess of Norway arrived at the White House; and in June, 1939, the King and Queen of England visited the United States at the invitation of the President and his First Lady.

Little Diana Hopkins, aged eight, was at that time living with her father at the White House. The only queens she had ever heard about were the fairy queens in her story books.

Through the thoughtfulness and kindness of Mrs. Roosevelt, little Diana (whose mother was dead) was permitted to get a glimpse of the Queen, beautiful in her white spangled dress and jeweled crown, on her way to a formal dinner at the British embassy. The King, splendid in his dress uniform, spoke kindly to the child, but she had eyes only for his lady. After they passed, a starry-eyed Diana rushed off to her father, Harry Hopkins, and said: "Oh, Daddy, I have just seen the Fairy Queen!"

In her unobtrusive way, Mrs. Roosevelt was constantly doing nice things for people in all walks of life. It was this kindness that led her to become interested in the young people of the American Youth Congress, an organization which was regarded by many as subversive. As soon as she was convinced that the American Youth Congress actually did have communistic leanings, she parted company with them. In her autobiography, Mrs. Roosevelt wrote:

> "I wish to make it clear that I felt a great sympathy for these young people, even though they often annoyed me. . . . I have never felt the slightest bitterness toward any of them, and as a matter of fact, I am extremely grateful for my experience with them. I learned what communist tactics are. I discovered for myself how infiltration of an organization is accomplished. I was taught how communists get themselves into positions of importance. I understand all their methods of objection and delay, the effort to tire out the rest of the group and carry the vote when all their companions have gone home. These tactics are now all familiar to me. I know that no defeat is final. In fact, I think my work with the American Youth

Congress was of infinite value to me in understanding some of the tactics I have had to meet in the United Nations."

On April 12, 1945, Franklin D. Roosevelt died at Warm Springs, Georgia. The following December, Eleanor Roosevelt was appointed United States representative in the General Assembly of the United Nations, and later became chairman of the Human Rights Commission. She continued in these assignments until January, 1953.

The first President's wife to devote herself to a career of social reform and political activity, she was also the first to accept public office after leaving the White House. Both in her official capacity and as a private citizen, Mrs. Roosevelt worked to promote social justice, peace, and understanding among the nations of the world, and to secure greater advantages and opportunities for women everywhere. From a shy, self-conscious, homely little child, and a First Lady who was often criticized and ridiculed, she emerged as one of the foremost women of our time in international affairs.

Eleanor Roosevelt died on November 7, 1962, after an illness of several months. Flags were ordered to fly at half-mast in our nation's capital and in other parts of the country, marking the first time in our history that this honor was accorded a former First Lady. The entire civilized world mourned the passing of a great humanitarian. She was buried beside her husband in the rose garden at Hyde Park, New York.

Elizabeth Virginia Wallace Truman

FIRST LADY FROM INDEPENDENCE, MISSOURI

IT was Spring in our nation's capital. Reflected in the still waters of the Tidal Basin, Washington's famous cherry trees spilled the beauty of pale pink blossoms over the lengthening shadows of late afternoon. But the spirits of the people who saw them were not lifted by the promise of the new season. For the date was April 12, 1945, and in Warm Springs, Georgia, the President had just died.

In the Cabinet room of the White House executive office a brief and historic ceremony was about to begin. Two women entered the room quietly. They stood proudly erect, as they heard a dear and familiar voice repeat the words:

"I do solemnly swear that I will faithfully execute the Office of President of the United States, and will to the best of my ability preserve, protect, and defend the Constitution of the United States."

It was the voice of Harry S. Truman, new President of the United States. Mrs. Truman and their daughter, Margaret, as they stood there, realized the burden of responsibility which now rested upon his shoulders. To be Chief Executive of the nation in peace time is a serious and awesome undertaking. But in that year of 1945 the United States was still fighting World War II; and it was Harry Truman who, in the months ahead, would have to make the momentous decision to use the newly-developed atom bomb against our enemies.

The new President and the new First Lady had come a long way together since their carefree school days.

Mrs. Truman was born in Independence, Missouri, on February 13, 1885. She was christened Elizabeth Virginia, but her family and friends always called her Bess. The eldest of four children, and the only daughter of David Willock Wallace, a banker, Bess Wallace had the comfortable, happy childhood of the average American girl.

Independence was a warm-hearted community, where everybody knew everybody else. Blue-eyed, fair-haired Bess, with her sunny disposition and ready smile, had many friends. She particularly enjoyed outdoor sports. Like most of the other children, she went to grade school and high school, and later she attended for a year the Barstow School for Girls, in Kansas City, Missouri.

By that time she was a popular young lady, and foremost among her admirers was Harry S. Truman. Bess and Harry had grown up together. And from the time he was six or seven, when he first caught a glimpse of Bess in Sunday school, Harry Truman thought she was the sweetest, prettiest girl he had ever seen. There was less than a year's difference in their ages, and from the fifth grade until both were graduated from the Independence High School in 1901, they had been in the same classes.

During World War I, Harry Truman served overseas, taking part in the Meuse-Argonne and St. Mihiel actions. Several months after the war was over he returned to Missouri, and he and Bess Wallace were married on June 28, 1919, at the Episcopal Church. In 1924, their first and only child was born, and they named her Mary Margaret.

Though the Trumans were far from wealthy in those years, they were ideally happy in their devotion to each other and their delight over their baby daughter. For a number of years they continued to live in Independence. Then on November 6, 1934, the Democratic party elected Mr. Truman to the United States Senate, and they moved to Washington, D.C.

There they rented an apartment; and, as the wife of a senator, Bess Truman enjoyed life in the nation's capital. At the beginning of her husband's second term in the Senate (he was re-elected in 1940), World War II was being fought in Europe and a huge defense program was under way in the United States. On December 7, 1941, when Pearl Harbor was bombed by the Japanese, our country again became involved in global war. The Washington that Bess Truman knew changed quickly into a crowded, frantically busy nation's capital, united in a single objective: the vanquishing of a powerful enemy.

When the Democratic National Convention met in 1944, President Franklin D. Roosevelt wanted Harry Truman for his running mate. When the votes were counted, the President was re-elected for a fourth term and Senator Truman became Vice President. A few months later, upon the death of Roosevelt, Vice President Truman succeeded to the office of Chief Executive of the United States, and in 1948 he was elected in his own right.

For more than three and a half years while Bess Truman was First Lady, she and her family were deprived of the pleasure of living in the White House. After a century and a half of constant use by large crowds of people, the old mansion literally was falling apart. Its floors creaked, its plaster was cracking, its ceilings sagged dangerously, and it was considered unsafe for occupancy.

A week before the 1948 election, the Trumans moved over to Blair House, where the First Lady set up smaller editions of the Red, Blue, and Green Rooms of the White House; also a small state dining room.

After experts had estimated the repairs and improvements that would have to be made to the White House, there was considerable argument in Congress in favor of tearing down the ancient structure and building a new Executive Mansion. But the Trumans, along with many other Americans, felt strongly that no new building could possibly have the historic significance of the original.

Unlike her predecessor, Eleanor Roosevelt, Mrs. Truman did not hold weekly press conferences; reporters were kept informed of her social engagements through her secretary. But the First Lady, who so rarely expressed her opinions publicly, sent a special message to the press, saying that the White House walls should be saved.

The long job of restoring the Executive Mansion cost more than five and one-half million dollars. It was the most thorough and the most costly renovation in the nation's history. While the original shell of the White House was saved, new foundations were installed two floors below the old ones, and new walls were raised. Furnishings were removed and refurbished, many pieces of historic furniture were re-installed, and valuable pieces were acquired, so that the transformed building could be completely furnished in eighteenth-century style, in harmony with the Georgian architecture.

Every room was air-conditioned, and a broadcasting room was installed on the ground floor, complete with equipment for sending out radio and television programs. The modernization also included an all-electric mechanized kitchen, a barber shop, a theater, offices for doctor and dentist, public rest rooms, and self-operated elevators.

Mrs. Truman chose plum as the predominating color in her bedroom and sitting room and Margaret Truman selected green for the walls of her sitting room.

In March, 1952, the rejuvenation of the old mansion was declared complete and on March 27th, President and Mrs.

Truman and their family moved back into a White House more beautiful and more convenient for comfortable, gracious living than ever before in its long history. Two days later, on the evening of March 29, 1952, at the annual Jefferson-Jackson Day dinner, President Truman made the announcement that he would not run for another term.

Throughout her years as First Lady, Mrs. Truman was a gracious hostess, cheerfully performing all official duties, shaking hands with thousands of visitors, and presiding over numerous dinners, teas, and other social functions. But the lives of our First Ladies are not easy, and the responsibilities are great. It was well known in Washington circles that Mrs. Truman was happy in the contemplation of a return to private life.

On December 1, 1952, she was all smiles as she welcomed Mrs. Dwight D. Eisenhower on the steps of the White House, to show her over the premises.

Hatless, wearing a becoming dress of her favorite blue, and with a short black Persian lamb jacket thrown over her shoulders, Mrs. Truman stood patiently while photographers snapped pictures. She was nearing her sixty-eighth birthday, and the burden of official responsibilities would soon be turned over to another.

Elizabeth Virginia Wallace Truman's blue eyes were bright with pleasant anticipation, for on January 20, 1953, she was going home to Independence, Missouri—home to the place she loved best.

Mamie Geneva Doud Eisenhower

A LIGHTHEARTED FIRST LADY

WHEN on November 4, 1952, General Dwight D. Eisenhower was elected President of the United States, and friends began addressing the new First Lady as Mrs. Eisenhower, she looked at them with a merry smile, and said: "Just call me Mamie." That informal equivalent for Mary captured the imagination of the entire nation, as the First Lady herself captured its heart. For her remark was not a carefully considered bid for popularity, or the gracious gesture of a social leader. It was the spontaneous friendly response so typical of the girl from Colorado. As a round-faced, rosy-cheeked youngster she ran out to greet the postman each morning; as a lively teen-ager sitting on the top step of her front porch, she was always surrounded by a group of adoring young men. She had an enormous liking for people.

That characteristic, one of Mrs. Eisenhower's most charming assets, undoubtedly helped to smooth the way when she accompanied her husband from army post to army post in many parts of the world. Since her marriage she has moved twenty-five times. One of those moves took her to a chateau in France; another to a suite in a Manila hotel, where the walls were lined with satin and tremendous crystal chandeliers were suspended from the high ceilings. When her husband was stationed in Panama, they lived in a thinly planked house with a sheet-iron roof that was sweltering in the tropic sun by day, and was infested with bats by night. Mrs. Eisenhower herself says that she has lived in everything from shacks with cracks to palaces. But wherever the Eisenhowers found themselves and no matter how short their stay, the warmth of Mamie's personality and her ability as a hostess won friends and made any quarters homelike.

Mamie Geneva Doud was born in Boone, Iowa, on November 14, 1896; but Denver, Colorado, is the place she claims as home, for the Douds moved there when she was nine. There, in the shadow of the Rockies, she went to elementary school, high school, and to Sunday School at the Presbyterian church. She traces her ancestry on her father's side back to Guilford, England, from which the Douds emigrated to this country, helping to found the town of Guilford, Connecticut, in 1639. One grandfather, Royal H. Doud, moved from Rome, New York, to Chicago in 1876, where he went into the business of meat packing. Her other grandfather, Carl Carlson, was born in Sweden. In 1868 he arrived in Portland, Maine, moving later to Boone County, Iowa, where he operated a grain mill.

Mamie Doud's Denver childhood was happy and carefree. The Douds were devoted to one another. They all loved parties and good times, and were never happier than when they were together. They lived in a fine big cream-colored brick house on Lafayette Street, and on bright sunny week ends when the children were little, John Doud with his wife and four daughters, Mamie, Eleanor, Buster, and Mike, climbed into their car and started off on a picnic in the country or went to City Park to listen to the band concerts. John Doud died in 1951 at the age of eighty. His wife, Elivera Doud, although she spent much of her time at the White House, continued to maintain the old home on Lafayette Street until her death in September, 1960.

Mamie still remembers the fun she had as a young girl when, with her friends, she visited an amusement park on the edge of town. They traveled by trolley car and laughed as it went swinging along at the then exciting speed of twenty miles an hour. At the park they wandered through the zoo, rode on the merry-go-round and the miniature train, and danced at the pavilion. Later, when she was attending Miss Wolcott's School, Mamie drove around Denver in the family car, an electric brougham elegantly upholstered in plum-colored broadcloth. In the evenings, the boys and girls in the neighborhood gathered on the front porch at the Douds', and all up and down Lafayette Street their young voices could be heard lifted in songs and laughter. Mamie had many beaux, but though she liked them all, none won her heart completely.

When she was eighteen she met "Ike" Eisenhower at Fort Sam Houston, Texas. It was October, 1915, and with her family she had driven down from Denver to spend the winter in San Antonio. One day friends persuaded Mamie to visit the Fort with them, and there she first saw the young officer with the ruddy face and the disarming grin. In the weeks that followed Ike and Mamie spent much time together. She was a fun-loving girl, with a pert, slightly turned-up nose, light brown hair, and deep violet eyes. A double row of dimples appeared when she smiled—which was often. She liked to dance and sing, and she played the piano, partly by ear. With Ike and other young people, she sang such popular songs of the day as "A Little Love, a Little Kiss," and "When You Know You're Not Forgotten By the Girl You Can't Forget." And it soon became evident that Ike couldn't forget the girl from Colorado any more than she could forget him.

Mrs. Eisenhower still treasures the pink and green cretonne dress she was wearing when she first met Second Lieutenant Dwight D. Eisenhower, who had just been graduated from West Point. In February of the following year they became engaged; and on July 1, 1916, they were married in Denver—and her husband was promoted to first lieutenant. His pay was raised to $161.67 a month.

Their first home was in Eisenhower's two-room quarters at Fort Sam Houston. Mamie knew almost nothing about cooking. About all she could make, she confessed to her young husband, was fudge. He, however, enjoyed cooking. They started with a minimum of kitchen equipment—a toaster, a percolator, an electric grill, and a chafing dish. Ike prepared the meals, while Mamie conscientiously set herself to learning how to keep house. Her greatest ambition, then and all through her married life, was to be a good wife and to make a happy home for her husband. At Fort Sam Houston there was no rent to pay. They rented a piano for $5 per month. Mamie quickly made friends with other army couples, and life was good and gay.

Their first sorrow came when their son, a boy of three, died at Camp Meade, Maryland, where they were then living. The second son, John Sheldon Doud Eisenhower, was born in Denver on August 3, 1922. He served overseas during World War II and later in Korea. Young Major Eisenhower married Barbara Jean Thompson in 1947. Their four children, Dwight David, Barbara Anne, Susan Elaine, and Mary Jean, often visited the White House with their mother and father. No other First Lady in America's history has gone into such a complete and perfectly equipped White House as did Mrs. Eisenhower. During the latter part of the Truman administration it had been enlarged, rebuilt, and completely renovated and redecorated. Mamie called it "simply beautiful." With a personal secretary, a social secretary, four or five aides to help answer her mail, and a staff of some seventy-two people to attend to the cooking and housekeeping, Mrs. Eisenhower quickly mastered the complexities of White House entertaining. During the time that General Eisenhower was Supreme Commander of NATO (North Atlantic Treaty Organization), Mamie had entertained and been entertained by all the highest dignitaries abroad. During that period the Eisenhowers lived in a beautiful villa in Versailles, and Mamie flew everywhere with Ike. They went to Sweden, Norway, Denmark, England, and Holland, and she became accustomed to dining with kings, queens, and prime ministers. She learned, too, a great deal about the art of formal entertaining. Before she had been in the White House very long, official Washington began to notice that functions at the Executive Mansion were imbued with the warmth of her personality and her flair for making people feel at home.

When she walked into the White House to take charge in January, 1953, she broke a precedent by changing the staging of state dinners. She arranged to sit beside her husband at the head of the table, rather than at the opposite end. While she kept a close and competent eye on all social functions, she found time for many family reunions. Birthdays and holidays meant happy family gatherings with the children and grandchildren, where the President had a chance to relax and enjoy himself. Mrs. Eisenhower was responsible, too, for reviving the annual Easter egg-rolling contest, when the White House lawn is thrown open to the public. This custom, started by Dolley Madison, had lapsed during the years of World War II.

Mrs. Eisenhower took many duties off the shoulders of the President by making personal appearances, receiving various groups and delegations at the White House, presiding at benefit luncheons, opening charity drives, entertaining Boy and Girl Scouts, being photographed for worthy causes, and being interviewed by the press. Those who met her on such occasions came away with pleasant memories of her cordiality. It is said that she has shaken hands with more than a hundred thousand people. Highly gregarious, she frankly enjoyed life in Washington.

Mrs. Eisenhower likes smart, comfortable clothes. She is especially fond of earrings and of her charm bracelets, which jingle with symbols of her husband's career. She adores tiny hats, and wears her slightly graying brown hair in bangs. Five feet four inches tall, and weighing 138 pounds, the First Lady worries like any other woman about getting stout, but even though a grandmother, she is still decidedly attractive, with a youthful figure and trim ankles.

Her greatest trial came in the autumn of 1955, when President Eisenhower was stricken with a heart attack while visiting at the Doud home in Denver. He was taken to the army hospital, where his wife stayed beside him during many anxious weeks. When he was able to be moved, she went with him to their Gettysburg farm. There she watched over him and was overjoyed when his health began to improve. For a time Gettysburg, Pennsylvania, became the little capital of the United States; but by October 11, 1955, President Eisenhower again began to take an active part in public affairs. Later, after his doctors assured him that he was physically fit to remain in office for a second term, the President announced that he would run again.

On Election Day, November 7, 1956, President Eisenhower was re-elected by a "landslide" over his Democratic opponent, Adlai Stevenson.

Before she went to the White House for the first term,

Mamie Eisenhower declared that she was counting on seeing more of her husband than she did when he was a General of the Army. But she soon found that a First Lady must make many sacrifices. She must accept the fact that her hours alone with her husband will be few and far between and that their privacy may be invaded at any time.

Mrs. Eisenhower also found that the President's official duties would often take him to far places. During his eight years in office, he traveled more than three hundred thousand miles by air around the world on diplomatic missions. Mamie was always timid about flying; she worried constantly for his safety. The President suffered a mild stroke in September, 1957, and after a brief recuperation resumed his missions to promote peace and justice among men. Then Mamie worried about his health, but she realized that he must continue to serve his country.

Now and then she had a little leisure to visit with her grandchildren, practice on her electric organ, and arrange family parties. But running the White House, with its one hundred and thirty-two rooms and an estimated six hundred thousand visitors annually, was not easy. Each week she answered at least a thousand letters. Each month she shook hands with thousands of people who swarmed through the public rooms. There were frequent bazaars, lunches, and receptions for many delegations from all over the United States. Mamie posed willingly for photographs, and greeted visitors warmly.

The grounds around the Executive Mansion, long known as the President's Garden, delighted her, with its eighteen acres of green lawns, winding paths, historic trees, and beautiful flowers. Every First Lady, since Abigail Adams planted old-fashioned roses beside the doorstep, has left some mark of her personality there. Among the more modern tree-roses in the President's Garden, Mamie Eisenhower placed a neat metal sign, which reads:

"The kiss of the sun for pardon,
The song of the birds for mirth;
One is nearer God's heart in a garden
Than anywhere else on earth."

President Eisenhower had little spare time to enjoy the garden; but his wife—or his "best girl," as he often referred to her—tried to get him to relax whenever possible. When he was not away and there were no state banquets scheduled, Mamie had their dinner served on trays while they watched television in the comfortable family living room. Sometimes, when the weather was pleasant, they sat on the upstairs balcony President Truman had built, and enjoyed the cool breezes from the Potomac.

Porch-sitting was a family tradition with the Eisenhowers. A favorite spot at their Gettysburg Farm was a glass-enclosed, air-conditioned back porch, where they could get a fine view of the surrounding hills. General Eisenhower had bought the 189-acre farm in 1950, and he and Mamie regarded it as their first real, permanent home; but they had not been able to spend much time there.

Built more than a century ago, the old red brick farmhouse stands on a hill with the Blue Ridge Mountains in the background. From the front porch, there is a view of Cemetery Ridge, where General Pickett launched his history-making charge during the Civil War. The Eisenhowers have never regarded the Gettysburg property as a show place. It is a real, working farm with acres of wheat, oats, and barley, a collection of livestock, and a small pond stocked with fish.

As January 20, 1961, drew near and Washington buzzed with preparations for the advent of President-elect John F. Kennedy and his wife, Mamie thought more and more about the farm. Eagerly she looked forward to the moment of their returning, when they could lead their own private lives again and Ike could fish and hunt, get back to his hobby of painting, and write his memoirs at leisure.

When inauguration day arrived, the nation's capital was aglitter with sparkling white in the morning sun. Some fourteen inches of snow had fallen during the night. A biting wind was blowing and the weather was intensely cold, but Mamie's heart was warm and gay. She smiled, shook hands, greeted friends, posed for the photographers, and listened intently as John F. Kennedy took the solemn oath of office. But as soon as the ceremony was over, the Eisenhowers slipped away unobtrusively and joined a group of old friends for a farewell luncheon.

Late that afternoon Ike helped Mamie into their waiting car and drove off through the snow toward the farm. There was no motorcycle escort; no sirens were screaming; no secret service men hovered near. Mamie and Ike, after many long years of public service, were private citizens now and they were filled with happiness.

Soon Washington and its crowded streets lay behind. The noise, clamor, and confusion were gone. Ahead, serene and quiet in the winter twilight, they could see the snow-covered hills and the softly lighted houses of the little town of Gettysburg.

Ike and Mamie were going home, to the first real home they had ever known.

Jacqueline Lee Bouvier Kennedy

FIRST FIRST LADY BORN IN THE
TWENTIETH CENTURY

IT was close to Christmas, and the nation's capital buzzed with holiday activity. All over the city the sound of carols and chimes filled the wintry air with music. Christmas trees were green and fragrant outside the shops. Hurrying people, their arms filled with bundles, smiled shyly at one another, a little of the magic starshine of the holy season in their eyes. Airports, railroad depots, and bus terminals were crowded with men, women, and children going home for Christmas.

But the chestnut-haired, dark-eyed young woman sitting in the office of the editor of the *Washington Times-Herald* wasn't thinking of the happy holidays. Other things occupied her mind; she wanted a job.

"Do you want to go into journalism, or do you just want to hang around here until you get married?" asked the editor sternly.

"No, sir," replied the applicant. "I want to make a career."

The editor hesitated only briefly. Here was a businesslike little girl—nice, quiet, concentrated, obviously very, very much in earnest.

"Well," he continued more amiably, "if you're serious, I'll be serious. Come back after the holidays and I'll put you to work."

"Thank you," said the girl.

"But don't you come to me in six months and say you're engaged," was the editor's parting shot.

"No, sir!" murmured the girl, and she stepped out into the cold fresh air looking for all the world as though someone had just handed her the best Christmas gift ever. As she walked swiftly down the Avenue, stars in her big eyes and her cheeks as scarlet as the holly berries all over town, people turned to look at her before she was lost in the crowds. For she was pleasant to look at—a vibrantly pretty girl of medium height and slender figure; a girl of twenty-two who had just landed her first job.

The year was 1951. The girl was Jacqueline Lee Bouvier, who had not the remotest idea at that moment that she would some day become First Lady of the land.

Born into a wealthy family of high social rank, Jacqueline was blessed since the day of her birth with everything money can buy—and it can buy a great deal in the way of clothes, education, travel, and other material comforts. But it cannot buy beauty, grace, and charm plus the ambition to accomplish something useful in one's own right. These are outstanding qualities possessed by Jacqueline Kennedy. Early in life, she distinguished herself for talent and brains. She was an honor student at Vassar; was voted the most beautiful debutante of 1948; was an excellent horsewoman; a writer of poetry and prose, with a flair for painting and sketching; and in that first job on the *Washington Times-Herald* proved herself a clever, resourceful, and highly original reporter-photographer.

Jacqueline was born on July 28, 1929, in Southampton, Long Island, where her parents, John Vernon Bouvier III and Janet Lee Bouvier, had their summer home. She was not really a pretty baby; she looked somewhat frail and wan. She was named for her father, who was known to his friends as "Jack"; and was christened at the Church of St. Ignatius Loyola in New York.

Jacqueline's mother was twenty-one. A handsome brunette and member of the old Lee family of Virginia, she had been the belle of her debutante season. She was small and very feminine, but was a renowned horsewoman. Jack Bouvier III was thirty-seven and, until his marriage, had been considered one of social New York's most popular bachelors. He was tall, dark, and good-looking. Mr. and Mrs. Bouvier were regarded as the handsomest couple on Long Island. Their daughter, Jacqueline, would start life with every asset.

Almost as soon as the little one could walk, she was introduced to her mother's favorite sport. At first she rode ponies, but at the age of five she was competent to handle a good-sized thoroughbred horse; and she was also exhibiting her black Scotch terrier, Hootchie, at local dog shows. Winters were spent in a Park Avenue apartment, and Central Park was young Jackie's favorite playground. By that time she had blossomed into an attractive little girl with big brown eyes and softly curling almost black hair, with an independent spirit and an inquiring mind.

One day when, with her nurse and baby sister, Jackie had gone to the Park, Mrs. Bouvier at home answered the telephone. "We have a little girl here," said a masculine voice. "We can't understand her name, but she knows her telephone number. Could she be yours?" It was the police. Frantically Mrs. Bouvier hurried to the station house where she found Jackie chatting amiably with the Lieutenant. "Hello, Mummy," she said, as if it were the most natural thing in the world to meet her mother in the police station. The officer on the Central Park beat told the story. He had noticed the little girl walking alone down a path. When he paused to question her, she stated flatly, "My nurse is lost!"

Jacqueline's education began with kindergarten at Miss Yates's preschool class. The following year she attended Miss Chapin's school to learn good citizenship and good manners, along with regular studies. She must have been quite a handful, for the headmistress later reported to her mother, "I mightn't have kept Jacqueline, except that she has the most inquiring mind we've had in this school in thirty-five years!"

More serious than in her days at Miss Chapin's, Jacqueline enjoyed her two years at Holton-Arms, a private school in Washington, D.C., and she admitted that she "adored" Latin. She had been studying French since early childhood. Later she mastered Spanish and Italian.

When Jacqueline was fifteen, she became a first-year student at Miss Porter's school in Farmington, Connecticut. She also studied ballet, wrote poetry, and tried her hand at sketching. She and her sister, Lee, saw a great deal of their parents and felt secure in love and affection. This did not change when Jack Bouvier and his wife decided to live separately. The girls and their mother moved into a smaller apartment, and Jackie and Lee spent Sundays and summer vacations with their father, whom they idolized. He encouraged his girls to climb trees, to ride bicycles, and to love all animals; and now and then he took Jackie downtown to lunch and to the New York Stock Exchange. Jack Bouvier, who never remarried, died in 1957, and this was Jackie's first real sorrow. She felt as though she had lost part of her heart.

Mrs. Bouvier had remarried in June, 1942, when Jackie was not quite thirteen. A new phase then began for the children. Jacqueline and Lee joined their mother and new stepfather, Hugh D. Auchincloss, living in winter at "Merrywood," a gracious Georgian house in the Virginia countryside across the Potomac from Washington. In summer they lived at Hammersmith Farm, a large Victorian house with seventy-five acres of land on the outskirts of fashionable Newport. Hugh Dudley Auchincloss was a kindly, steadfast man, whom Jackie often said was "a wonderful stepfather."

Those were happy times for young Jacqueline. She was in that dreamy stage of reading Shakespeare and Byron, and doubtless Rupert Brooke, Swinburne, and Shelley, as so many young girls do. She had a great zest for living, yet there was a spiritual quality about her that belied her prankish tomboy nature. One of the many poems she wrote during this period includes the following verses:

"I love the autumn
And yet I cannot say
All the thoughts and things
That make me feel this way.

"I love walking on the shore
To watch the angry sea,
Where summer people were before
And now there's only me.

"I love wood fires at night
That have a ruddy glow;
I stare into the flames
And think of long ago.

"The tangy taste of apples,
The snowy mist at morn,
The wanderlust inside you
When you hear the huntsman's horn.

"Nostalgia—that's the autumn
Dreaming through September

Just a million things I
Always will remember."

Jacqueline chose Vassar to complete her education and passed her aptitude test in the top group. Masculine callers flocked to Vassar to see the glamour girl who had been elected queen debutante of the year. Weekends she visited her family or went to dances at Yale and Harvard, but during the week she applied herself to learning about literature, art, and the history of religion.

The summer after her first year at college, Jacqueline with a group of other girls, chaperoned by a teacher, made the "grand tour" of Europe. They sailed on the *Queen Mary;* attended a Royal Garden Party at Buckingham Palace; met Winston Churchill; then headed for Paris, the chateau country, the French Riviera, Switzerland, and Italy.

Jacqueline fell in love with Paris at first sight. With the permission of her teachers, she spent her junior college year there to perfect her French. She studied at the Sorbonne and lived with a family where only French was spoken. The family was poor, and there was so little heat that Jacqueline had to wrap up in sweaters and scarves and study in bed. A single bathroom was available for seven people, and hot water was a rare luxury, but Jacqueline seemed to care little for creature comforts. She never complained.

The following year she won *Vogue* magazine's annual *Prix de Paris,* which offered the winner a six-months' job on *Vogue* in Paris and a similar span in New York. Contestants had to submit four technical papers on fashion; a personal profile; the plan for a complete issue of *Vogue;* and five hundred words on "People I Wish I Had Known." Jacqueline, who by then had returned from Paris and was polishing off her college career at George Washington University, turned down the first prize. Her mother thought she had been away from home long enough.

In 1950 she joined her stepbrother for a tour of Ireland and Scotland. And on her second holiday, Jackie acted as guide to her younger sister, Lee, on the latter's first trip abroad. The girls hired a drive-yourself car and traveled from Paris to Spain and through Italy.

Early in 1952, mindful of the promise of the editor of the *Washington Times-Herald,* Jacqueline was back in Washington, hard at work on her first job as the Inquiring Camera Girl. She had assured the editor she could handle a camera, and she could; but she knew nothing about the cumbersome Graflex used by professional photographers. Undismayed, she looked up a camera school and proceeded to learn her new trade. Her first week's pay was the magnificent sum of $42.50, but later she was given a number of small raises which boosted her salary to $56.75 a week.

In the course of her work she interviewed and photographed men and women in the street, busmen, housewives, and children; and up on the "Hill" asked leading questions of congressmen, senators, page boys, and others. One of those she interviewed was John Fitzgerald Kennedy, a young congressman who had recently defeated Senator Henry Cabot Lodge and had become Senator from Massachusetts. Another of her scoops was Vice-President Nixon. When Jacqueline was sent to see young John Kennedy, the editor told her: "You behave yourself. Don't get your hopes up. He's too old for you—besides he doesn't want to get married." The mischievous Inquiring Camera Girl rolled her eyes, said nothing, and went out on her assignment.

Early in 1953 Jacqueline was again aboard the *Queen*

Mary, on her way to the coronation of Queen Elizabeth. She reported the event for the *Times-Herald* and her attractive sketches and colorful stories made the front pages of her paper again and again. When the coronation was over, Jacqueline and an older companion, Aileen Bowdoin, had a fun-filled week in Paris; then they flew home. Young Miss Bouvier had to pay more than a hundred dollars in excess fare for her heavy, book-filled suitcases. The volumes were a present for a friend of hers—Senator Kennedy.

The returning plane touched down in Boston before proceeding to New York, and the girls stepped out for a brief walk around. In the waiting room, leaning casually against a counter, was Senator John Fitzgerald Kennedy.

Not long afterward, Jacqueline called her aunt on long distance telephone. "Aunt Maudie," she said, "I just want you to know that I'm engaged to Jack Kennedy, but you can't tell anyone for a while, because it wouldn't be fair to *The Saturday Evening Post.*"

Aunt Maudie was mystified. "What," she asked, "has *The Saturday Evening Post* to do with your engagement?"

Jackie laughed. "The *Post* is coming out tomorrow," she said, "with an article, and the title is on the cover. It's 'Jack Kennedy—the Senate's Gay Young Bachelor.' "

John Fitzgerald Kennedy and Jacqueline Lee Bouvier were married on September 12, 1953. Both families, wealthy and socially prominent, were delighted over the match. Jacqueline was then twenty-four, and her bridegroom was thirty-six. Their vows were taken at St. Mary's Church in fashionable Newport, and the wedding and reception which followed left society columnists breathless over the splendor and lavishness of the affair. There were twenty-six groomsmen and bridesmaids and seven hundred distinguished guests, with an additional two hundred at the reception. A mob of three thousand spectators broke through police lines and nearly crushed the bride.

Jacqueline was radiant in her white silk taffeta gown and an exquisite rose-point lace bridal veil that had been worn by her maternal grandmother at the time of her own marriage. When the festivities were finally over, and the bridal couple waved their goodbyes, they started off on a honeymoon that would take them to Mexico and then on a leisurely motor trip up the California Coast.

Upon their return to Washington, Senator and Mrs. Kennedy bought a farmhouse in McLean, Virginia, in which to live. But Jack's senatorial duties kept him away from home so much of the time that Jacqueline often felt lonely and isolated. Caroline was born late in 1957, and when she was three weeks old, the John Kennedys moved into a red brick house in the Georgetown section of Washington. They became very fond of the unpretentious dwelling, with its little back garden. While her husband was still a Senator, Jacqueline Kennedy said: "My sweet little house leans slightly to one side, and the stairs creak." It was a three-story house with four bedrooms, comfortably furnished with a mixture of contemporary and French furniture. Art books were piled on almost every table, fresh flowers were everywhere, and the lovely pictures on the walls were carefully chosen by Mrs. Kennedy. She wanted everybody to be happy and at ease in the old house and to love it as she did.

In July of 1960 Senator Kennedy was nominated as the Democratic party's candidate for President, with Lyndon Johnson as his running mate. Toward the end of the Presidential campaign, when Mrs. Kennedy was awaiting the arrival of their second child (John Fitzgerald Kennedy, Jr., who was born in Georgetown on Thanksgiving Eve), she held television parties to watch her husband's debates with Vice President Nixon. She also wrote a daily newspaper column appealing especially to women. She asked them to write and let her know their views so that she could pass them on to her husband.

When John F. Kennedy was elected President, Jacqueline naturally was delighted, because she knew it was the goal he so greatly desired; but she left politics strictly to him and devoted herself to his personal comfort. "I want to take such good care of my husband," she said, "that, whatever he is doing, he can do it better because he has me." About her children, when questioned, she replied, "People have too many theories about raising children. I believe simply in love, security, and discipline."

Jacqueline was well fitted by birth and education for the position of First Lady. Her years of entertaining and being entertained in the highest circles, both at home and abroad, supplemented the social graces in which she had been trained since early childhood.

Among her initial activities as First Lady, Mrs. Kennedy took up the tremendous task of restoring the White House to the historic grandeur of early Presidential days. She made a careful study of those times, established a Fine Arts Committee to help her, and brought to light many beautiful pieces which had been hidden in White House storerooms for decades. She also sought and received from all parts of the United States gifts of authentic period furniture, bric-a-brac, and china. Some items which she particularly wanted were purchased. She secured the Nelly Custis sofa, the Dolley Madison sofa, and other valuable antiques. Her interest drew to the White House thousands of tourists eager to see the results of her labors.

In February, 1962, she appeared in a nationally televised tour of the Executive Mansion, which stimulated an increase in the number of visitors. For their benefit, Mrs. Kennedy prepared a colorful guide book, giving the facts on the furnishings and the history of the White House. Under her direction a catalog system was also set up, listing every book, painting, piece of furniture, and other property within its walls.

But that was only the beginning. Before she went to the White House, Washington had been regarded as having very few cultural advantages, beyond its museums and occasional concerts. Jacqueline Kennedy proceeded to change all that. She brought the best in music, ballet, drama, and poetry to the nation's capital. Not since the era of Thomas Jefferson had culture found such a cordial reception there. Carl Sandburg, Gian Carlo Menotti, Pablo Casals, Robert Frost, Leonard Bernstein, Igor Stravinsky, George Balanchine, Elia Kazan, Sir Ralph Richardson, and many other notables were invited to the White House by the Kennedys. Some people thought at first that what they called the "arty atmosphere" might hurt the President politically, but apparently it served to enhance his popularity and that of Jacqueline.

Mrs. Kennedy also accomplished much in addition to her unofficial role as "minister of culture." In the spring of 1961 she traveled to Europe with her husband, and together this handsome and dedicated couple captured the imagination of young and old. Queen Elizabeth and Prince Philip, along with all other Britons, were enchanted by the lovely Jacqueline. President de Gaulle of France was touched and captivated when she talked fluently with him in his native tongue.

Even Premier Khrushchev and his wife greeted her affectionately when the two leaders met in Vienna.

Wherever she went, enthusiastic crowds applauded and called out her name; and women of many countries imitated her hair styles, her clothes, her regal way of walking—even her manner of speaking.

Despite her many other duties, Mrs. Kennedy never neglected her children, Caroline and young John-John, as his father called him. A nursery and first-grade school were established at the White House for some twenty youngsters, so that Caroline would have playmates and as normal a childhood as possible. There were gay little parties for special occasions, and each evening before bedtime (and sometimes during the day), the children enjoyed a romp with their beloved and loving father.

Summers at Hyannisport were a delight to the entire family. They went swimming, sailing, and fishing and enjoyed long, happy days together on the beaches and in the waters surrounding Cape Cod.

At home in the White House, Mrs. Kennedy put an end to the old and tiring custom of having long lines of guests at huge receptions, who traditionally waited to shake hands with the President and his First Lady. Instead, upon arrival, guests were shown into the East Room where refreshments were served before their hosts appeared. Later, the Kennedys circulated informally among those present, chatting and making everybody feel at ease. At state dinners, instead of assigning guests to places at the huge banquet table which could seat ninety people, Jacqueline favored a number of smaller round tables, each seating ten or twelve. These tables were usually covered with pretty pastel-colored cloths and decorated with bouquets of fresh flowers.

In cool weather Jackie arranged to have fireplaces glowing cheerfully. When the weather was warm and fine, parties were often moved out to the gardens (also completely restored by the Kennedys). When darkness came there was a gleam of candlelight, and sometimes displays of fireworks. Mrs. Kennedy left nothing to chance. She supervised even the smallest details. She was a brilliant conversationalist, and could converse with honored guests in French, Spanish, and Italian. Parties at the White House changed from solemn rituals to gatherings of light-hearted people who enjoyed themselves thoroughly.

Sorrow marked the otherwise happy lives of President and Mrs. Kennedy during the summer of 1963. On August 7, Mrs. Kennedy bore a baby son, who was christened Patrick Bouvier Kennedy; but within two days the little one was dead of a respiratory illness. Both father and mother were deeply saddened by their loss.

But another blow, an unbelievable tragedy, was in store for Jacqueline Kennedy—and the entire nation as well. Late in November the President was to make a brief trip to Texas. Mrs. Kennedy did not often accompany him on such trips, but she was to go with him on this one.

On Friday, November 22, 1963, the President and Mrs. Kennedy were in Dallas, riding through the crowded streets of the city in an open car with Governor Connally and his wife.

It was a lovely sunny day. President Kennedy was hatless as usual, and the Governor's wife was just remarking to him, "You can't say Dallas hasn't greeted you with open arms," when three shots rang out. At first those in the slow-moving motorcade and the cheering crowds on the sidewalks thought it must be a backfire, or firecrackers. But they were real bullets. Fired from an upper floor of a building along the line of

348

march, they struck both Governor Connally and President Kennedy, who, fatally wounded, slumped into the arms of his wife. Her pink suit and the roses she carried were stained with streams of blood.

Secret Service men swarmed into action. Speedily the President's car left the parade and raced against time to Parkland Memorial Hospital.

At the hospital, the dreaded announcement finally came. President John F. Kennedy was dead. Throughout the ordeal Jacqueline Kennedy's only recorded cry of pain was "Oh, no!" which she uttered when her husband fell into her arms. From that moment on, she faced the horrible fact of the assassination with stoic strength. She stood, tearless, still, beside Lyndon B. Johnson, in the plane that had brought her husband and her to Texas, while the oath of office was administered making Vice President Johnson President of the United States. On the flight back to Washington, with the new President and his wife, and the body of her husband in the forward compartment, Jacqueline Kennedy had time to think.

Meanwhile, all over the United States and many other parts of the world, millions watching television or listening to radio were plunged into grief and uncertainty. It seemed impossible that this man with the sunny personality, the vigor, and the intellectual grasp of the problems that faced him was suddenly gone from our midst. Men and women cried openly in the streets; the faithful thronged to their churches and prayed.

The assassination of the President was the first of a chain of almost incredible events. As Lyndon Johnson was taking the oath of office, Lee Harvey Oswald, the accused assassin, was being arrested by Dallas police. Before he was captured he had shot and killed Officer J. D. Tippit, who had attempted to question him. Two days later, on November 24, Oswald himself was shot to death by Jack Ruby, a Dallas nightclub operator, while being transferred from the city to the county jail. Ruby was immediately taken into custody.

From the moment she arrived back in Washington, Jacqueline Kennedy, a quiet, tearless monument of fortitude, made detailed plans for a funeral that would be a fitting tribute to her husband's memory. With his brothers, Robert and Edward, beside her, she did not falter or rest. There was much to be done, and Mrs. Kennedy studied the reports of the funeral of President Lincoln, using the procedure in some respects as a guide.

On Monday morning, November 25, the day of her husband's funeral, Mrs. Kennedy carried out a precedent-shattering decision by electing to walk behind her husband's casket as it was borne from the White House to St. Matthew's Cathedral, some half mile distant. As the cortege wound away from the Executive Mansion for the last time, Jacqueline clung momentarily to the hand of Robert Kennedy. Then she resolutely straightened, threw back her shoulders, and let go of his hand. Her step was firm and her face composed as they strode along, followed by some two hundred dignitaries, including Prince Philip, Charles de Gaulle, President de Valera of Ireland, Japanese Premier Hayato Ikeda, and many others.

Within the cathedral, there was almost unbearable poignancy. Cardinal Cushing was present to say the Mass—the old family friend who had married John and Jacqueline some ten years before, who had christened their two children, and buried the infant son they had lost during the summer. Luigi Vena of Boston was there to sing "Ave Maria" as he had sung it at their wedding. The entire Kennedy family was gathered in the first pews, except John Kennedy's father, who had never completely recovered from a stroke suffered some time before. Caroline sat beside her mother, quiet and serious. Young John-John, who was three years old that very day, was kept occupied at the rear of the church with some religious picture books.

At the end of the impressive service, Jacqueline led both children to the door of the cathedral. As the flag-draped casket was borne down the steps, Mrs. Kennedy leaned over and whispered to the little boy, and John-John lifted his chubby right hand to his forehead and saluted smartly as his father's body was carried to the caisson.

The slow procession, with its traditional riderless horse, took an hour to reach Arlington National Cemetery. Jet fighters roared over the grave site on a hillside in front of the Custis-Lee mansion, and after them Air Force One, the plane President Kennedy had loved so much, flew over, dipping its wings in salute as it passed. There were final prayers, the muffled beat of drums, the lonely bugle sound of taps, and the sharp crack of a rifle volley. The honor guard folded the flag which had covered the coffin and gave it to Mrs. Kennedy. Then, with Robert and Edward Kennedy to help, Jacqueline lighted the eternal flame which was her own idea of "something living forever" at the grave. One by one foreign kings, ambassadors, premiers, and other dignitaries paused at the new grave for a moment before they left. There were unshed tears in Jacqueline's eyes, behind the heavy black veil, but she held them bravely back and walked down the little hill, hand in hand with Robert Kennedy. The last act of the tragic drama that had gripped the nation for four terrible days had come to an end.

But for Jacqueline Kennedy all was not yet over; there was

one more task to be performed. Her unerring sense of social fitness told her she must receive and thank the many men and women who had journeyed across the world to attend the funeral. "It would be most ungrateful of me not to invite these people to the White House," she said. So, within minutes of her return from Arlington, she was greeting Emperor Haile Selassie of Ethiopia, Prince Philip of England, Queen Frederika of Greece, and other distinguished visitors who had honored her husband and the nation by coming here.

Very late that evening, she left the White House with Robert Kennedy, to stand again by the now lonely grave in Arlington and leave a spray of lilies of the valley.

Jacqueline Kennedy remained in the White House only a few days longer, and then moved to Georgetown, not far from where she and her husband had lived when he was a senator. Up to the last moment before she left the Executive Mansion she did everything she could to make sure that the era of John Fitzgerald Kennedy would close with dignity and grace. She sent flowers and a message to the family of Officer Tippit; she bade good-by to White House aides, secretaries, telephone operators, and other workers, and presented many of them with keepsakes that had belonged to her husband; she left a bouquet and a note for the new First Lady, Mrs. Lyndon Johnson.

Mrs. Kennedy declared for herself a year of mourning, during which she accepted no public engagements. With the help of friends she answered more than 800,000 letters of condolence. Then there was work to be done in planning the John F. Kennedy Memorial Library, and, more than anything else, she wanted to devote more time to her children.

Eulogies have been written about Jacqueline Kennedy in practically every magazine and newspaper in the United

States, and from England came this tribute: "Jacqueline Kennedy has given the American people from this day on one thing they have always lacked—majesty."

All over the world, people echoed the praises of Mrs. Kennedy. From that incredible moment when an assassin's senseless and cruel deed cut down her husband to the final tragic moment when John Fitzgerald Kennedy was laid to rest, his widow was a tower of strength, poise, and self-control. With past great women of the world, Jacqueline Lee Bouvier Kennedy takes her distinguished place. She is a First Lady in the highest sense of the title. She has added her own regal "profile in courage" to the annals of America's history and has been an inspiration to the entire nation in its time of great tragedy.

Claudia Alta Taylor Johnson

FIRST FIRST LADY FROM TEXAS

Mrs. Lyndon Baines Johnson was catapulted so suddenly and under such tragic conditions into her new role of First Lady that she scarcely had time to realize the immensity of the task which lay before her.

It was November 22, 1963, the day of the assassination of President Kennedy in Dallas, Texas. What were the feelings of this woman familiarly known to the nation as "Lady Bird," wife of the Vice President? Talking things over some weeks later with a reporter, Mrs. Johnson confided: "I felt a torrent of emotion. I felt the deepest admiration for the discipline and courage of Mrs. Kennedy. But, for my husband, because I have been close enough to know the magnitude of the job— I felt a sense of compassion."

Regardless of her feelings, however, from the moment she stood beside her husband in the plane where he hastily took the oath of office as President of the United States, Lady Bird Johnson moved calmly and efficiently. She had an assurance acquired during some twenty-nine years of official and public life beside her husband, first when he was a representative and a senator, and later when he was Vice President. Then, by the accident of death, came the new challenge for both of them.

President Johnson has been described as probably the best-prepared President ever to enter the White House; and his wife with her long experience in Washington circles was also well equipped for her duties as our First Lady. With her wide knowledge of politics, it was predicted by many that she would be extremely active as a working partner with her husband. She herself put her aims very modestly. In an early statement to the press, our new First Lady said:

"I will try to be balm, sustainer and sometimes critic for my husband; to help my children look at this job with all the reverence due it, to get from it the knowledge their unique vantage point gives them, and to retain the light-heartedness to which every teen-ager is entitled. For my own self, my role must emerge in deeds, not words."

Before the Johnsons had been in the White House six weeks, however, Lady Bird was playing a somewhat more active role than "balm and sustainer." On January 11, 1964, she was off by air to Wilkes-Barre and Scranton, Pennsylvania, to see for herself one of the "pockets of poverty," where the jobless rate was nearly double the nation's average. During her flight she jotted down notes and readied herself for speeches. Before that trip she had sat in the gallery of the Congress and heard her husband declare war on poverty in the United States, and she had made up her mind to get him a first-hand report from the mining area.

At the airport she was greeted with cheers and applause, and she shook hands with hundreds of people, charming the crowds with her warm smile and friendly southern drawl. At Wilkes College, one of the places where she spoke, a poster on a dormitory proclaimed: "Ashley Hall Welcomes Y'all."

Mrs. Johnson also gave talks in the central squares of Wilkes-Barre and Scranton and toured a vocational school and a textile plant. Many people who saw her for the first time were surprised that she was so small. Mrs. Johnson is 5 feet 4 inches tall and weighs about 110 pounds. Her hair is dark brown; her expressive eyes are an amber hue. She leans toward bright colors in clothes, and her husband chooses most of her outfits.

Her independent traveling and speechmaking were reminiscent of another First Lady, Eleanor Roosevelt, and left no doubt that if President Johnson were to run in the next Presidential election, Lady Bird would hit the campaign trail eagerly and perhaps with more assurance of success than she had done in 1960.

Mrs. Johnson was not always such a willing public speaker. As a little child and later in her school and college days, she was shy and retiring. She was born on December 22, 1912, in the village of Karnack, Texas, which in those days was a raw frontier town of less than one hundred people. Lady Bird's mother, the beautiful, dashing, and well-educated Minnie Pattillo Taylor, was the daughter of one of the first families of Alabama and a woman of cultivation and taste, as well as a crusader for woman suffrage.

Lady Bird was christened Claudia Alta Taylor, but when she was two years old a chance remark of her nurse saddled her with a nickname she has never liked. "She's as purty as a little lady bird," the nurse said, and the name caught on. The child's mother died before Claudia Alta reached her fifth birthday, and Aunt Effie, her mother's maiden sister, came from Alabama to become companion and protector.

The little girl's father, a big, powerfully built man, ran two country stores and some cotton gins several miles from town. A sign over one of his establishments read: "Thomas Jefferson Taylor, Dealer in Everything." He called his daughter "Lady," and lavished affection upon her. But he was a busy man and there were many lonely hours for the motherless girl.

When she attended high school in Jefferson, Texas, Aunt Effie moved there to look after her. In Lady Bird's senior year she transferred to Marshall High School and commuted fourteen miles every day from the brick house where she was born. After graduation she enrolled at St. Mary's Episcopal

School in Dallas. Later, when she became a student at the University of Texas School of Journalism, she found a whole new world opened up to her. She did not have an active social life, but she studied hard, stood high scholastically, and was graduated with honors.

Her father gave her a trip to New York and Washington, and after that she had no plans except to keep house for him. It was about that time, though, that she met Lyndon Baines Johnson, who was on a business trip to Texas, and it appeared at once that this persuasive young man had very definite plans for Miss Lady Bird. The next time he visited Texas, it was especially to see the girl from Karnack. He wanted to marry her; he wouldn't take no for an answer; and he wouldn't wait, either. They were married on November 17, 1934, when Lady Bird was not quite twenty-two.

Eight months later, Lyndon Johnson became Texas State Administrator for Franklin D. Roosevelt's National Youth Administration. Less than two years after that, he was elected to Congress.

Being a politician's wife frightened young Mrs. Johnson at first, but Lyndon believed in her ability. He expected great things of her. And, wanting to please him, she surprised herself by forgetting her shyness and becoming his partner in politics, as well as his wife and homemaker. In the years that followed she campaigned for him, acted as official greeter, and made speeches. In the 1960 election she traveled 35,000 miles in seventy-one days on her own campaign trail on behalf of her husband's cause. After he became Vice President she covered 120,000 miles in thirty foreign countries by his side.

In 1942, with money left her through her mother's estate, Lady Bird Johnson bought radio station KTBC in Austin, Texas. From a small station badly in debt she converted it

into a flourishing radio and television station today worth
several million dollars. Until she became First Lady, she was
active in running the business. But when she went to the
White House her properties were turned over to a trusteeship
to avoid any possible criticism that she or her family might
profit from their connection with the highest office in the
land.

Her two attractive daughters keep Mrs. Johnson young.
When their father became President, Lynda Bird was nineteen. She had been a student at the University of Texas in
Austin while her father was Vice President, but she transferred to George Washington University in the nation's capital soon after the family moved to the White House. The
younger daughter, Luci Baines, was sixteen at that time and
a junior at the National Cathedral School for Girls in
Washington.

Even though Mrs. Johnson had spent many years in Washington's political and social circles, she soon realized that
being a First Lady was a full-time job. She missed her Texas
home and the carefree informality of the ranch. While cop-
ing with an unceasing round of engagements and acting as
hostess to foreign dignitaries from all over the world, as well
as handling the social routine of the capital, she became increasingly aware of the fact that she had to sacrifice most of
her privacy. What she said, what she wore, how she dressed
her hair—almost every detail of her personal life—was sure
to be discussed in homes throughout our nation.

As time went on she worried, too, about her husband,
fearing that the pressure of the Presidency would be too
heavy for him, and that he might have another heart attack
such as he had had in previous years. President Johnson
worked from twelve to fifteen hours each day, and more

often than not he and his wife were rudely awakened from sleep at three or four o'clock in the morning with the clanging of a telephone bell that almost always seemed to be a portent of bad news.

The ever-escalating war in Vietnam; the fearful increase in crime; race riots, poverty, crippling strikes, and other grave problems weighed constantly upon the President's mind.

In November 1964 Lyndon Baines Johnson was elected President in his own right. In January of the following year, he spelled out to the nation his aspirations for what he hoped would become "The Great Society." Through the difficult months and years that followed, Lady Bird Johnson was a ready consultant when her husband discussed his problems with her. The President himself, when asked by a reporter whether he listened to his wife's advice, replied: "All the time, I listen to her more than to any other person I know."

Mrs. Johnson enjoyed a close companionship with her daughters, both of whom were happily married during the White House years. Luci, the younger, became a Catholic on July 2, 1965, and in June 1966 (shortly after her nineteenth birthday) was married to Patrick John Nugent.

The wedding ceremony was witnessed by more than seven hundred guests, and took place in the largest Roman Catholic church in the United States—the beautiful hilltop Shrine of the Immaculate Conception. It was a ceremony unmatched in splendor and ritual by the wedding of any other President's daughter in American history. President Johnson looked serious as he walked down the aisle with the radiant little Luci on his arm; but after the ceremony, he was smiling and jubilantly greeting friends and relatives, as the young couple and their guests adjourned to the White House for an elegant and gay reception.

Lynda, the older daughter, born on March 19, 1944, was married on December 9, 1967, to Captain Charles Spittal Robb of the U.S. Marine Corps. Their wedding was charming; Lynda and Charles took their vows in the huge and beautiful East Room of the Executive Mansion, which was decorated with holly and other Christmas greens.

It was the first time in fifty-three years that the daughter of a President had been married in the White House. Woodrow Wilson gave away both his daughters there—one in 1913, the second in 1914. At the wedding of Lynda Johnson, her bridegroom, Captain Robb, was in dress uniform, as were the other marine officers in attendance; they formed the traditional arch of swords over the newlyweds. But there was a subdued air among those present, because the bridegroom and three of his fellow-officers were scheduled to leave for Vietnam within a few months.

On June 21, 1967, at Austin, Texas, Luci Baines Nugent gave birth to the President's first grandchild—a lively, husky little boy who was named Patrick Lyndon. Then, on Friday, October 25, 1968, Lynda Bird Robb bore a lovely little girl. Two days later, when the proud mother talked with her husband in Vietnam by long-distance telephone, they decided to call the baby Lucinda Desha.

With happily married daughters and two little grandchildren, Mrs. Johnson's personal life appeared to be all that anybody could wish. But political life at the White House was troubled. President Johnson had made great progress in helping the underprivileged; he enforced equal-rights legislation; he sponsored Medicare for the aged and increased Social Security benefits. But the war in Vietnam had been escalated to a point where more than half a million young Americans were fighting on the other side of the world—a war not only involving billions of dollars, but, more importantly, taking the lives of untold Americans. In the meantime, crime had risen to a new high in the United States. People throughout the world were protesting America's part in the Vietnam war. At home they were questioning the precarious state of the budget, and were suggesting that the nation spend less on foreign affairs and more on making our country a better place in which to live.

President Johnson himself realized that his efforts had failed to achieve all he had envisioned. On November 4, 1968, in a televised speech that astonished the world, he announced: "I shall not seek, and I will not accept, the nomination of my party for another term as your President."

Mrs. Johnson seemed to be relieved that her husband's burden was lifted and that they could once more return to private life. During her own stay at the White House she had been unfailingly gracious, and a charming hostess. She had done much to lift the spirits of the nation by making the United States a more beautiful place in which to live. Natural beauty and conservation had been her watchwords. Flowers and trees grew and blossomed all over our nation's capital where only dry grass and weeds had flourished before. Because of her efforts and the cooperation of garden clubs everywhere, gas stations, school playgrounds, factory sites, and public parks had become pleasant sights on the landscape.

On November 4, 1969, Richard Milhous Nixon was elected President of the United States, defeating his Democratic opponent, Hubert Humphrey.

On Inauguration Day, January 20, 1969, Mrs. Johnson looked supremely happy. For five years she had fulfilled her duties as First Lady, and now an important phase of her life was over. While she might miss the magnetic attractions of public life, she knew a satisfying future awaited her. She and her husband were going home—home to their sprawling, peaceful acres and their many Texas friends.

Pat (Thelma Catherine) Ryan Nixon

FIRST FIRST LADY FROM NEVADA

IN the long procession of First Ladies since America's beginnings, probably none has been better equipped to preside over the Executive Mansion than Mrs. Richard Nixon. From the time her husband became a congressman in 1946, her training began. When he made his remarkable rise to the Vice Presidency in 1952, she accompanied him on diplomatic travels around the world that, at the behest of President Eisenhower, included fifty-four countries. During Eisenhower's Presidency, incidentally, Mrs. Nixon often presided at the White House on state occasions when Mamie Eisenhower was not well.

Mrs. Nixon was at her husband's side during his Presidential-campaign travels in 1960, when he was defeated by the late John F. Kennedy. And in 1962 she campaigned for her husband in his unsuccessful race for governor of California, even though she had opposed his running. In 1968, although she was also much opposed to his running again for the Presidency, she traveled more than 40,000 miles with Richard Nixon, smiling, gracious, untiring, as he campaigned, this time successfully, for the highest office in the land.

Life was not always this exciting for Thelma Catherine Ryan, whose Irish father insisted on calling her Pat, because she was born on St. Patrick's Eve. The time was fifty-six years ago (in 1913); the place was the little town of Ely, Nevada, where her father worked as a miner. Soon after her birth the family moved to a truck farm in Artesia, California, then a primitive little place without any modern conveniences. Here, before Pat was thirteen, her mother died, leaving the child to keep house, cook, scrub, and sew for her father and two older brothers. She also was out in the fields at harvest time, helping with the crops.

Not long after her mother passed away, her father died, following a painful illness, during which Pat cared for him all by herself. Life wasn't much fun for the youthful, but ambitious, Pat in those days. But nothing daunted her, and in the years that followed she struggled to get a college education.

She worked her way through the University of Southern California, doing all sorts of part-time jobs, ranging from work in the college library to various small jobs as a movie-extra and as a department-store salesgirl. She was graduated with honors, which helped her to secure a teaching job in the high school at Whittier, California.

There, in 1938, she met Richard Milhous Nixon, a young lawyer who had worked his own way through college. He proposed to her on their first date, but it wasn't until two years later that they were married. Shortly afterward, on December 7, 1941, came the shocking news of Pearl Harbor, and the devastating bombing by Japan of our fleet in the Pacific. Richard Nixon became a commissioned officer in the Navy, and during his separation from his young bride, she kept busy most of the time working, and trying to build up a nest egg for a permanent home for them when he returned.

But politics had lured Richard Nixon ever since he was a small boy, when he pored over one American history book after another. After the war was over, he was elected to Congress, and Pat Nixon began to learn about protocol and political life in the nation's capital. And except for the few recent years when her husband became a partner in a New York City law firm, the Nixons have been immersed in politics ever since.

Their two daughters—Tricia, a pretty blonde, and Julie, a

lovely brunette—have lived in a political atmosphere all their lives, and they seem to have thrived on it.

One of the very happy occasions for President-elect Nixon and Pat was the marriage on December 22, 1968, of Julie to young David Eisenhower, grandson of the former President. It was an exciting and gala affair, with a church wedding at the Marble Collegiate Church in New York City. Julie wanted her wedding to be held before the family took up residence in the White House in January. But it was her sister, Tricia, who caught the bridal bouquet Julie tossed as she and her new husband left the wedding reception. So perhaps there will be a White House wedding, after all.

President Nixon, his wife, and their two daughters are all members of the Society of Friends in East Whittier, California. And it is certain that Pat Nixon will preside over the Executive Mansion as graciously and successfully as did another charming Quaker lady, Dolley Madison, long, long ago.

BIBLIOGRAPHY

BOOKS

CHARLES FRANCIS ADAMS, *Familiar Letters of John Adams and His Wife,* Houghton Mifflin Company, 1875.

FREDERICK LEWIS ALLEN, *The Big Change,* Harper & Brothers, New York, 1952.

FREDERICK LEWIS ALLEN, *Only Yesterday,* Harper & Brothers, New York, 1931.

CHARLES M. ANDREWS, *The Colonial Period of American History,* vol. IV, Yale University Press, 1938.

PAUL M. ANGLE, *The Lincoln Reader,* Rutgers University Press, 1947.

KATHERINE ANTHONY, *Dolly Madison, Her Life and Times,* Doubleday & Co., Garden City, New York, 1949.

RAY STANNARD BAKER, *Woodrow Wilson,* vol. 7, Doubleday, Doran & Company, Inc., 1939.

MARSTON BALCH, (edited) *Modern Short Biographies and Autobiographies,* New York, Harcourt, Brace and Company, 1949.

AARON BANCROFT, D. D., *Life of Washington,* Philadelphia: Porter & Coates (Alta Edition—no date.)

CHARLES A. BEARD and MARY R. BEARD, *America In Midpassage,* The Macmillan Company, New York, 1946.

CHARLES A. BEARD and MARY R. BEARD, *The Beards' Basic History of the United States,* Doubleday, Doran & Company, New York, 1944.

DOROTHIE BOBBÉ, *Mr. and Mrs. John Quincy Adams,* Minton, Balch & Company, New York, 1930.

GAMALIEL BRADFORD, *Wives,* Harper & Brothers, New York and London, 1925.

VAN WYCK BROOKS, *The Flowering of New England 1815-1865,* E. P. Dutton & Co., Inc., 1937.

MITCHELL V. CHARNLEY, *The Boys' Life of Herbert Hoover,* Harper & Brothers, New York, 1931.

EDNA M. COLMAN, *Seventy-five Years of White House Gossip, from Washington to Lincoln,* Doubleday Page and Company, New York, 1925.

WILLIAM PENN CRESSON, *James Monroe,* The University of North Carolina Press, Chapel Hill, 1946.

ALICE CURTIS DESMOND, *Glamorous Dolly Madison,* Dodd, Mead & Co., New York, 1946.

JOSEPH F. DINEEN, *The Kennedy Family,* Little, Brown and Company, Boston, Toronto, 1959.

JANE TAYLOR DUKE, *Kenmore and the Lewises,* Doubleday & Company, Inc., Garden City, New York, 1949.

ALICE MORSE EARLE, *Colonial Dames and Good Wives,* Houghton Mifflin Company, The Riverside Press, Cambridge, 1895.

MRS. ELLET, *Queens of American Society,* Porter & Coates, Phila., Charles Scribner & Co., 1867.

MARGARET AXSON ELLIOTT, *My Aunt Louisa and Woodrow Wilson,* University of North Carolina Press, 1944.

MARY EVANS, *Costume Throughout the Ages,* 1930.

DOUGLAS SOUTHALL FREEMAN, *George Washington, Planter and Patriot* (vol. 3), Charles Scribner's Sons, 1951.

JOHN FROST, L.L.D., *Lives of the Presidents,* Boston, Phillips, Sampson and Company, 1855.

BESS FURMAN, *White House Profile,* The Bobbs-Merrill Company, Inc., Indianapolis—New York, 1951.

PHEBE A. HANAFORD, *Daughters of America or Women of the Century,* Boston: B. B. Russell, 57 Cornhill. 1883.

ALDEN HATCH, *Red Carpet for Mamie,* Henry Holt & Co., New York, 1954.

BIBLIOGRAPHY

Paul Leland Haworth, *George Washington, Country Gentleman,* The Bobbs-Merrill Company, 1915.

Deane and David Heller, *Jacqueline Kennedy,* Monarch Books, Inc., Derby, Connecticut, 1961.

Laura C. Holloway, *Ladies of the White House,* Bradley & Co., Philadelphia, 1881.

Herbert Hoover, *Memoirs of Herbert Hoover,* vol. I, (1951) vol. II, (1952), The Macmillan Company, New York, 1951, 1952.

William Henry Jackson, *Time Exposure, the Autobiography of William Henry Jackson,* G. P. Putnam's Sons, New York, 1940.

Marie Kimball, *The Martha Washington Cook Book,* Coward-McCann, 1940.

H. H. Kohlsaat, *From McKinley to Harding,* Charles Scribner's Sons, New York—London, 1923.

Lloyd Lewis, *Captain Sam Grant,* Little, Brown and Company, Boston, 1950.

Mrs. John A. Logan, *Thirty Years in Washington,* A. D. Worthington & Co., Publishers, Hartford, Conn., 1901.

Joe McCarthy, *The Remarkable Kennedys,* The Dial Press, New York, 1960.

Jane and Burt McConnell, *Presidents of the United States,* New York, Thomas Y. Crowell Company, 1951.

Silas Bent McKinley, *Old Rough and Ready, the Life and Times of Zachary Taylor,* Vanguard Press, New York, 1946.

Meade Minnigerode, *Some American Ladies,* G. P. Putnam's Sons, New York and London, 1926.

Frank Monaghan and Marvin Lowenthal, *This Was New York,* Doubleday, Doran & Co., Inc., Garden City, New York, 1943.

Charles Moore, *The Family Life of George Washington,* Houghton Mifflin Company, Boston and New York, 1926.

James Morgan, *Our Presidents,* The Macmillan Company, New York, 1949.

SAMUEL WHITE PATTERSON, *Old Chelsea And Saint Peter's Church,* The Friebele Press, New York, 1935.

KATHLEEN PRINDIVILLE, *First Ladies,* The Macmillan Company, New York, 1947.

MARY RANDOLPH, *Presidents and First Ladies,* D. Appleton–Century Company Incorporated, New York, 1936, London.

JAMES FORD RHODES, L.L.D., *The McKinley and Roosevelt Administrations,* The Macmillan Company, New York, 1922.

ELEANOR ROOSEVELT, *This Is My Story,* Harper & Brothers, New York, 1937.

ELEANOR ROOSEVELT, *This I Remember,* Harper & Brothers, New York, 1949.

MRS. THEODORE ROOSEVELT, SR., MRS. KERMIT ROOSEVELT, RICHARD DERBY, KERMIT ROOSEVELT, *Cleared for Strange Ports,* Charles Scribner's Sons, New York, 1927.

SARAH ROYCE, *A Frontier Lady,* Yale University Press, 1933.

CARL SANDBURG, *Mary Lincoln, Wife and Widow,* part I. Part II, Letters, Documents & Appendix by Paul M. Angle, Harcourt, Brace and Company, New York, 1932.

IRVING STONE, *The President's Lady,* Doubleday & Co., Garden City, 1951.

MRS. WILLIAM HOWARD TAFT, *Recollections of Full Years,* Dodd, Mead & Company, New York, 1914.

WILLIAM M. THAYER, *From Log-Cabin to the White House,* Boston, James H. Earle, Publisher, 178 Washington Street, 1886.

CARL VAN DOREN, *The Great Rehearsal,* The Viking Press, New York, 1948.

ANNE HOLLINGSWORTH WHARTON, *Women of Colonial and Revolutionary Times—Martha Washington,* Charles Scribner's Sons, New York, 1897.

JANET PAYNE WHITNEY, *Abigail Smith Adams,* Little, Brown & Co., Boston, 1947.

MARY ORMSBEE WHITTON, *First First Ladies,* Hastings House, 1948.

Gilson Willetts, *Inside History of the White House*, Christian Herald, 1908.

Edith Bolling Wilson, *My Memoir*, The Bobbs-Merrill Company, New York, 1938.

John S. Wise, *The End of An Era*, Houghton Mifflin Company, Boston and New York, The Riverside Press, 1899.

MAGAZINES

American Weekly, December 11, 1960 ("Your Child's World," by Jacqueline Kennedy).

The Atlantic Monthly, March 1923.

Collier's, March 6, 1920; March 4, 1922; March 6, 1926; October 4, 1952.

Cosmopolitan, May, 1952.

Delineator, July, 1912; October, 1928.

Good Housekeeping, March, 1913; April, 1930.

Harper's Bazaar, February, 1961.

Ladies' Home Journal, July, 1918; August, 1921; March, 1929; September, 1930; February and March, 1961.

Lippincott's Magazine, January, 1881.

Literary Digest, July 3, 1915; November 24, 1928.

McCall's Magazine, January–December, 1952; January, 1953 ("If You Ask Me," feature by Eleanor Roosevelt); March, 1961.

Red Book, November, 1960.

Saturday Evening Post, June 9, 1928.

Survey, October 3, 1914.

Time, December 5, 19, 1960; January 20, February 3, 19, 1961.

Woman's Home Companion, April, 1928; March, 1929.

World's Work, May, 1921; June, 1929.

INDEX